Theory Test for Car Drivers

The official revision questions and answers for car drivers

Up to **£40 off** your
first 10 hours of lessons*
Call 0800 107 2045

Driving School

AA

Published by AA Publishing (a trading name of AA Media Limited, whose registered office is
Fanum House, Basing View, Basingstoke, Hampshire RG21 4EA; registered number 06112600).

ISBNs: 978-0-7495-7838-1 and 978-0-7495-7698-1 (SS)

Printed and bound in China by Leo Paper Products

A05458

For more driving products, visit AA Publishing at www.theaa.com/shop
For driving lessons, visit AA Driving School at www.theaa.com/driving-school

Contents

Introduction	8
About the theory test	11
Understanding the theory test	21
Theory test revision questions	53
Alertness	54
Attitude	61
Safety and your vehicle	71
Safety margins	89
Hazard awareness	101
Vulnerable road users	122
Other types of vehicle	141
Vehicle handling	148
Motorway rules	161
Rules of the road	176
Road and traffic signs	193
Documents	230
Incidents, accidents and emergencies	238
Vehicle loading	253
Glossary	257
Answers to questions	265

Getting your licence

You want to pass your driving test and take advantage of the freedom and mobility that driving a car can give you. The following three things will help you to achieve your goal.

- Acquire knowledge of the rules of the road by learning *The Highway Code*.
- Take the right attitude. Be careful, courteous and considerate to all other road users.
- Learn and understand the skills of driving by taking lessons from a trained and qualified driving instructor.

This book has been designed to help you become a careful and safe driver and help you take the first steps towards achieving your goal – preparing for your theory test.

Six essential steps to getting your licence

1 Get your provisional licence

You can apply online for your provisional licence at www.gov.uk/apply-first-provisional-driving-licence or apply using form D1 available from Post Offices.

The driving licence is issued as a photocard.

You must be at least 17 before you can legally begin learning to drive and you must be in possession of the correct licence documents. Take care when completing all the forms. Many licences

cannot be issued for the required date because of errors or omissions on the application. You will need to provide proof of identity, such as a UK passport.

2 Learn *The Highway Code*

The Highway Code is essential reading for all drivers and not just those learning to drive. It sets out all the rules for good driving, as well as the rules for other road users such as pedestrians and motorcycle riders. When you have learned the rules you will be able to answer most of the questions in the theory test and be ready to start learning the driving skills you will need to pass your practical test.

3 Apply for and take the theory test

The driving test is in two parts, the theory test and the practical test. Once you have a valid provisional licence you may take the theory test at any time, but you must pass it before you are allowed to apply for the practical test. It is important, however, not to take your theory test too early in your course of practical lessons. This is because you need the experience of meeting real hazards while you are learning to drive, to help you pass the hazard perception element of the theory test.

You can book your theory test online or by phone. You will need your Driver and Vehicle Licensing Agency (DVLA) licence number and your debit or credit card details to hand.

Online: www.gov.uk/book-theory-test
Enquiries and booking support:
    0300 200 1122
Welsh speakers: 0300 200 1133
Textphone: 0300 200 1166
Lines are open Monday to Friday, from 8am to 4pm
Post: DVSA, PO Box 381, M50 3UW

4 Learn to drive

It is recommended that you learn to drive with an Approved Driving Instructor (ADI). Only an ADI may legally charge for providing tuition. A fully qualified ADI must display a green badge on the windscreen of the car while teaching you. Some trainee driving instructors display a pink badge on the windscreen.

Choose an instructor or driving school by asking friends or relatives for recommendations. Price is important, so find out whether the school offers any discounts for blocks or lessons paid in advance; if you decide to pay in advance, make sure the driving school is reputable. If lesson prices are very low, ask yourself 'why?' Check how long the lesson will last. Ask about the car you'll be learning to drive in. Is it modern and reliable? Is it insured? Does it have dual controls?

The most efficient and cost-effective way to learn to drive is to accept that there is no short-cut approach to learning the necessary skills. Agree with your instructor on a planned course of tuition suited to your needs, take regular lessons, and don't skip weeks and expect to pick up where you left off. Ensure the full official syllabus is covered and, as your skills develop, get as much driving practice on the road as possible with a relative or friend. Ensure they are legally able to supervise you; they must be over 21 years of age and have held a full driving licence for at least three years.

5 Apply for and take the practical test

Once you have passed the theory test, and with your instructor's guidance based on your progress, you can plan ahead for a suitable test date for the practical test. You can book your practical test online or by phone.

Online: www.gov.uk/book-driving-test
Enquiries and booking support:
    0300 200 1122
Lines are open Monday to Friday, from 8am to 12pm

Make sure you have the following details to hand when booking your practical test:

- theory test pass certificate number
- driver number shown on your licence
- driving school code number (if known)
- your preferred date
- unacceptable days or periods
- if you can accept a test at short notice
- disability or any special circumstances
- your credit/debit card details (the person who books the test must be the cardholder)

If you need to, you can change your practical test appointment online.

Saturday and weekday evening tests are available at some driving test centres. The fee is higher than for a driving test during normal working hours on weekdays. Evening tests are available during the summer months only.

6 Apply for your full driving licence

If you have a photocard provisional driving licence issued after 1 March 2004, and pass your driving test, the examiner can issue your full driving licence immediately. The DVLA will send your new full licence by post within four weeks of passing your practical test.

If you don't have a photocard provisional driving licence, you need to send your Pass Certificate and your provisional licence to the DVLA in Swansea, within two years of passing your practical test.

After the practical test

Drivers may wish to enhance their basic skills and widen their experience by taking further training in the form of the Pass Plus scheme.

This is a six-module syllabus that covers town and rural driving, night driving, driving in adverse weather conditions and driving on dual carriageways and motorways. It offers you the opportunity to gain more driving experience with the help of an instructor. Insurance companies may be prepared to offer discounts to new drivers who have completed the course. There is no test to take at the end of the course.

More information

For more information on learning to drive, including the theory test, the practical test and Pass Plus, visit www.gov.uk/browse/driving.

About the
theory test

Revising for the theory test

The theory test is all about making you a safer driver and it is a good idea to prepare for the theory test at the same time as you develop your skills behind the wheel for the practical test. By preparing for both tests at the same time, you will reinforce your knowledge and understanding of all aspects of driving and improve your chances of passing both tests first time.

How to use this book

This book is designed to help you prepare for the multiple-choice questions part of the theory test and contains all the official revision questions from the DVSA. The theory test consists of 50 unseen theory test questions based on the topics in this book (see pages 53–256). The real test questions are no longer published, but you can use this book to help you revise for the test.

To help you study for the test, the questions are arranged into the theory test topics. Each topic has its own colour band to help you find your way through the book.

Start your revision by picking a topic; you don't have to study the topics in order. Study each question carefully to make sure you understand what it is asking you. Look carefully at any diagram or photograph before reading the explanatory information and deciding on your answer.

All the answers are given in the back of this book (see pages 265–270).

Remember

- Learning *The Highway Code* and taking lessons with an ADI (approved driving instructor) are the best way to prepare for your theory test.
- Don't attempt too many questions at once.
- Don't try to learn the questions and answers by heart; the real test questions are not available for you to practice and are different from the revision questions given in this book.

Questions marked NI are **not** found in theory tests in Northern Ireland.

1 Study the question carefully and make sure you understand what it is asking you.

27 Mark *one* answer

You're waiting to emerge from a junction. The windscreen pillar is restricting your view. What should you be particularly aware of?

3 Look carefully at any photograph, symbol or diagram given within the question.

☐ **A** Lorries
☐ **B** Buses
☐ **C** Motorcyclists
☐ **D** Coaches

2 Read through all the possible answers.

Windscreen pillars can completely block your view of pedestrians, motorcyclists and cyclists. You should make a particular effort to look for these road users; don't just rely on a quick glance.

4 Each question in this book is accompanied by an explanation that will help you understand the theory behind the question and what answer may be appropriate. Make sure you read through this text before answering the question. This text will not appear in your actual theory test.

What to expect in the theory test

The theory test consists of two parts: 50 multiple-choice questions and hazard perception. You have to pass both parts in order to pass your theory test. You will receive your test scores at the end of the test. Even if you only failed on one part of the theory test, you still have to take both parts again next time.

Multiple-choice questions

You will have 57 minutes to complete the question part of the test using a touch-screen and all the questions are multiple-choice. The 50 questions appear on the screen one at a time and you can return to any of the questions within the 57 minutes to re-check or change your answers. You have to score a minimum of 43 out of 50 to pass. The Government may change the pass mark from time to time. Your driving school or the DVSA will be able to tell you if there has been a change.

Each question has four possible options. You must select the one correct answer. Don't worry about accidentally missing marking an answer because you'll be reminded that you haven't chosen an answer before moving on to the next question.

Study each question carefully and look carefully at any diagram, drawing or photograph. Before you look at the options given, decide what you think the correct answer might be. Read through the options and then select the answer that matches the one you had decided on. If you follow this system, you will avoid being confused by answers that appear to be similar.

You can answer the questions in any order you choose by moving forwards and backwards through the questions. You can also change your answer if necessary and flag questions you're unsure about, then go back to them later in the test. Your remaining time is shown on the screen.

Case study questions

Typically, five of the 50 questions will take the form of a case study. All five questions will be based on a single driving situation and appear one at time.

Case studies are designed to test that you not only know your car theory but also that you understand how to apply your knowledge when faced with a given driving situation.

The case study in your theory test could be based on any driving scenario and ask questions from a range of topics in the DVSA's database of questions.

The sample case study on the following pages demonstrates how the case study questions may appear in your live test, so you'll know what to expect.

CASE STUDY 1

You need to go to the airport to pick up a relative that has been on holiday. The journey will take you on various roads including both A-roads and motorways.

As you start your journey it begins to rain and continues to get heavier as you drive.

You have not driven to the airport before but you have planned your route before leaving and feel confident about the journey.

1. You are following a vehicle on a wet road. You should leave a time gap of at least

Mark one answer

☐ one second

☐ two seconds

☐ three seconds

☐ four seconds

| Back | Flag | Review | Next |

CASE STUDY 1

You need to go to the airport to pick up a relative that has been on holiday. The journey will take you on various roads including both A-roads and motorways.

As you start your journey it begins to rain and continues to get heavier as you drive.

You have not driven to the airport before but you have planned your route before leaving and feel confident about the journey.

2. What does this sign mean?

Mark one answer

☐ you have priority

☐ no motor vehicles

☐ two-way traffic

☐ no overtaking

| Back | Flag | Review | Next |

CASE STUDY 1

You need to go to the airport to pick up a relative that has been on holiday. The journey will take you on various roads including both A-roads and motorways.

As you start your journey it begins to rain and continues to get heavier as you drive.

You have not driven to the airport before but you have planned your route before leaving and feel confident about the journey.

3. You have just gone through deep water. To dry off the brakes you should

Mark one answer

☐ accelerate and keep to a high speed for a short time

☐ go slowly while gently applying the brakes

☐ avoid using the brakes at all for a few miles

☐ stop for at least an hour to allow them time to dry

Back   Flag   Review   Next

CASE STUDY 1

You need to go to the airport to pick up a relative that has been on holiday. The journey will take you on various roads including both A-roads and motorways.

As you start your journey it begins to rain and continues to get heavier as you drive.

You have not driven to the airport before but you have planned your route before leaving and feel confident about the journey.

4. A bus has stopped at a bus stop ahead of you. Its right-hand indicator is flashing. You should

Mark one answer

☐ flash your headlights and slow down

☐ slow down and give way if it is safe to do so

☐ sound your horn and keep going

☐ slow down and then sound your horn

Back   Flag   Review   Next

CASE STUDY 1

You need to go to the airport to pick up a relative that has been on holiday. The journey will take you on various roads including both A-roads and motorways.

As you start your journey it begins to rain and continues to get heavier as you drive.

You have not driven to the airport before but you have planned your route before leaving and feel confident about the journey.

5. Where you see street lights but no speed limit signs the limit is usually

Mark one answer

☐ 30mph

☐ 40mph

☐ 50mph

☐ 60mph

| Back | Flag | Review | Next |

Answers to sample case study questions:
1 D **2** D **3** B **4** B **5** A

Hazard perception

The video clip element of the theory test is known as hazard perception. Its aim is to find out how good you are at noticing hazards developing on the road ahead. The test will also show how much you know about the risks to you as a driver, the risks to your passengers and the risks to other road users.

Who do you think have the most accidents – new or experienced drivers? New drivers have just had lessons, so they should remember how to drive safely, but in fact new drivers have the most accidents.

Learner drivers need training in how to spot hazards because they are often so busy thinking about the car's controls that they forget to watch the road and traffic. Losing concentration for even a second could prove fatal to you or another road user.

Proper training can help you to recognize more of the hazards that you will meet when driving and to spot those hazards earlier, so you are less likely to have an accident.

Your driving instructor has been trained to help you learn hazard perception skills and can give you plenty of practice in what to look out for when driving, how to anticipate hazards, and what action to take to deal with hazards of all kinds.

What is a hazard?

A hazard is anything that might cause you to change speed or direction when driving. The hazard perception element of the theory test is about spotting developing hazards. This is one of the key skills of good driving and is also called anticipation. Anticipating hazards, such as car doors opening or children running into the road, means looking out for them in advance and taking the appropriate action.

As you get more driving experience you will start to learn about the times and places where you are most likely to meet hazards. An example of this is the rush hour. You know people take more risks when they are in a hurry. Maybe they have to drop their children at school before going to work. Perhaps they are late for a meeting or want to get home. So you have to be prepared for bad driving, for example another driver pulling out in front of you.

You won't be able to practise with the real clips used in the official test, of course, but training books and practice software are widely available.

What to expect in the hazard perception test

After answering the multiple-choice questions, you will be given a short break before you begin the hazard perception part of the test. The hazard perception test lasts for about 20 minutes. Before you start you will be given some instructions explaining how the test works; you'll also get a chance to practise with the computer and mouse before you start. This is to make sure that you know what to expect on the test and that you are happy with what you have to do.

Next you will see 14 clips of street scenes with traffic such as cars, cyclists, pedestrians etc. The scenes are from the point of view of a driver in a car. You have to notice potential hazards that are developing on the road ahead – that is, problems that could lead to an incident. As soon as you notice a hazard developing, click the mouse. You will have plenty of time to see the hazard and the sooner you notice it, the more marks you score.

Each clip has at least one hazard in it but some clips may have more than one hazard. You have to score a minimum of 44 out of 75 to pass, but the pass mark may change so check with your instructor or the DVSA before sitting your test.

Note that the computer has checks built in to show anyone trying to cheat – for example someone who keeps

Above: Click the mouse when you spot potential hazards – the tractor emerging from the side road (ringed in red).

clicking the mouse all the time. Be aware that, unlike the theory test questions, you will not have an opportunity to go back to an earlier clip and change your response, so you need to concentrate throughout the test.

You responded to this clip in an unacceptable manner. You will score zero for this clip.

Further information

For more practical information on learning to drive including the theory test, practical test and Pass Plus visit www.gov.uk/browse/driving.

Left: You may see a warning screen similar to this one if the computer detects a clicking pattern or you click the mouse constantly.

Understanding the theory behind the test

Contents   Page

Alertness   22

Attitude   23

Safety and your vehicle   25

Safety margins   26

Hazard awareness   29

Vulnerable road users   34

Other types of vehicle   37

Vehicle handling   38

Motorway rules   40

Rules of the road   43

Road and traffic signs   45

Documents   47

Incidents, accidents   49
and emergencies

Vehicle loading   51

Section 1
Alertness

The first section in the theory test revision questions is headed ALERTNESS. Alertness is a short section and is a good place to start.

- Alertness means being wide awake and concentrating on what you are doing – driving – not being distracted by mobile phones or loud music
- Alertness means looking out for hazards
- Alertness means noticing all road signs and road markings, and acting on the instructions and information they give

Are you fit to drive?
'Fit' can mean:
- Did you have any alcoholic drinks before you set out?
- Are you under the influence of illegal substances (drugs)?
- Are you feeling groggy or unwell?
- Are you taking prescription medicine that could affect your ability to control the car?
- Are you too tired to drive?

It's unwise to set out on a journey if you're not well, on the basis of 'I'll see how I go – I'll probably be all right':
- Your reactions are likely to be slower
- You may be unable to judge distances properly
- Your actions may be less well co-ordinated than usual and it's not legal

If you are tired, open the window for a few moments to let in some fresh air. If you drive when you are too tired, you risk falling asleep at the wheel – an all too common cause of serious accidents. Driving for long stretches on a motorway at night can be especially dangerous. If you sense that you are losing your concentration, then take a break at a motorway service station. Plan your journey ahead, giving yourself plenty of time for rest stops – at least every couple of hours.

Tackling the questions
Look at the questions in the Alertness section. You'll see that the Alertness questions are all about these:
- anticipation
- observation
- signalling
- reversing
- using your mirrors
- concentration
- getting distracted
- feeling sleepy
- using mobile phones

DID YOU KNOW?
The main causes of distraction are:
- Loud music in the car
- Passengers (usually children)
- Events happening outside (such as accidents)
- Using a mobile phone

Now test yourself on the questions on pages 54–60

Section 2
Attitude

The government road safety organisations believe that the ATTITUDE of learner drivers is extremely important for road safety.

Attitude means:
- Your frame of mind when you get in the car
- How you react when you meet hazards on the road
- How you behave towards other drivers

Attitude is a very important part of being a good driver. Your attitude when you are driving plays a big part in ensuring your safety and that of other road users.

Do you aim to be a careful and safe driver or a fast and skilful driver? If you don't want to end up as another road accident statistic, then carefully and safely is the way to go.

Remember that a car is not an offensive weapon, and often people don't realise what a potentially lethal machine they are in control of when they get behind the wheel. You only have to think about this to understand the importance of your attitude when driving.

You'll see that questions in this section are concerned with encouraging you to be a careful and safe driver, and cover:
- Tailgating
- Consideration for other road users, including pedestrians, buses, slow-moving vehicles and horse riders
- Driving at the right speed for the conditions

- When to flash headlights
- The right place, time and way to overtake

And remembering a few dos and don'ts will help you achieve the right attitude for driving and make passing this section of the test much easier.

Good drivers do:
- drive at the right speed and for the road and traffic conditions
- observe speed limits
- overtake only when it is safe to do so
- park in correct and safe places
- wait patiently if the driver in front is a learner or elderly or hesitant
- look out for vulnerable road users such as cyclists, pedestrians and children
- concentrate on their driving at all times
- plan their journey so that they have plenty of time to get to their destination

Good drivers don't:
- allow themselves to become involved in road rage
- break speed limits
- drive too fast, particularly in wet, foggy or icy weather
- accelerate or brake too harshly
- overtake and 'cut in', forcing others to brake sharply
- put pressure on other drivers by driving too close behind them (this is called 'tailgating'), flashing headlights or gesturing
- allow their attention to be distracted by passengers, mobile phones or loud music, or what is happening on the road, such as staring at an accident

Tailgating

Driving excessively close behind another vehicle is known as tailgating – and it's dangerous! The car in front may stop suddenly (to avoid hitting a child or animal that has dashed out into the road, for example); when this happens the car following runs the risk of crashing into it.

You should always leave enough space between your vehicle and the one in front, so that you can stop safely if the driver in front suddenly slows down or stops.

Rear-end shunts account for a large percentage of all accidents on the road. In these situations, the driver of the car behind is almost always judged to be the guilty party.

So tailgating is potentially expensive as well as dangerous.

Another time when drivers are tempted to tailgate is when attempting to pass a large, slow-moving vehicle. However, keeping well back will improve your view of the road ahead, so that you're better able to judge when it's safe to overtake and the driver of the large vehicle will also be able to see you.

Useful tip

If you are being followed too closely by another driver you should slow down and increase the distance between your vehicle and the one in front. If you slow down or have to stop suddenly, the driver behind may crash into you, but you will have increased your stopping distance and will not be pushed into the vehicle in front of you.

Always remember:

- Expect the unexpected, and make provision for the potential errors of other drivers – everyone makes mistakes sometimes.
- Don't create unnecessary stress for other drivers by showing your frustration in an aggressive manner.

If you are driving at the right speed for the road and weather conditions and a driver behind tries to overtake, you should pull back a bit from the vehicle in front so that if the driver behind insists on overtaking, there is less risk of an accident.

Do not try to stop the car behind from overtaking. Do not move into the middle of the road or move up close to the car in front. These actions could be very dangerous.

You should not give confusing signals such as indicating left or waving the other driver on.

Now test yourself on the questions on pages 61–70

Section 3
Safety and your vehicle

When you go through this section you will notice that the questions are a bit of a mixture. They cover a number of topics about SAFETY, including:

- Understanding the controls of your vehicle
- What the car's warning lights tell you
- Tyres – correct inflation, pressures and tread depths
- When to use hazard warning lights
- Passenger safety
- The environment
- Security and crime prevention

Many of the questions in this section are to do with 'legal requirements' and rules regarding parking your car and using lights. Look up all the sections in *The Highway Code* that deal with parking rules. Find out the rules for red routes, white lines and zigzag lines as well as yellow lines.

Seat belts

If any of your passengers are young people under 14, you are responsible for making sure that they wear seat belts. You are responsible for them by law, even if you are still a learner driver yourself.

Tips for this section

Learn *The Highway Code* and you will be able to answer most of the questions in this section. In particular make sure you know the rules regarding seat belts, tyres, and when to use your lights, including your hazard warning lights.

A confusing question

One of the most confusing questions in this section asks what kind of driving results in high fuel consumption. The answer, of course, is **bad** driving – especially harsh braking and acceleration. This means you will use more fuel than you should and therefore cause more damage to the environment than is necessary.

BUT many people read the word 'high' as meaning 'good' – as in a level of driving skill – and so pick the wrong answer.

Don't let it be you…

Now test yourself on the questions on pages 71–88

Section 4
Safety margins

Experienced drivers are usually better than new or learner drivers at leaving good SAFETY MARGINS. Learner drivers find it harder to keep their vehicle at a safe distance from the one in front. Therefore the questions in this section cover:
- safe stopping distances

and
- safe separation distances (these are the same as safety margins)

What is a safety margin?

A safety margin is the space that you need to leave between your vehicle and the one in front so that you will not crash into it if it slows downs or stops suddenly. They are also called 'separation distances' and are an important part of anticipating road and traffic hazards. When you are learning to drive, you can feel pressured to speed up by drivers behind you.

Don't let other drivers make you cut down on your safety margins. Stay a safe distance behind the vehicle in front. Then you will have time to anticipate and react to hazards.

The two-second rule

In traffic that's moving at normal speed, allow at least a two-second gap between you and the vehicle in front.

Stopping distances

Many people who are taking their theory test get confused about this. You will notice that some of the questions ask for your overall

stopping distance and others ask for your braking distance. These are different.

Overall stopping distance or stopping distance is not the same as braking distance. Stopping distance is made up of thinking distance + braking distance.

In other words, the time it takes to notice that there's a hazard ahead plus the time it takes to brake to deal with it.

Thinking distance

Thinking distance is sometimes called reaction time or reaction distance. If you are driving at 30mph, your thinking distance will be 30 feet (9 metres). That means your vehicle will travel 30 feet (9 metres) before you start braking.

The link between stopping distance and safety margins

You should always leave enough space between your vehicle and the one in front. If the other driver has to slow down suddenly or stop without warning, you need to be able to stop safely. The space is your safety margin.

Safety margins for other vehicles

Long vehicles and motorcycles need more room to stop – in other words, you must leave a bigger safety margin when following a long vehicle or motorbike. When driving behind a long vehicle, pull back to increase your separation distance and your safety margin so that you get a better view of the road ahead – there could be hazards developing and if you are too close he will

Thinking Distance   Braking Distance

20 mph
6 metres + 6 metres
= 12 metres (40 feet) or 3 car lengths

30 mph
9 metres + 14 metres
= 23 metres (75 feet) or 6 car lengths

40 mph
12 metres + 24 metres
= 36 metres (118 feet) or 9 car lengths

50 mph
15 metres + 38 metres
= 53 metres (175 feet) or 13 car lengths

60 mph
18 metres + 55 metres
= 73 metres (240 feet) or 18 car lengths

70 mph
21 metres + 75 metres
= 96 metres (315 feet) or 24 car lengths

be unable to see you in his rear view mirror. Strong winds can blow lorries and motorbikes off course. So leave a bigger safety margin.

Different conditions and safety margins

You may find that one or more questions in your theory test might be about driving in 'different conditions'. These questions aim to make sure you know what adjustments you should make to your driving when either road conditions are different from normal, for example, when parts of the road are closed off for roadworks or weather conditions affect your driving.

Roadworks

You should always take extra care when you see a sign warning you that there are roadworks ahead. Remember, roadworks are a hazard and you have to anticipate them.

If you see the driver in front of you slowing down, take this as a sign that you should do the same – even if you can't see a hazard ahead. You still need to keep a safe distance from him. Harassing the driver in front by 'tailgating' is both wrong and dangerous and so is overtaking to fill the gap. It's especially important that you know what to do when you see a sign for roadworks ahead on a motorway.

- There may be a lower speed limit than normal – keep to it
- Use your mirrors and indicators, and get into the correct lane in plenty of time
- Don't overtake the queue and then force your way in at the last minute (this is an example of showing an inconsiderate

attitude to other road users)
- Always keep a safe distance from the vehicle in front

Weather conditions

In bad weather (often called 'adverse' weather), you need to increase your safety margins.

When it's raining you need to leave at least twice as much distance between you and the vehicle in front. When there's ice on the road leave an even bigger gap because your stopping distance increases tenfold.

It's amazing how often drivers go too fast in bad weather. In adverse weather motorways have lower speed limits, but some drivers don't take any notice of them.

When it's icy you should multiply your two-second gap by ten.

Questions that look alike

There are a number of questions about anti-lock brakes in this section. Lots of questions look the same. Some are easy and some are hard. Some of them appear to be the same but they are not.

The questions test two things – your knowledge of the rules of the road and your understanding of words to do with driving.

Now test yourself on the questions on pages 89–100

Section 5
Hazard awareness

How often does a motorist protest that the accident happened before they had time to realise the person they hit was there? Some accidents will inevitably happen, but part of your instructor's job while teaching you to drive is to help you learn to anticipate problems before they happen.

What is the difference between Hazard Awareness and Hazard Perception?

- Hazard Awareness and Hazard Perception mean the same thing
- Hazard Perception is the name for the part of the theory test that uses video clips. This test is about spotting developing hazards. One of the key skills of good driving, this is called anticipation
- Anticipating hazards means looking out for them in advance and taking action now
- Hazard Awareness is about being alert whenever you are driving

That is why some of the questions in the HAZARD AWARENESS section deal with things that might make you less alert. For example feeling tired, feeling ill, taking medicines prescribed by your doctor, drinking alcohol or taking illegal drugs.

Other questions in Hazard Awareness cover noticing road and traffic signs as well as road markings, what to do at traffic lights and when to slow down for hazards ahead.

Why are young male drivers more at risk?

New drivers have a greater than average chance of being involved in accidents. Statistics show that young male drivers have the most accidents.

- Maybe it's because when they first get their licence they want to show off to other drivers
- Some people think that driving much too fast will earn them 'respect' from their friends
- Some people think that they are such good drivers that the rules of the road should not apply to them

Whatever the reason – drivers who don't watch out for hazards are at risk of being involved in an accident. The problem has a lot to do with people's attitude to driving. You'll find more about this aspect of driving in the Attitude part of the theory test.

We've already said that young drivers often don't learn to anticipate hazards until they are older and more experienced. The Hazard Perception test aims to 'fill the gap' in hazard perception for young drivers and other new drivers by making sure they have some proper training to make up for their lack of experience.

This should make them safer drivers when they start out on the road alone.

Looking for clues to hazards developing on the road

As you get more driving experience you will start to learn about the times and places where you are most likely to meet hazards. Think about some of these examples.

Rush hour

You know that people take more risks when driving in the rush hour. Maybe they have to drop their children off at school before going to work. Maybe they are late for a business meeting. So you have to be prepared for bad driving, such as other drivers pulling out in front of you.

Dustbin day

Drivers in a hurry may get frustrated if they are held up in traffic because of a hazard such as a dustcart. They may accelerate and pull out to overtake even though they cannot see clearly ahead. You should not blindly follow the lead of another driver. Check for yourself that there are no hazards ahead.

School children

Young children are often not very good at judging how far away a car is from them, and may run into the road unexpectedly. Always be on the lookout for hazards near a school entrance.

Parked cars

Imagine you are driving on a quiet one-way street with cars parked down each side of the road. You wouldn't expect to meet any vehicles coming the other way – but what about children playing? They might run out into the road after a football. It would be difficult to see them because of the parked cars, until they were in the road in front of you.

More examples of hazards

So, what kinds of hazards are we talking about? And what should you do about them?

Road markings and road signs sometimes highlight likely hazards for you.

The list below gives some of the hazards you should look out for when driving along a busy street in town.

After each hazard there are some ideas about what you should be looking out for, and what to do next.

- You see a bus which has stopped in a lay-by ahead

There may be some pedestrians hidden by the bus who are trying to cross the road, or the bus may signal to pull out. Be ready to slow down and stop.

- You see a white triangle painted on the road surface ahead

This is a hazard warning sign. It tells you that there is a 'Give Way' junction just ahead. Slow down and be ready to stop.

- You see a sign for a roundabout on the road ahead

Anticipate that other drivers may need to change lane, and be ready to leave them enough room.

- You come to some road works where the traffic is controlled by temporary traffic lights

Watch out for drivers speeding to get through before the lights change.

- You look in your rear view mirror and see an emergency vehicle with flashing lights coming up behind you

An emergency vehicle wants to pass, so get ready to pull over when it's safe.

- You see a small child standing with an adult near the edge of the pavement

Check if the child is safely holding the adult's hand. Be ready to stop safely if the child suddenly steps into the road.

- You notice dustbins or rubbish bags put out on the pavement

The dustcart could be around the next corner, or the bin men could be crossing the road with bags of rubbish. Be ready to slow down and stop if necessary.

- You hear a siren

Look all around to find out where the emergency vehicle is. You may have to pull over to let it pass.

You will find out more about the different types of hazards you may encounter, including what to look for when driving on narrow country roads, or in bad (adverse) weather conditions, in the Vehicle Handling section of this book.

> **Always expect the unexpected**
> Don't forget that not all hazards can be anticipated. There are bound to be some you haven't expected.

> **Red flashing warning lights**
> Level crossings, ambulance stations, fire stations and swing bridges all have red lights that flash on and off to warn you when you must stop.

Observation

Another word for taking in information through our eyes is observation. Observation is one of the three key skills needed in hazard perception. The three skills are:

- observation
- anticipation
- planning

An easy way to remember this is **O A P** for

Observe
Anticipate
Plan

Talk to yourself!

It's a good idea to 'talk to yourself' when you're learning to drive – and even after you've passed your test. Talk about all the things you see that could be potential hazards. Your driving instructor might suggest this as a way of making you concentrate and notice hazards ahead.

Even if you don't talk out loud, you can do a 'running commentary' in your head on everything you see around you as you drive.

For example, you might say to yourself – 'I am following a cyclist and the traffic lights ahead are red. *When the lights change I will allow him/her plenty of time and room to move off.'*
or
'The dual carriageway ahead is starting to look very busy. There is a sign showing that the right lane is closing in 800 yards. *I must get ready to check my mirrors and, if safe to do so, drop back to allow other vehicles to move into the left-hand lane ahead of me.'*

Note: Don't forget the mirrors! This way, you will notice more hazards, and you will learn to make more sense of the information that your eyes are taking in.

Scanning the road

Learner drivers tend to look straight ahead of their car and may not notice all the hazards that might be building up on both sides. You will spot more hazards when driving if you train yourself to scan the road.

- Practise looking up and ahead as far as possible
- Use all your mirrors to look out for hazards too
- Don't forget that you have 'blind spots' when driving – work out where they are and find safe ways of checking all round for hazards
- Ask your driving instructor to help you with all of this

Learn your road signs!

Notice the information at the bottom of the first page of traffic signs in *The Highway Code*. It explains that you won't find every road sign shown here.

You can buy a copy of *Know Your Road Signs* from a bookshop to see some of the extra signs that are not in *The Highway Code*.

Note: In Wales, some road signs include the Welsh spelling as well as the English, and in Scotland some signs are written using Gaelic spelling. You'll also see some 'old-style' road signs around, which are slightly different too.

How is learning to scan the road going to help me pass my theory test?

- The idea of the hazard perception element of the test is to encourage you to get some real experience of driving before you take the theory test
- If you meet real hazards on the road and learn how to anticipate them, you'll learn how to pass the hazard perception element of the test
- In the video test you may not be able to look all around you as you would when driving a car; but the clips will be as realistic as possible in giving you a wide 'view' of the road ahead

Observation questions

Study some of the pictures in the Hazard Awareness section.

They include photographs of scenes such as:

• a view of the road ahead with traffic building up where one lane is closing

Look out for situations like these when you are out driving with your instructor, and use the practice to improve your hazard awareness.

As well as photographs, there are pictures of road and traffic signs.

• a cyclist at traffic lights, seen from the viewpoint of a driver in a car behind the cyclist

What do these signs mean?

What actions should you take when you see these signs?

• what you see as a driver when you are approaching a level crossing

• If you are not sure, look them up in *The Highway Code*

• Think about why the square yellow sign with the two children is in the Vehicle Markings section and not with the rest of the road signs

• what you see when coming up to a 'blind bend'

Now test yourself on the questions on pages 101–21

Section 6
Vulnerable road users

Today's new vehicles are becoming safer all the time for the driver inside the car, but sadly this is not always the case for the pedestrian or cyclist outside. Many road users who are not driving cars have nothing to protect them if they are in an accident with a motor vehicle.

The questions in the VULNERABLE ROAD USERS section deal with the following:
- why different types of road users are vulnerable
- what you as a driver must do to keep them safe

Who are vulnerable road users?
You must drive with extra care when you are near the following vulnerable road users:
- pedestrians
- children
- elderly people
- people with disabilities
- cyclists
- motorcycle riders
- horse riders
- learner drivers and new drivers
- animals being herded along the road

Cyclists
Give cyclists plenty of room. Remember to keep well back from cyclists when you are coming up to a junction or a roundabout because you cannot be sure what they are going to do. On the roundabout they may go in any direction – left, right or straight ahead. They are allowed to stay in the left lane and

signal right if they are going to continue round. Leave them enough room to cross in front of you if they need to. Turn to the section headed Vulnerable Road Users in the theory test questions to see some pictures of this. You must also give way to cyclists at toucan crossings and in cycle lanes (see the rules for cyclists set out in *The Highway Code*).

Look out for cyclists!
- It can be hard to see cyclists in busy town traffic
- It can also be hard to see them coming when you are waiting to turn out at a junction. They can be hidden by other vehicles

Always be on the lookout for cyclists.

Especially, check your mirror to make sure you do not trap a cyclist on your left when you are turning left into a side road. Check your blind spots for cyclists, too.

Controlling your vehicle near cyclists
When you are following a cyclist, you must be able to drive as slowly as they do, and keep your vehicle under control. Only

overtake when you can allow them plenty of room, and it is safe to do so.

Cycle lanes

Cycle lanes are reserved for cyclists and car drivers should not use them. A cycle lane is marked by a white line on the road. A solid white line means you must not drive or park in the cycle lane during the hours it is in use. A broken white line means that you should drive or park in it only if there is no alternative. You should not park there at any time when there are waiting restrictions.

When you overtake a cyclist, a motorcyclist or a horse rider, give them at least as much room as you would give a car.

Cyclists and motorcycle riders

Cyclists and motorcycle riders are more at risk than car drivers because

- they are more affected by strong winds, or by turbulence caused by other vehicles
- they are more affected by an uneven road surface, and they may have to move out suddenly to avoid a pothole
- car drivers often cannot see them

Pedestrians

Pedestrians most at risk include elderly people and children. Elderly people and others who cannot move easily may be slower to cross roads – you must give them plenty of time. Children don't have a sense of danger on the road; they can't tell how close a car is, or how fast it is going. They may run out into the road without looking. Or they may step out behind you when you are reversing – you may not see them because they are small.

People who are unable to see and/or hear

A person who is blind will usually carry a white stick to alert you to their presence. If the stick has a red band, this means that the person is also deaf, so will have no warning of an approaching car either visually or from engine noise.

When to give way to pedestrians

At any pedestrian crossing, if a pedestrian has started to cross, wait until they have reached the other side. Do not harass them by revving your engine or edging forward.

At a crossing with lights (pelican, toucan or puffin crossings), pedestrians have priority once they have started to cross even if, when on a pelican crossing, the amber lights start flashing.

Once a pedestrian has stepped on to a zebra crossing, you must stop and wait for them to cross.

Note: It is courteous to stop at a zebra crossing if a pedestrian is waiting to cross.

When you take your practical driving test, you must stop for any pedestrians who are waiting on the pavement at a zebra crossing even if they haven't stepped on to the crossing yet. However, you must not wave to them to cross.

If you want to turn left into a side road and pedestrians have already started to cross the side road on foot, wait for them to finish crossing. People on foot have priority over car drivers.

DID YOU KNOW?

If a car hits a pedestrian at 40mph, the pedestrian will probably be killed. Even at 35mph, 50% of pedestrians hit by cars will be killed.

At 20mph, pedestrians have a better chance of surviving. This is why you will find 20mph limits and other things to slow traffic in some residential streets and near school entrances.

Other types of vulnerable road users

Be prepared to slow down for animals, learner drivers, and other more unusual hazards such as people walking along the road in organised groups (for example, on a demonstration, or a sponsored walk). There are rules in *The Highway Code* that walkers must follow. But even if they break the rules, make sure you keep to them.

Animals

Drive slowly past horses or other animals. Allow them plenty of space on the road. Don't frighten them by sounding your horn or revving your engine.

If you see a flock of sheep or a herd of cattle blocking the road, you must:
- stop
- switch off your engine
- and wait until they have left the road

People riding horses on the road are often children, so you need to take extra care; when you see two riders abreast, it may well be that the one on the outside is shielding a less experienced rider.

Traffic signs

Look up the Traffic Signs and Vehicle Markings sections in *The Highway Code* and find the following signs:
- pedestrians walking in the road ahead (no pavement)
- cycle lane and pedestrian route
- advance warning of school crossing patrol ahead
- school crossing patrol
- elderly or disabled people crossing
- sign on back of school bus or coach

Now test yourself on the questions on pages 122–40

Section 7
Other types of vehicle

We have already come across some of the other types of vehicle that share the road with you and your car including motorbikes and bicycles. The questions in this part of the theory test are mostly about long vehicles such as lorries. However, you also need to know what to do about:

- buses
- caravans
- trams
- tractors and other farm vehicles
- special vehicles for disabled drivers (powered invalid carriages)
- slow vehicles such as road gritters
- motorway repair vehicles

Important points to remember about these types of vehicle:
- Many of them can only move very slowly
- They cannot easily stop or change direction
- The driver's field of vision may be restricted – this means that car drivers have to allow them plenty of room

Motorcycles
- Motorcycles are easily blown off course by strong winds. If you see a motorcyclist overtaking a high-sided vehicle such as a lorry, keep well back. The lorry may shield the motorcyclist from the wind as it is overtaking, but then a sudden gust could blow the motorcyclist off-course
- It can be hard to see a motorcyclist when you are waiting at a junction. Always look out for them

- If you see a motorcyclist looking over their shoulder, it could mean that they will soon give a signal to turn right. This applies to cyclists too. Keep back to give them plenty of room
- Motorcyclists and cyclists sometimes have to swerve to avoid hazards such as bumps in the road, patches of ice and drain covers. As before – give them plenty of room

Long vehicles
- Like cyclists, long vehicles coming up to roundabouts may stay in the left lane even if they intend to turn right. This is because they need lots of room to manoeuvre. Keep well back so they have room to turn
- Take great care when overtaking long or high-sided vehicles. Before you pull out to overtake, make sure you have a clear view of the road ahead
- A long vehicle that needs to turn left off a major road into a minor road may prepare to do so by moving out towards the centre of the road, or by moving across to the other side

If you're following them:
- Give way, and don't try to overtake – on the right or the left
- You might need to slow down and stop while the driver of the long vehicle makes the turn

Buses and trams
- Always give way to buses when they signal to pull out
- Always give way to trams as they cannot steer to avoid you
- Don't try to overtake a tram

Trams are **quiet** vehicles – you cannot rely on approaching engine noise to warn you that a tram is coming.

Take extra care when you see this sign, because trams are sometimes allowed to go when car drivers are not.

Tractors and slow-moving vehicles

• Always be patient if you are following a slow vehicle

Drivers of slow vehicles will usually try to find a safe place to pull in to let the traffic go past. In the meantime you should keep well back, so that you can see the road ahead. Allow a safe distance in case they slow down or stop.

Slow vehicles are not allowed on motorways because they cannot keep up with the fast-moving traffic. Vehicles not allowed on motorways include:

• motorcycles under 50cc
• bicycles
• tractors and other farm vehicles
• powered invalid carriages

Now test yourself on the questions on pages 141–47

Section 8
Vehicle handling

The questions in this section test how much you know about controlling your vehicle on different road surfaces and in different weather.

Your control is affected by:

• the road surface – is it rough or smooth? Are there any holes or bumps? Are there any 'traffic-calming' measures, such as humps or chicanes?
• the weather conditions – you have to drive in different ways when there is fog, snow, ice or heavy rain

Other questions in this section cover driving on country roads – on narrow and one-way roads, humpback bridges, steep hills, fords. Other questions need practical knowledge, for example, on engine braking, brake fade, and coasting your vehicle – use the Glossary.

This section also has some questions on overtaking and parking.

Road surface

The condition of the road surface can affect the way your vehicle handles. Your vehicle handles better on a smooth surface than on a surface that is damaged, bumpy or full of holes. If you have to drive on an uneven surface, keep your speed down so that you have full control of your vehicle, even if your steering wheel is jolted.

Take care also where there are tramlines on the road. The layout of the road affects the way your vehicle handles.

You may have to adjust your driving for traffic-calming measures, such as traffic humps (sometimes called 'sleeping policemen') and chicanes. These are double bends that have been put into the road layout to slow the traffic down. The sign before the chicane tells you who has priority.

Traffic calming measures are often used in residential areas or near school entrances to make it safer for pedestrians.

Weather conditions

Bad weather (adverse weather) such as heavy rain, ice or snow affects the way your vehicle handles. If you drive too fast in adverse weather, your tyres may lose their grip on the road when you try to brake. This means the car may skid or 'aquaplane'. Aquaplaning means sliding out of control on a wet surface.

Driving in snow

In snow, the best advice is do not drive at all unless you really have to make a journey. If you have to drive in snowy conditions, leave extra time for your journey and keep to the main roads. You can fit snow chains to your tyres to increase their grip in deep snow.

Driving in fog

In fog your field of vision can be down to a few metres. Your vehicle is fitted with fog lights to help you see and be seen in fog. But you must know how and when to use them. Look up the three rules about fog lights in *The Highway Code*. You'll see that the key points to remember are:

- Don't dazzle other road users with your fog lights
- Switch them off as soon as you can see better (as soon as the fog starts to clear)

Remember the two-second rule
You should double the two-second gap to four seconds when driving in rain, and increase the gap by as much as ten times when there is ice on the road.

Country driving

If you have had most of your driving lessons in a town, you need to know how to drive on narrow country roads. Some are only wide enough for one vehicle ('single-track'), and some are on very steep hills.

Your control of the gears, clutch and brakes will be important if you have to follow a tractor very slowly up a hill. On a steep downward slope you have to make sure your vehicle does not 'run away'.

On country roads you might find humpback bridges and fords. The signs below warn you of these hazards.

- Find out what you must do first after you have driven through a ford

Technical knowledge

We have already mentioned engine braking. Understanding how engine braking works is part of good vehicle handling.

Note: If you press the footbrake constantly on a long hill, you may get brake fade. If you're not sure, check what that means in the Glossary near the back of this book.

Use the gears to control your vehicle on a downhill slope (or 'gradient'). If you put the vehicle in 'neutral', or drive with the clutch down (called coasting), your vehicle will increase speed beyond what is safe and will not be under proper control.

This sign warns you of a steep hill downwards.

- Travelling in neutral for long distances (known as coasting) is wrong and dangerous – you should not be tempted to do it and it doesn't save fuel

Remember that if there is sudden heavy rain after a dry hot spell, the road surface can get very slippery.

Now test yourself on the questions on pages 148–60

Section 9
Motorway rules

Learner drivers aren't allowed on motorways, so you can't get experience of what it's like to drive on them until you've passed your test. However, you do need to know all about MOTORWAY RULES before taking your practical test, and your theory test will most likely include a question about motorways.

As soon as you pass your driving test you will be legally allowed to drive on motorways. You need to know all the motorway rules in advance, so that you are confident and ready to cope with motorway driving when you pass your test.

There are some major roads and dual carriageways that learners can drive on which are very much like motorways. You may drive on some of these fast roads during your driving test, so that your examiner can see how well you cope with hazards at higher speeds.

When driving on these fast roads you will need some of the very same skills that you will need for motorway driving – for example, using lanes properly, knowing when it is safe to overtake, and controlling your vehicle at speed.

If you are learning to drive with a driving school, you will have the chance to book a motorway lesson with your instructor after you have passed your test. It makes sense to take up this offer before you drive on a motorway alone for the first time.

Motorways and other roads

- On a motorway traffic is moving at high speed all the time
- All lanes are in use
- No stopping is allowed on a motorway – traffic only slows or comes to a stop because of accidents or other types of hold-up
- Some road users are not allowed on motorways. These include:
  - pedestrians, cyclists and learner drivers
  - horses and other animals
  - motorcycles under 50cc
  - slow-moving vehicles, tractors and farm vehicles and invalid carriages
- You always enter and leave a motorway on the left, via a slip road
- To the left of the inside lane (left-hand lane) on a motorway is the hard shoulder. You can only drive on this in an emergency
- Special signs and signals are used on motorways. These include signs above the road on overhead gantries, signs on the central reservation, and amber and red flashing lights

Checks before your journey

Be extra careful about doing all your regular checks before you set out on a motorway journey. You cannot stop on the motorway to fix small problems, and no one wants to break down in the middle of fast traffic. Always check:

- oil and coolant levels, screen wash container
- tyres and tyre pressures
- fuel gauge
- that all mirrors and windows are free of dirt and grease
- that the horn works

Many of these checks are legally necessary, as well as important for your safety.

How to move on to a motorway

- Join the motorway by building up your speed on the slip road to match the speed of traffic in the left lane of the motorway
- Use MSM (Mirrors – Signal – Manoeuvre) and move into the flow of traffic when it is safe to do so

Changing lanes and overtaking

Driving on a motorway needs all the skills you have learned about anticipation and forward planning.

You should:
- make good use of all mirrors, and check your blind spots
- signal to move out in plenty of time
- look out for hazards ahead in the lane you want to move to
- not go ahead if it will force another vehicle to brake or swerve
- keep a safe distance from the vehicle in front

Take a break

When you drive on motorways you will sometimes see signs that say 'Tiredness can kill – take a break!' This is very good advice. Motorways are monotonous – boring to drive, with long stretches of road that look the same for miles. A major cause of accidents is drivers falling asleep at the wheel. Plan your journey so that you have time to get out, stretch your legs and have a drink or snack.

The rules you need to know:

- Keep to the left-hand lane unless you are overtaking and move back to the left lane as soon as it is safe to do so. Sometimes you need to stay in the centre lane for a time – for example, when a line of lorries is travelling up a hill in the left lane. Stay in the centre lane until you have passed the hazard, then signal left and return to the left lane
- NEVER reverse, park, walk or drive in the wrong direction on a motorway
- Don't exceed the speed limit. This is normally 70mph, but lower speed limits may be signed when the road is busy, or in bad weather
- Keep to the correct separation distance (see Safety Margins)
- Don't overtake on the left.
  If traffic is moving slowly in all three lanes you may find that the lane on the left is moving faster than the one to its right for a short time. Or the left lane may be signed for traffic turning off at the next junction only. But these are exceptions to the rule
- If luggage falls from your vehicle, do not get out to pick it up. Stop at the next emergency phone and tell the Highways Agency or the police. Posts on the edge of the motorway show the way to the nearest emergency phone. You should use these phones rather than your mobile phone, because the emergency phone connects directly to the Highways Agency or the police and tells them exactly where you are calling from on the motorway
- Don't stop on the hard shoulder except in an emergency. The hard shoulder is an extremely dangerous place, as many as one in eight road deaths happen there

Traffic signs and road markings

Light signals

In *The Highway Code* you'll find the light signals only seen on motorways. Signs above the roadway or on the central reservation are activated as needed to warn of accidents, lane closures or weather conditions. Overhead gantries display arrows or red crosses showing which lanes are open or

closed to traffic and which lanes to move to when motorways merge or diverge. They may also show temporary speed limits.

Direction signs

Direction signs on motorways are blue and those on other major roads are green – other direction signs are white with black print.

Reflective studs

It's useful to know the colours of studs on a motorway; this can help in working out which part of the road you're on if it's dark or foggy. White studs mark lanes or the centre of the road and red studs mark the left edge of the carriageway.

Amber studs are used alongside the central reservation and green studs mark the entry to a slip road.

Note: These markings are also found on some dual carriageways.

Using the hard shoulder

- Stop as far to the left as possible and, if you can, near an emergency phone
- Emergency phones are situated 1 mile apart and have blue and white marker posts every 100 metres. An arrow on the posts points the direction of the nearest phone
  - If you are using a mobile phone you can identify your location from the number on the post
- Switch on your hazard warning lights
- Use the left-hand door to get out of the vehicle, and make sure your passengers do too
- Get everyone away from the road – if possible, behind the barrier or up the bank
- Leave animals in the vehicle unless they aren't safe there
- Phone the Highways Agency or the police with full details of where you are, then go back and wait in a safe place near your vehicle

Section 10
Rules of the road

'Rules of the Road' is a good way to describe what is in *The Highway Code*.

The questions that come under this heading in the theory test include several on road signs and road markings. There are many more road sign questions in the section on Road and Traffic Signs. Several of the topics listed in this section have already come up.

Other questions in this section cover:
- speed limits
- overtaking
- parking
- lanes and roundabouts
- clearways
- box junctions
- crossroads
- pedestrian crossings
- towing caravans and trailers

Speed limits

Driving too fast for the road, traffic or weather conditions causes accidents. Make sure that you keep below the speed limit shown on the signs for the road that you are on.

Now test yourself on the questions on pages 161–75

| 30mph in a built-up area | 50mph on a long, twisty country road | or as low as 20mph in a residential area with speed humps or traffic-calming measures |

The national speed limit for cars on a dual carriageway is 70mph.
This is also the maximum speed for motorway driving.

National speed limit

When you leave a built-up area you will usually see this sign.

- This sign tells you that the national speed limit for this type of road applies here
- The national speed limit for cars on a normal road (single carriageway outside a built-up area) is 60mph. So on this road you must drive below 60mph even if it is straight and empty

Street lights usually mean that a 30mph limit applies, unless there are signs showing other limits.

The right speed for the conditions

If it is raining or there is snow and ice on the road or if you are driving in a high wind you will have to drive more slowly than the maximum speed limit. This will keep you and other road users safe.

- Remember – you have to double the time you allow for stopping and braking in wet weather. Allow even more time in snow and ice
- You need to be extra careful when driving in fog

The right speed for your vehicle

Some other vehicles have lower speed limits than cars. You can find out more about speed limits from the table in *The Highway Code*.

Parking rules

There are some general rules about parking that all drivers should know:

- Whenever you can, you should use off-street car parks, or parking bays. These are marked out with white lines on the road
- Never park where your vehicle could be a danger to other road users

Look for special signs that tell you that you cannot park there at certain times of the day or that only certain people may park in that place. Examples include signs showing bus lanes, cycle lanes, residents' parking zones and roads edged with red or yellow lines.

Blue badges are given to people with disabilities. Do not park in a space reserved for a driver with a disability, even if that is the only place left to park. A driver with a disability may need to park there. You will break the law if you park in that space.

Parking at night

- If you park at night on a road that has a speed limit higher than 30mph, you must switch on your parking lights. You must switch on your parking lights even if you have parked in a lay-by on this type of road
- When parking at night, always park facing in the same direction as the traffic flow
- If your vehicle has a trailer, you must switch on parking lights, even if the road has a 30mph speed limit

Where not to park

You are not permitted to park:

- on the pavement
- at a bus stop
- in front of someone's drive
- opposite a traffic island
- near a school entrance
- on a pedestrian crossing (or inside the zigzag lines either side of it)
- near a junction
- on a clearway
- on a motorway

Now test yourself on the questions on pages 176–92

Section 11

Road and traffic signs

When you look up the chapter on ROAD AND TRAFFIC SIGNS in the theory test questions you will see that it takes up a lot of pages. This is because most of the questions have a picture of a road sign or marking. You will also see that a lot of questions ask 'What does this sign mean?'

But however differently the questions are worded, it all comes down to how well you know *The Highway Code*. You can try to learn as much of *The Highway Code* as possible, but there are other ways you can get to know the road signs.

As you walk or drive around, look at the road signs you see in the street, and the different markings painted on the road surface.

On foot

Look at the signs and signals that all road users must obey, whether they are in a car or walking. For example, when you use a pedestrian crossing, check what kind of crossing it is (such as a pelican, toucan or zebra crossing).

Check whether you know the following:

- What are the rules for pedestrians and drivers coming up to the crossing?
- What kinds of crossings are controlled by traffic lights?
- What is different about a zebra crossing?

During your driving lessons

If you are having a driving lesson look well ahead so that you see all the signs that tell you what to do next. Obey them in good time.

During your test

When you take your test the examiner will tell you when to move off, when to make a turn and when to carry out one of the set manoeuvres. The examiner will expect you to watch out for lane markings on the road, and signs giving directions, and to decide how to react to these yourself.

Signs

If you see several signs all on the same post, it can be confusing. The general rule is to start at the top and read down the post. The sign at the top tells you about the first hazard you have to look out for.

If you are a passenger in a car on a motorway, look at the motorway signs, because you need to know them, even though you can't drive on a motorway yet yourself.

Check that you can answer the following:
- What colour are the signs at the side of the motorway?
- What do the light signals above the road tell you?
- What signs tell you that you are coming to an exit?

Shapes of signs

Road and traffic signs come in three main shapes. Get to know them. You must learn what the signs mean.

Circles

Signs in circles tell you to do (blue) or not do (red) something – they give orders.

Triangles

Signs in triangles tell you of a hazard ahead – they give warnings.

Rectangles

Signs in rectangles tell you about where you are or where you are going – they give information.

There is only one sign which is octagonal – that is, it has eight sides. This is the sign for STOP. The eight-sided shape makes the sign stand out.

Now test yourself on the questions on pages 193–229

Section 12
Documents

This is quite a short section in the theory test questions. It is also different from the other sections, because it does not deal with either your driving skills or knowledge of *The Highway Code*.

It covers all the paperwork and the laws that you need to know about when you start learning to drive.

In this section there are questions about:
- driving licences
- insurance
- MOT certificate
- Vehicle Excise Duty (road tax)
- Vehicle Registration Document (log book)

This section also covers who can supervise a learner driver and changes you must tell the licensing authority about.

Driving licence

If you are learning to drive, you'll need a provisional licence.
- You must have a valid licence to drive legally
- The driving licence consists of a photocard (see example, above) – keep it with you at all times
- Your signature appears on the licence
- Take good care of your provisional licence. If you lose it by mistake, you can get another one but you will have to pay a fee, and wait for the new licence to come
- When you pass your test you can apply for a full licence

Insurance

You must have a valid insurance certificate that covers you at least for third party liability. If you are learning with a driving school, you are covered by their insurance while you are in the driving school car. When you are in your own or anybody else's car, you must have insurance. Third party insurance cover usually comes as 'Third Party, Fire and Theft'. It is a basic insurance policy that will pay for repairs to another person's car and allows you to claim on the other driver's insurance if you are in an accident that was not your fault. If you have comprehensive insurance, the policy will pay for repairs to your vehicle even when the accident was your fault.

MOT certificate

Cars and motorcycles must have their first MOT test three years (four years in Northern Ireland) after they are new and first registered. After that, they must have an MOT test every year.

The MOT test checks that your vehicle:
- is roadworthy – that is, all the parts work properly and the vehicle is safe to drive
- keeps to the legal limits for exhaust emissions – that is, the level of poisons in the gas that comes from the exhaust of your vehicle

If your vehicle is more than three years old you must not drive it without a valid MOT certificate – unless you are on your way to get an MOT and you have booked it in advance.

Vehicle Excise Duty

Vehicle Excise Duty is the tax that the government charges you to drive your vehicle on the roads. It is also sometimes called road tax.

To drive or keep a vehicle on the road you must get vehicle tax. The DVLA will send you a reminder when your tax is due to expire. When you buy a vehicle, any existing tax cannot be transferred with the vehicle.

Your vehicle must have valid insurance cover before you can tax it. If required, it will also need to have a valid MOT certificate. You can tax your vehicle online, by phone or at certain post offices.

If you want to keep a vehicle off the public road you must inform the DVLA by completing a Statutory Off Road Vehicle Notification (SORN). It is an offence not to do so. You then won't have to pay vehicle excise duty (road tax). The SORN is valid until your vehicle is taxed, sold or scrapped.

Vehicle Registration Certificate

The Vehicle Registration Certificate has all the important details about you and your vehicle, such as the make and model of the vehicle. It also has your name and address as the registered keeper of the vehicle. It is a record of the vehicle's history and is sometimes called 'the log book'.

DVLA

The Driver and Vehicle Licensing Agency is known as the DVLA. You must tell the DVLA if you are going to keep your car off road and are not renewing your vehicle excise duty (car tax), when you buy or sell a car and if you change your name or your address.

This is because your details go on to the Vehicle Registration Certificate and you are legally responsible for the vehicle (car tax, parking fines, etc) until you have notified the DVLA that it is off road or you have sold it.

Supervising a learner driver

As a learner driver you cannot drive on your own. If you are not with your driving instructor, you must be supervised by a person who is at least 21 years old, has a full licence for the kind of car you drive and has had that licence for at least three years. Note that if a person has a licence to drive an automatic car only, they cannot supervise a learner in a manual car.

Now test yourself on the questions on pages 230–37

Section 13
Incidents, accidents and emergencies

The questions in this section are about helping anyone who is hurt in a road accident. Some people think they might do more harm than good if they try to help. But if you have a basic knowledge of first aid you won't panic and if you are first on the scene at an accident, you could even save a life. Look up 'First Aid on the road' in *The Highway Code*.

The theory test questions in this section cover:
- what to do when warning lights come on in your vehicle
- what to do if you break down
- safety equipment to carry with you
- when to use hazard warning lights
- what to do – and what not to do – at the scene of an accident
- what to do in tunnels

Basic first aid
What to do at an accident scene:
- Check that you are not putting yourself in danger before you go to help somebody else. You may need to warn other drivers of the accident
- Check all vehicle engines are switched off
- Make sure no one is smoking
- Move people who are not injured to a safe place. If the accident has happened on a motorway, if possible get uninjured people away from the hard shoulder, behind the barrier or on to the bank
- Call the emergency services. You will need to tell them exactly where you are, and how many vehicles are involved in

the accident. On motorways, use the emergency phone which connects directly to the Highways Agency or the police and tells them exactly where you are
- Do not move injured people – unless there is a risk of fire or of an explosion
- Give essential first aid to injured people (see Annexe 7 of *The Highway Code*)
- Stay there until the emergency services arrive

Other ways to help:
- Do speak in a calm way to the injured person
- Do try to keep them warm and as comfortable as possible
- Do not give them anything to drink
- Do not give them a cigarette
- Don't let injured people wander into the road

Advice on safety if you break down
If you are on a non-motorway road:
- Try to get your vehicle off the main road. At least, get it right to the side of the road or on to the verge
- If the vehicle is in a place where it might be hit by another vehicle, get any passengers out and to a safer place
- Switch on the hazard warning lights to warn other drivers
- If you have a red warning triangle, place it at least 45 metres behind your car to warn other traffic (but don't use it on a motorway)
- If you are a member of a motoring organisation, call them and tell them where you are and what has happened. Wait with your vehicle until the patrol arrives

If you are on a motorway:

- If possible, leave the motorway at the next exit. If you can't get that far, drive on to the hard shoulder. Stop far over to the left, and switch on your hazard warning lights
- Get everyone out of the vehicle, using the nearside doors (but leave pets in the vehicle). Get them to sit on the bank, well away from the traffic
- Use the nearest orange emergency phone to call the emergency services and tell them where you are and what has happened (for your safety, face the oncoming traffic while you are on the phone)
- Go back to your vehicle and wait on the bank near by until help arrives
- Do not cross the motorway on foot or try to do repairs yourself – even changing a wheel. This is too dangerous on a motorway

DID YOU KNOW?

Before driving into a tunnel you should tune into a local radio station and listen to the traffic reports in case there are any accidents or problems in the tunnel.

Now test yourself on the questions on pages 238–52

Section 14
Vehicle loading

This last section, called VEHICLE LOADING, is the shortest of all. It covers a mixture of the following:
- how to load your vehicle safely
- using a roof rack
- towing caravans and trailers
- child restraints and safety locks

When you have passed your test you can tow a trailer, if the combined weight of the vehicle and trailer is less than 3,500kg. So you need to know the rules about towing.

Towing

When you get your first full driving licence, check it to see how much you are allowed to tow. Do not tow any trailer that comes to more than that weight. The weight of a trailer should be no more than 85% of the weight of the car that is to pull it. But it is best to stay well below that top weight, because towing a trailer will affect the way your vehicle handles. When you are towing, you need to allow more room when overtaking and more time to brake and stop.

When you are turning at a roundabout or junction you will need to think about where you are on the road.

When towing a heavy load, you might need to blow your tyres up to more than the normal pressures. Check your vehicle's handbook for advice. Remember to change back to the normal tyre pressures when you finish your journey.

Roof racks

If you attach a roof rack to your car, it will make a difference to the way in which your vehicle handles. Any load that is carried on a roof rack must be tied down securely.

- The roof rack makes your vehicle taller, so more vulnerable to strong winds
- You will increase your fuel consumption
- You need to change the way you drive to allow for the extra weight

To find out more, look up the parts of *The Highway Code* that deal with 'Loads and Towing'.

Loading a trailer

If the weight of the load is arranged properly, this should cut down the risk of losing control, swerving and snaking.
- Try to spread the weight evenly when you load your trailer. Do not put more weight towards the front, or the back, or to one side
- It is against the law to have a load that is sticking out in a dangerous way
- Don't forget that if you park a vehicle with a trailer overnight, it must have lights

A vehicle towing a trailer:
- must not go over a maximum speed limit of 60mph
- must not use the right (outside) lane on a motorway

If you are going to buy a trailer, make sure it fits your car's tow bar. Tow bars must keep to EU regulations, and must have electric sockets to connect to the lights on the trailer.

Snaking

'Snaking' means moving from side to side. A caravan will snake if it is not properly attached or loaded, or if the car pulling it is going too fast.

If you are towing a caravan or trailer and it starts to snake:
- slow down – stop pressing the accelerator (do not brake suddenly)
- get back in control of the steering
- then brake gently

You are responsible for passengers in your vehicle

There are also questions in the Vehicle Loading section about the safety of passengers. As the driver, you are responsible for making sure your vehicle is not overloaded – and this applies to people and animals as well as to luggage. Remember that all passengers must wear a seat belt (unless they have a medical certificate saying they should not wear one) and that all children under the age of 14 must wear a seat belt or be strapped into a child seat or other 'restraint' suitable for their age. (See the section on 'Child Restraints' in *The Highway Code*).

Children

Children must not sit in the space behind the back seat of a hatchback car, and no passengers should sit in a caravan while it is being towed.

Pets

Pets should be kept under careful control. You might keep them and you safe with a special harness, or if they are kept behind a screen in a hatchback which would stop them being thrown forward in the event of an accident.

Now test yourself on the questions on pages 253–56

Theory test revision questions

Contents | Page

Alertness	54
Attitude	61
Safety and your vehicle	71
Safety margins	89
Hazard awareness	101
Vulnerable road users	122
Other types of vehicle	141
Vehicle handling	148
Motorway rules	161
Rules of the road	176
Road and traffic signs	193
Documents	230
Incidents, accidents and emergencies	238
Vehicle loading	253

1 Mark *one* answer
What should you do before making a U-turn?

- ☐ **A** Give an arm signal as well as using your indicators
- ☐ **B** Check signs to see that U-turns are permitted
- ☐ **C** Look over your shoulder for a final check
- ☐ **D** Select a higher gear than normal

If you have to make a U-turn, slow down and ensure that the road is clear in both directions. Make sure that the road is wide enough for you to carry out the manoeuvre safely.

2 Mark *one* answer
What should you do as you approach this bridge?

- ☐ **A** Move to the right
- ☐ **B** Slow down
- ☐ **C** Change gear
- ☐ **D** Keep to 30 mph

You should slow down and be cautious. The bridge is narrow and there may not be enough room for you to pass an oncoming vehicle at this point. Also, there's no footpath, so be aware of pedestrians in the road.

3 Mark *one* answer
In which of these situations should you avoid overtaking?

- ☐ **A** Just after a bend
- ☐ **B** In a one-way street
- ☐ **C** On a 30 mph road
- ☐ **D** Approaching a dip in the road

As you begin to think about overtaking, ask yourself whether it's really necessary. If you can't see well ahead, stay back and wait for a safer place to pull out.

4 Mark *one* answer
What does this road marking mean?

- ☐ **A** Traffic should use the hard shoulder
- ☐ **B** The road bends to the left
- ☐ **C** Overtaking traffic should move back to the left
- ☐ **D** It's safe to overtake

In this picture, the road marking shows that overtaking drivers or riders need to return to the left before they reach the hatch markings ahead. The hatch markings are designed to separate opposing streams of traffic; for example, approaching some junctions or dual carriageways.

5 Mark *one* answer

Your mobile phone rings while you're travelling. What should you do?

☐ **A** Stop immediately
☐ **B** Answer it immediately
☐ **C** Ignore it
☐ **D** Pull up at the nearest kerb

It's illegal to use a hand-held mobile or similar device when driving or riding, except in a genuine emergency. The safest option is to switch off your mobile phone before you set off, and use a message service. If you've forgotten to switch your phone off and it rings, you should ignore it. When you've stopped in a safe place, you can see who called and return the call if necessary.

6 Mark *one* answer

Why are these yellow lines painted across the road?

☐ **A** To help you choose the correct lane
☐ **B** To help you keep the correct separation distance
☐ **C** To make you aware of your speed
☐ **D** To tell you the distance to the roundabout

These lines are often found on the approach to a roundabout or a dangerous junction. They give you extra warning to adjust your speed. Look well ahead and do this in good time.

7 Mark *one* answer

What should you do when you're approaching traffic lights that have been on green for some time?

☐ **A** Accelerate hard
☐ **B** Maintain your speed
☐ **C** Be ready to stop
☐ **D** Brake hard

The longer traffic lights have been on green, the sooner they'll change. Allow for this as you approach traffic lights that you know have been on green for a while. They're likely to change soon, so you should be prepared to stop.

8 Mark *one* answer

Which of the following should you do before stopping?

☐ **A** Sound the horn
☐ **B** Use the mirrors
☐ **C** Select a higher gear
☐ **D** Flash the headlights

Before pulling up, check the mirrors to see what's happening behind you. Also assess what's ahead and make sure you give the correct signal if it will help other road users.

9 Mark *one* answer
You're following a large vehicle. Why should you stay a safe distance behind it?

☐ **A** You'll be able to corner more quickly
☐ **B** You'll help the large vehicle to stop more easily
☐ **C** You'll allow the driver to see you in their mirrors
☐ **D** You'll keep out of the wind better

If you're following a large vehicle but are so close to it that you can't see its exterior mirrors, the driver won't be able to see you. Keeping well back will also allow you to see the road ahead by looking past on either side of the large vehicle.

10 Mark *one* answer
When you see a hazard ahead, you should use the mirrors. Why is this?

☐ **A** Because you'll need to accelerate out of danger
☐ **B** To assess how your actions will affect following traffic
☐ **C** Because you'll need to brake sharply to a stop
☐ **D** To check what's happening on the road ahead

You should be constantly scanning the road for clues about what's going to happen next. Check your mirrors regularly, particularly as soon as you spot a hazard. What's happening behind may affect your response to hazards ahead.

11 Mark *one* answer
You're waiting to turn right at the end of a road. Your view is obstructed by parked vehicles. What should you do?

☐ **A** Stop and then move forward slowly and carefully for a clear view
☐ **B** Move quickly to where you can see so you only block traffic from one direction
☐ **C** Wait for a pedestrian to let you know when it's safe for you to emerge
☐ **D** Turn your vehicle around immediately and find another junction to use

At junctions, your view is often restricted by buildings, trees or parked cars. You need to be able to see in order to judge a safe gap. Edge forward slowly and keep looking all the time. Don't cause other road users to change speed or direction as you emerge.

12 Mark *one* answer
What may happen if you hang objects from your interior mirror?

☐ **A** Your view could be obstructed
☐ **B** Your sun visor might get tangled
☐ **C** Your radio reception might be affected
☐ **D** Your windscreen might mist up

Ensure that you can see clearly through the windscreen of your vehicle. Stickers or hanging objects could obstruct your view or draw your attention away from the road.

13 Mark *one* answer

You're on a long motorway journey. What should you do if you start to feel sleepy?

☐ **A** Play some loud music
☐ **B** Stop on the hard shoulder for a rest
☐ **C** Drive faster to complete your journey sooner
☐ **D** Leave the motorway and stop in a safe place

If you feel sleepy, you should leave the motorway at a service area or at the next exit and stop in a safe place to rest. A supply of fresh air can help to keep you alert before you reach the exit, but it isn't a substitute for stopping and resting.

14 Mark *one* answer

Why should you switch your lights on when it first starts to get dark?

☐ **A** To make your dials easier to see
☐ **B** So others can see you more easily
☐ **C** So that you blend in with other drivers
☐ **D** Because the street lights are lit

Your headlights and tail lights help others on the road to see you. It may be necessary to turn on your lights during the day if visibility is reduced; for example, due to heavy rain. In these conditions, the light might fade before the street lights are timed to switch on. Be seen to be safe.

15 Mark *one* answer

What is most likely to distract you while you're driving?

☐ **A** Using a mobile phone
☐ **B** Using the windscreen wipers
☐ **C** Using the demisters
☐ **D** Checking the mirrors

It's easy to be distracted. Planning your journey before you set off is important. A few sensible precautions are to tune your radio to stations in your area of travel, take planned breaks, and plan your route. Except for emergencies, it's illegal to use a hand-held mobile phone while driving. Even using a hands-free kit can severely distract your attention.

16 Mark *one* answer

When may you use a hand-held mobile phone in your car?

☐ **A** When receiving a call
☐ **B** When suitably parked
☐ **C** When driving at less than 30 mph
☐ **D** When driving an automatic vehicle

It's illegal to use a hand-held mobile phone while driving, except in a genuine emergency. Even using a hands-free kit can distract your attention. Park in a safe and convenient place before receiving or making a call or using text messaging. Then you'll also be free to take notes or refer to papers.

17 Mark *one* answer

You're driving on a wet road. You have to stop your vehicle in an emergency. What should you do?

☐ **A** Apply the handbrake and footbrake together
☐ **B** Keep both hands on the steering wheel
☐ **C** Select reverse gear
☐ **D** Give an arm signal

As you drive, look well ahead and all around so that you're ready for any hazards that might develop. If you have to stop in an emergency, react as soon as you can while keeping control of the vehicle. Keep both hands on the steering wheel so you can control the vehicle's direction of travel.

18 Mark *one* answer

What should you do when moving off from behind a parked car?

☐ **A** Give a signal after moving off
☐ **B** Check both interior and exterior mirrors
☐ **C** Look around after moving off
☐ **D** Use the exterior mirrors only

Before moving off, you should use both the interior and exterior mirrors to check that the road is clear. Look around to check the blind spots and, if necessary, give a signal to warn other road users of your intentions.

19 Mark *one* answer

You're travelling along this narrow country road. How should you pass the cyclist?

☐ **A** Sound your horn as you pass
☐ **B** Keep close to them as you pass
☐ **C** Leave them plenty of room as you pass
☐ **D** Change down one gear before you pass

Allow the cyclist plenty of room in case they wobble or swerve around a pothole or raised drain. Look well ahead before you start to overtake, because you'll need to use all of the road. Look for entrances to fields where tractors or other farm machinery could be waiting to pull out.

20 Mark *one* answer

Your vehicle is fitted with a hand-held telephone. What should you do to use the phone?

☐ **A** Reduce your speed
☐ **B** Find a safe place to stop
☐ **C** Steer the vehicle with one hand
☐ **D** Be particularly careful at junctions

Never attempt to use a hand-held phone while you're driving, except in a genuine emergency. It's illegal and will take your attention away from driving, putting you at greater risk of causing a collision.

21 Mark *one* answer

You lose your way on a busy road. What is the best action to take?

☐ **A** Stop at traffic lights and ask pedestrians
☐ **B** Shout to other drivers to ask them the way
☐ **C** Turn into a side road, stop and check a map
☐ **D** Check a map, and keep going with the traffic flow

It's easy to lose your way in an unfamiliar area. If you need to check a map or ask for directions, first find a safe place to stop.

22 Mark *one* answer

When do windscreen pillars cause a serious obstruction to your view?

☐ **A** When you're driving on a motorway
☐ **B** When you're driving on a dual carriageway
☐ **C** When you're approaching a one-way street
☐ **D** When you're approaching bends and junctions

Windscreen pillars can obstruct your view, particularly at bends and junctions. Look out for other road users – especially cyclists, motorcyclists and pedestrians – as they can easily be hidden by this obstruction.

23 Mark *one* answer

You can't see clearly behind when reversing. What should you do?

☐ **A** Open the window to look behind
☐ **B** Open the door to look behind
☐ **C** Look in the nearside mirror
☐ **D** Ask someone to guide you

If you want to turn your car around, try to find a place where you have good all-round vision. If this isn't possible, and you're unable to see clearly, then get someone to guide you.

24 Mark *one* answer

What does the term 'blind spot' mean for a driver?

☐ **A** An area covered by your right-hand mirror
☐ **B** An area not covered by your headlights
☐ **C** An area covered by your left-hand mirror
☐ **D** An area not covered by your mirrors

Modern vehicles provide the driver with well-positioned mirrors which are essential to safe driving. However, they can't see every angle of the scene behind and to the sides of the vehicle. This is why it's essential that, when necessary, you look around to check those areas not visible in your mirrors.

25 Mark *one* answer
What is likely to happen if you use a hands-free phone while you're driving?

- ☐ **A** It will improve your safety
- ☐ **B** It will increase your concentration
- ☐ **C** It will reduce your view
- ☐ **D** It will divert your attention

Talking to someone while you're driving can distract you and, unlike someone in the car with you, the person on the other end of a mobile phone is unable to see the traffic situations you're dealing with. They won't stop speaking to you even if you're approaching a hazardous situation. You need to concentrate on your driving all of the time, but especially so when dealing with a hazard.

26 Mark *one* answer
You're turning right onto a dual carriageway. What should you do before emerging?

- ☐ **A** Stop, apply the handbrake and then select a low gear
- ☐ **B** Position your vehicle well to the left of the side road
- ☐ **C** Check that the central reservation is wide enough for your vehicle
- ☐ **D** Make sure that you leave enough room for a vehicle behind

Before emerging right onto a dual carriageway, make sure that the central reservation is deep enough to protect your vehicle. If it isn't, you should treat the dual carriageway as one road and check that it's clear in both directions before pulling out. Neglecting to do this could place part or all of your vehicle in the path of approaching traffic and cause a collision.

27 Mark *one* answer
You're waiting to emerge from a junction. The windscreen pillar is restricting your view. What should you be particularly aware of?

- ☐ **A** Lorries
- ☐ **B** Buses
- ☐ **C** Motorcyclists
- ☐ **D** Coaches

Windscreen pillars can completely block your view of pedestrians, motorcyclists and cyclists. You should make a particular effort to look for these road users; don't just rely on a quick glance.

28 Mark *one* answer
How should you use a satellite navigation system so that it doesn't distract you when you're driving?

- ☐ **A** Turn it off while driving in built-up areas
- ☐ **B** Choose a voice that you find calming
- ☐ **C** Only set the destination when you're lost
- ☐ **D** Stop in a safe place before programming the system

Vehicle navigation systems can be useful when driving on unfamiliar routes. However, they can also distract you and cause you to lose control if you look at or adjust them while driving. Pull up in a convenient and safe place before adjusting them.

29 Mark *one* answer
At a pelican crossing, what must you do when the amber light is flashing?

- ☐ **A** Stop and wait for the green light
- ☐ **B** Stop and wait for the red light
- ☐ **C** Give way to pedestrians waiting to cross
- ☐ **D** Give way to pedestrians already on the crossing

Pelican crossings are signal-controlled crossings operated by pedestrians. Push-button controls change the signals. Pelican crossings have no red-and-amber stage before green; instead, they have a flashing amber light. This means you must give way to pedestrians who are already on the crossing. If the crossing is clear, however, you can continue.

30 Mark *one* answer
Why should you never wave people across at pedestrian crossings?

- ☐ **A** Another vehicle may be coming
- ☐ **B** They may not be looking
- ☐ **C** It's safer for you to carry on
- ☐ **D** They may not be ready to cross

If people are waiting to use a pedestrian crossing, slow down and be prepared to stop. Don't wave them across the road, because another driver may not have seen them, may not have seen your signal, and may not be able to stop safely.

31 Mark *one* answer
What does 'tailgating' mean?

- ☐ **A** Using the rear door of a hatchback car
- ☐ **B** Reversing into a parking space
- ☐ **C** Following another vehicle too closely
- ☐ **D** Driving with rear fog lights on

'Tailgating' is the term used when a driver or rider follows the vehicle in front too closely. It's dangerous because it restricts their view of the road ahead and leaves no safety margin if the vehicle in front needs to slow down or stop suddenly. Tailgating is often the underlying cause of rear-end collisions or multiple pile-ups.

32 Mark *one* answer
Why is it unwise to follow this vehicle too closely?

- ☐ **A** Your brakes will overheat
- ☐ **B** Your view ahead will be increased
- ☐ **C** Your engine will overheat
- ☐ **D** Your view ahead will be reduced

Staying back will increase your view of the road ahead. This will help you to see any hazards that might occur and give you more time to react.

33 Mark *one* answer

What is the minimum time gap you should leave when following a vehicle on a wet road?

☐ **A** One second
☐ **B** Two seconds
☐ **C** Three seconds
☐ **D** Four seconds

Water will reduce your tyres' grip on the road. The safe separation gap of at least two seconds in dry conditions should be doubled, to at least four seconds, in wet weather.

34 Mark *one* answer

A long, heavily laden lorry is taking a long time to overtake you. What should you do?

☐ **A** Speed up
☐ **B** Slow down
☐ **C** Hold your speed
☐ **D** Change direction

A long lorry with a heavy load will need more time to pass you than a car, especially on an uphill stretch of road. Slow down and allow the lorry to pass.

35 Mark *one* answer

Which vehicle will use a blue flashing beacon?

☐ **A** Motorway maintenance
☐ **B** Bomb disposal
☐ **C** Snow plough
☐ **D** Breakdown recovery

Emergency vehicles use blue flashing lights. If you see or hear one, move out of its way as soon as it's safe and legal to do so.

36 Mark *one* answer

You're being followed by an ambulance showing flashing blue lights. What should you do?

☐ **A** Pull over as soon as it's safe to do so
☐ **B** Accelerate hard to get away from it
☐ **C** Maintain your speed and course
☐ **D** Brake harshly and stop well out into the road

Pull over in a place where the ambulance can pass safely. Check that there are no bollards or obstructions in the road that will prevent it from passing.

37 Mark *one* answer

What type of emergency vehicle is fitted with a green flashing beacon?

☐ **A** Fire engine
☐ **B** Road gritter
☐ **C** Ambulance
☐ **D** Doctor's car

A green flashing beacon on a vehicle means the driver or passenger is a doctor on an emergency call. Give way to them if it's safe to do so. Be aware that the vehicle may be travelling quickly or may stop in a hurry.

38 Mark *one* answer
Who should obey diamond-shaped traffic signs?

- ☐ **A** Tram drivers
- ☐ **B** Bus drivers
- ☐ **C** Lorry drivers
- ☐ **D** Taxi drivers

These signs apply only to tram drivers, but you should know their meaning so that you're aware of the priorities and are able to anticipate the actions of the driver.

39 Mark *one* answer
On a road where trams operate, which of these vehicles will be most at risk from the tram rails?

- ☐ **A** Cars
- ☐ **B** Cycles
- ☐ **C** Buses
- ☐ **D** Lorries

The narrow wheels of a bicycle can become stuck in the tram rails, causing the cyclist to stop suddenly, wobble or even lose balance altogether. The tram lines are also slippery, which could cause a cyclist to slide or fall off.

40 Mark *one* answer
What should you use your horn for?

- ☐ **A** To alert others to your presence
- ☐ **B** To allow you right of way
- ☐ **C** To greet other road users
- ☐ **D** To signal your annoyance

Your horn mustn't be used between 11.30 pm and 7 am in a built-up area or when you're stationary, unless a moving vehicle poses a danger. Its function is to alert other road users to your presence.

41 Mark *one* answer
You're in a one-way street and want to turn right. There are two lanes. Where should you position your vehicle?

- ☐ **A** In the right-hand lane
- ☐ **B** In the left-hand lane
- ☐ **C** In either lane, depending on the traffic
- ☐ **D** Just left of the centre line

When you're in a one-way street and want to turn right, you should take up a position in the right-hand lane. This will allow other road users not wishing to turn to pass on the left. Indicate your intention and take up the correct position in good time.

42 Mark *one* answer

You wish to turn right ahead. Why should you take up the correct position in good time?

☐ **A** To allow other drivers to pull out in front of you
☐ **B** To give a better view into the road that you're joining
☐ **C** To help other road users know what you intend to do
☐ **D** To allow drivers to pass you on the right

If you wish to turn right into a side road, take up your position in good time. Move to the centre of the road when it's safe to do so. This will allow vehicles to pass you on the left. Early planning will show other traffic what you intend to do.

43 Mark *one* answer

At which type of crossing are cyclists allowed to ride across with pedestrians?

☐ **A** Toucan
☐ **B** Puffin
☐ **C** Pelican
☐ **D** Zebra

A toucan crossing is designed to allow pedestrians and cyclists to cross at the same time. Look out for cyclists approaching the crossing at speed.

44 Mark *one* answer

You're driving at the legal speed limit. A vehicle comes up quickly behind you, flashing its headlights. What should you do?

☐ **A** Accelerate to make a gap behind you
☐ **B** Touch the brakes sharply to show your brake lights
☐ **C** Maintain your speed to prevent the vehicle from overtaking
☐ **D** Allow the vehicle to overtake

Don't enforce the speed limit by blocking another vehicle's progress. This will only lead to the other driver becoming more frustrated. Allow the other vehicle to pass when you can do so safely.

45 Mark *one* answer

When should you flash your headlights at other road users?

☐ **A** When showing that you're giving way
☐ **B** When showing that you're about to turn
☐ **C** When telling them that you have right of way
☐ **D** When letting them know that you're there

You should only flash your headlights to warn others of your presence. Don't use them to greet others, show impatience or give priority to other road users, because they could misunderstand your signal.

46 Mark *one* answer

You're approaching an unmarked crossroads. How should you deal with this type of junction?

- ☐ **A** Accelerate and keep to the middle
- ☐ **B** Slow down and keep to the right
- ☐ **C** Accelerate and look to the left
- ☐ **D** Slow down and look both ways

Be cautious, especially when your view is restricted by hedges, bushes, walls, large vehicles, etc. In the summer months, these junctions can become more difficult to deal with, because growing foliage may further obscure your view.

47 Mark *one* answer

The conditions are good and dry. When should you use the 'two-second rule'?

- ☐ **A** Before restarting the engine after it has stalled
- ☐ **B** When checking your gap from the vehicle in front
- ☐ **C** Before using the 'Mirrors – Signal – Manoeuvre' routine
- ☐ **D** When traffic lights change to green

In good conditions, the 'two-second rule' can be used to check the distance between your vehicle and the one in front. This technique works on roads carrying faster traffic. Choose a fixed object, such as a bridge, sign or tree. When the vehicle ahead passes this object, say to yourself 'Only a fool breaks the two-second rule.' If you reach the object before you finish saying this, you're too close.

48 Mark *one* answer

At a puffin crossing, which colour follows the green signal?

- ☐ **A** Steady red
- ☐ **B** Flashing amber
- ☐ **C** Steady amber
- ☐ **D** Flashing green

Puffin crossings have infra-red sensors that detect when pedestrians are crossing and hold the red traffic signal until the crossing is clear. The use of a sensor means there's no flashing amber phase as there is with a pelican crossing.

49 Mark *one* answer

You're in a line of traffic. The driver behind you is following very closely. What action should you take?

- ☐ **A** Ignore the following driver and continue to travel within the speed limit
- ☐ **B** Slow down, gradually increasing the gap between you and the vehicle in front
- ☐ **C** Signal left and wave the following driver past
- ☐ **D** Move over to a position just left of the centre line of the road

If the driver behind is following too closely, there's a danger they'll collide with the back of your car if you stop suddenly. You can reduce this risk by slowing down and increasing the safety margin in front of you. This reduces the chance that you'll have to stop suddenly and allows you to spread your braking over a greater distance. This is an example of defensive driving.

50 Mark *one* answer

You're driving on a clear night. There's a steady stream of oncoming traffic. The national speed limit applies. Which lights should you use?

☐ **A** Full-beam headlights
☐ **B** Sidelights
☐ **C** Dipped headlights
☐ **D** Fog lights

Use the full-beam headlights only when you can be sure that you won't dazzle other road users.

51 Mark *one* answer

You're driving behind a large goods vehicle. What should you do if it signals left but steers to the right?

☐ **A** Slow down and let the vehicle turn
☐ **B** Drive on, keeping to the left
☐ **C** Overtake on the right of it
☐ **D** Hold your speed and sound your horn

Large, long vehicles need extra room when making turns at junctions. They may move out to the right in order to make a left turn. Keep well back and don't attempt to pass them on their left.

52 Mark *one* answer

You're driving along this road. The red van cuts in close in front of you. What should you do?

☐ **A** Accelerate to get closer to the red van
☐ **B** Give a long blast on the horn
☐ **C** Drop back to leave the correct separation distance
☐ **D** Flash your headlights several times

There are times when other drivers make incorrect or ill-judged decisions. Be tolerant and try not to retaliate or react aggressively. Always consider the safety of other road users, your passengers and yourself.

53 Mark *one* answer

You're waiting in a traffic queue at night. How can you avoid dazzling drivers behind you?

☐ **A** Use the parking brake only
☐ **B** Use the footbrake only
☐ **C** Use the clutch with the accelerator
☐ **D** Use the parking brake with the footbrake

In queuing traffic, your brake lights can dazzle drivers behind you. If you apply your parking brake, you can take your foot off the footbrake. This will deactivate the brake lights.

54 Mark *one* answer

You're driving in traffic at the speed limit for the road. What should you do if the driver behind is trying to overtake?

☐ **A** Move closer to the car ahead, so the driver behind has no room to overtake
☐ **B** Wave the driver behind to overtake when it's safe
☐ **C** Keep a steady course and allow the driver behind to overtake
☐ **D** Accelerate to get away from the driver behind

Keep a steady course to give the driver behind an opportunity to overtake safely. If necessary, slow down. Reacting incorrectly to another driver's impatience can lead to danger.

55 Mark *one* answer

There's a bus lane on your left. The signs show no times of operation. What does this mean?

☐ **A** The lane isn't in operation
☐ **B** The lane is only in operation at peak times
☐ **C** The lane is in operation 24 hours a day
☐ **D** The lane is only in operation in daylight hours

Bus-lane signs show the vehicles allowed to use the lane and also its times of operation. Where no times are shown, the bus lane is in operation 24 hours a day.

56 Mark *one* answer

What should you do when a person herding sheep asks you to stop?

☐ **A** Ignore them as they have no authority
☐ **B** Stop and switch off your engine
☐ **C** Continue on but drive slowly
☐ **D** Try to get past quickly

If someone in charge of animals asks you to stop, you should do so and switch off your engine. Animals are unpredictable and startle easily; they could turn and run into your path or into the path of another moving vehicle.

57 Mark *one* answer

What should you do when you're overtaking a horse and rider?

☐ **A** Sound your horn as a warning
☐ **B** Go past as quickly as possible
☐ **C** Flash your headlights as a warning
☐ **D** Go past slowly and carefully

Horses can be startled by the sound of a car engine or the rush of air caused by a vehicle passing too closely. Keep well back and only pass when it's safe. Leave them plenty of room; you may have to use the other side of the road to go past safely.

58 Mark *one* answer

You're approaching a zebra crossing. Pedestrians are waiting to cross. What should you do?

☐ **A** Give way to the elderly and infirm only
☐ **B** Slow down and prepare to stop
☐ **C** Use your headlights to indicate they can cross
☐ **D** Wave at them to cross the road

As you approach a zebra crossing, look for pedestrians waiting to cross. Where you can see them, slow down and prepare to stop. Be especially careful of children and older people, who may have difficulty judging when it's safe to cross.

59 Mark *one* answer

A vehicle pulls out in front of you at a junction. What should you do?

☐ **A** Swerve past it and sound your horn
☐ **B** Flash your headlights and drive up close behind
☐ **C** Slow down and be ready to stop
☐ **D** Accelerate past it immediately

Try to be ready for the unexpected. Plan ahead and learn to anticipate hazards. You'll then give yourself more time to react to any problems that might occur. Be tolerant of other road users who don't behave correctly.

60 Mark *one* answer

You're approaching a red light at a puffin crossing. Pedestrians are on the crossing. When will the red light change?

☐ **A** When you start to edge forward onto the crossing
☐ **B** When the pedestrians have cleared the crossing
☐ **C** When the pedestrians push the button on the far side of the crossing
☐ **D** When a driver from the opposite direction reaches the crossing

A sensor will automatically detect that the pedestrians have reached a safe position. Don't drive on until the green light shows and it's safe for you to do so.

61 Mark *one* answer

Which instrument-panel warning light would show that headlights are on full beam?

☐ **A**   ☐ **B**

☐ **C**   ☐ **D**

You should be aware of all the warning lights and visual aids on the vehicle you're driving. If you're driving a vehicle for the first time, you should familiarise yourself with all the controls, warning lights and visual aids before you set off.

62 Mark *one* answer

In which conditions should you leave at least a two-second gap between your vehicle and the one in front?

☐ **A** wet   ☐ **B** good
☐ **C** damp   ☐ **D** foggy

In good, dry conditions, a driver needs to keep a distance of at least two seconds from the car in front. This should allow enough space for you to stop if the driver in front has to stop suddenly.

63 Mark *one* answer

You're driving at night on an unlit road, following another vehicle. What should you do?

☐ **A** Flash your headlights
☐ **B** Use dipped headlights
☐ **C** Switch off your headlights
☐ **D** Use full-beam headlights

If you follow another vehicle with your headlights on full beam, they could dazzle the driver. Leave a safe distance and make sure that the light from your dipped beam falls short of the vehicle in front.

64 Mark *one* answer

You're driving a slow-moving vehicle on a narrow, winding road. What should you do?

☐ **A** Keep well out to stop vehicles overtaking dangerously
☐ **B** Wave following vehicles past you if you think they can overtake quickly
☐ **C** Pull in when you can, to let following vehicles overtake
☐ **D** Give a left signal when it's safe for vehicles to overtake you

If you're driving a slow-moving vehicle along a narrow road, try not to hold up faster traffic. If you see vehicles following behind, pull over in a safe place and let the traffic pass before continuing. Don't wave other traffic past – this could be dangerous if you or they haven't seen any hazard that's hidden from view.

65 Mark *one* answer

What can a loose filler cap on your diesel fuel tank cause?

☐ **A** It can make the engine difficult to start
☐ **B** It can make the roads slippery for other road users
☐ **C** It can improve your vehicle's fuel consumption
☐ **D** It can increase the level of exhaust emissions

Diesel fuel can spill out if your filler cap isn't secured properly. This is most likely to occur on bends, junctions and roundabouts, where it will make the road slippery, especially if it's wet. At the end of a dry spell of weather, the road surfaces may have a high level of diesel spillage that hasn't been washed away by rain.

66 Mark *one* answer
After refuelling your vehicle, what should you do to avoid spillage?

☐ **A** Check that your tank is only three-quarters full
☐ **B** Check that you've used a locking filler cap
☐ **C** Check that your fuel gauge is working
☐ **D** Check that your filler cap is securely fastened

When learning to drive, it's a good idea to practise filling your car with fuel. Ask your instructor if you can use a petrol station and fill the fuel tank yourself. You need to know where the filler cap is on the car you're driving, so you know which side of the pump to park at. Take care not to overfill the tank and make sure you secure the filler cap correctly, so that no fuel leaks onto the road while you're driving.

67 Mark *one* answer
What style of driving causes increased risk to everyone?

☐ **A** Considerate
☐ **B** Defensive
☐ **C** Competitive
☐ **D** Responsible

Competitive driving increases the risks to everyone and is the opposite of responsible, considerate and defensive driving. Defensive driving is about questioning the actions of other road users and being prepared for the unexpected. Don't be taken by surprise.

68 Mark *one* answer
What is badly affected if the tyres are under-inflated?

☐ **A** Braking
☐ **B** Indicating
☐ **C** Changing gear
☐ **D** Parking

Your tyres are your only contact with the road. To prevent problems with braking and steering, keep your tyres free from defects; they must have sufficient tread depth and be correctly inflated. Correct tyre pressures help reduce the risk of skidding and provide a safer and more comfortable drive or ride.

69 Mark *one* answer
When mustn't you sound your vehicle's horn?

☐ **A** Between 10.00 pm and 6.00 am in a built-up area
☐ **B** At any time in a built-up area
☐ **C** Between 11.30 pm and 7.00 am in a built-up area
☐ **D** Between 11.30 pm and 6.00 am on any road

Every effort must be made to prevent excessive noise, especially in built-up areas at night. Don't rev your engine or sound the horn unnecessarily. It's illegal to sound your horn in a built-up area between 11.30 pm and 7.00 am, except when another road user poses a danger.

70 Mark *one* answer
What makes the vehicle in the picture 'environmentally friendly'?

☐ **A** It's powered by gravity
☐ **B** It's powered by diesel
☐ **C** It's powered by electricity
☐ **D** It's powered by unleaded petrol

Trams are powered by electricity and therefore don't emit exhaust fumes. They ease traffic congestion by offering drivers an alternative to using their car, particularly in busy cities and towns.

71 Mark *one* answer
Why have 'red routes' been introduced in major cities?

☐ **A** To raise the speed limits
☐ **B** To help the traffic flow
☐ **C** To provide better parking
☐ **D** To allow lorries to load more freely

Inconsiderate parking can obstruct the flow of traffic and so make traffic congestion worse. Red routes are designed to prevent this by enforcing strict parking restrictions. Driving slowly in traffic increases fuel consumption and causes a build-up of exhaust fumes.

72 Mark *one* answer
What is the purpose of road humps, chicanes and narrowings?

☐ **A** To separate lanes of traffic
☐ **B** To increase traffic speed
☐ **C** To allow pedestrians to cross
☐ **D** To reduce traffic speed

Traffic-calming measures help to keep vehicle speeds low in congested areas where there are pedestrians and children. A pedestrian is much more likely to survive a collision with a vehicle travelling at 20 mph than they are with a vehicle travelling at 40 mph.

73 Mark *one* answer
What is the purpose of a catalytic converter?

☐ **A** To reduce fuel consumption
☐ **B** To reduce the risk of fire
☐ **C** To reduce harmful exhaust gases
☐ **D** To reduce engine wear

Catalytic converters reduce a large percentage of harmful exhaust emissions. They work more efficiently when the engine has reached its normal working temperature

74 Mark *one* answer
It's essential that tyre pressures are checked regularly. When should this be done?

☐ **A** After any lengthy journey
☐ **B** After travelling at high speed
☐ **C** When tyres are hot
☐ **D** When tyres are cold

Check the tyre pressures when the tyres are cold. This will give you a more accurate reading. The heat generated on a long journey will raise the pressure inside the tyre.

75 Mark *one* answer
When will your vehicle use more fuel?

☐ **A** When its tyres are under-inflated
☐ **B** When its tyres are of different makes
☐ **C** When its tyres are over-inflated
☐ **D** When its tyres are new

Check your tyre pressures frequently – normally once a week. If they're lower than those recommended by the manufacturer, there will be more 'rolling resistance'. The engine will have to work harder to overcome this, leading to increased fuel consumption.

76 Mark *one* answer
How should you dispose of a used vehicle battery?

☐ **A** Bury it in your garden
☐ **B** Put it in the dustbin
☐ **C** Take it to a local-authority site
☐ **D** Leave it on waste land

Batteries contain acid, which is hazardous, and they must be disposed of safely. This means taking them to an appropriate disposal site.

77 Mark *one* answer
What is most likely to cause high fuel consumption?

☐ **A** Poor steering control
☐ **B** Accelerating around bends
☐ **C** Staying in high gears
☐ **D** Harsh braking and accelerating

Accelerating and braking gently and smoothly will help to save fuel and reduce wear on your vehicle. This makes it better for the environment too.

78 Mark *one* answer
The fluid level in your battery is low. What should you top it up with?

☐ **A** Battery acid
☐ **B** Distilled water
☐ **C** Engine oil
☐ **D** Engine coolant

Some modern batteries are maintenance-free. Check your vehicle handbook and, if necessary, make sure that the plates in each battery cell are covered with fluid.

79 Mark *one* answer
You're parked on the road at night. Where must you use parking lights?

☐ **A** Where there are continuous white lines in the middle of the road
☐ **B** Where the speed limit exceeds 30 mph
☐ **C** Where you're facing oncoming traffic
☐ **D** Where you're near a bus stop

When parking at night, park in the direction of the traffic. This will enable other road users to see the reflectors on the rear of your vehicle. Use your parking lights if the speed limit is over 30 mph.

80 Mark *one* answer
How can you reduce the environmental harm caused by your motor vehicle?

☐ **A** Only use it for short journeys
☐ **B** Don't service it
☐ **C** Drive faster than normal
☐ **D** Keep engine revs low

Engines that burn fossil fuels produce exhaust emissions that are harmful to health. The harder you make the engine work, the more emissions it will produce. Engines also use more fuel and produce higher levels of emissions when they're cold. Anything you can do to reduce your use of fossil fuels will help the environment.

81 Mark *one* answer
What can cause excessive or uneven tyre wear?

☐ **A** A faulty gearbox
☐ **B** A faulty braking system
☐ **C** A faulty electrical system
☐ **D** A faulty exhaust system

If you see that parts of the tread on your tyres are wearing before others, it may indicate a brake, steering or suspension fault. Regular servicing will help to detect faults at an early stage and this will avoid the risk of minor faults becoming serious or even dangerous.

82 Mark *one* answer
You need to top up your battery. What level should you fill it to?

☐ **A** The top of the battery
☐ **B** Halfway up the battery
☐ **C** Just below the cell plates
☐ **D** Just above the cell plates

Top up the battery with distilled water and make sure each cell plate is covered.

83 Mark *one* answer
Before starting a journey, it's wise to plan your route. How can you do this?

☐ **A** Look at a map
☐ **B** Contact your local garage
☐ **C** Look in your vehicle handbook
☐ **D** Check your vehicle registration document

Planning your journey before you set out can help to make it much easier and more pleasant, and may help to ease traffic congestion. Look at a map to help you do this. You may need maps of different scales, depending on where and how far you're going. Printing or writing out the route can also help.

84 Mark *one* answer
Why is it a good idea to plan your journey to avoid busy times?

☐ **A** You'll have an easier journey
☐ **B** You'll have a more stressful journey
☐ **C** Your journey time will be longer
☐ **D** It will cause more traffic congestion

No-one likes to spend time in traffic queues. Try to avoid busy times related to school or work travel.

85 Mark *one* answer
You avoid busy times when travelling. How will this affect your journey?

☐ **A** You're more likely to be held up
☐ **B** Your journey time will be longer
☐ **C** You'll travel a much shorter distance
☐ **D** You're less likely to be delayed

If possible, avoid the early morning, late afternoon and early evening 'rush hour'. Doing this should allow you to travel in a more relaxed frame of mind, concentrate solely on what you're doing and arrive at your destination feeling less stressed.

86 Mark *one* answer
It can be helpful to plan your route before starting a journey. Why should you also plan an alternative route?

☐ **A** Your original route may be blocked
☐ **B** Your maps may have different scales
☐ **C** You may find you have to pay a congestion charge
☐ **D** You may get held up by a tractor

It can be frustrating and worrying to find your planned route is blocked by roadworks or diversions. If you've planned an alternative, you'll feel less stressed and more able to concentrate fully on your driving or riding. If your original route is mostly on motorways, it's a good idea to plan an alternative using non-motorway roads. Always carry a map with you just in case you need to refer to it.

87   Mark *one* answer

You're making an appointment and will have to travel a long distance. How should you plan for the journey?

- ☐ **A** Allow plenty of time for the trip
- ☐ **B** Plan to travel at busy times
- ☐ **C** Avoid roads with the national speed limit
- ☐ **D** Prevent other drivers from overtaking

Always allow plenty of time for your journey in case of unforeseen problems. Anything can happen; for example, punctures, breakdowns, road closures, diversions and delays. You'll feel less stressed and less inclined to take risks if you aren't 'pushed for time'.

88   Mark *one* answer

What can rapid acceleration and heavy braking lead to?

- ☐ **A** Reduced pollution
- ☐ **B** Increased fuel consumption
- ☐ **C** Reduced exhaust emissions
- ☐ **D** Increased road safety

Using the controls smoothly can reduce fuel consumption by about 15%, as well as reducing wear and tear on your vehicle. Plan ahead and anticipate changes of speed well in advance. This will reduce the need to accelerate rapidly or brake sharply.

89   Mark *one* answer

Which of these, if allowed to get low, could cause you to crash?

- ☐ **A** Anti-freeze level
- ☐ **B** Brake fluid level
- ☐ **C** Battery water level
- ☐ **D** Radiator coolant level

You should carry out frequent checks on all fluid levels but particularly brake fluid. As the brake pads or shoes wear down, the brake fluid level will drop. If it drops below the minimum mark on the fluid reservoir, air could enter the hydraulic system and lead to a loss of braking efficiency or even complete brake failure.

90   Mark *one* answer

What can cause excessive or uneven tyre wear?

- ☐ **A** Faults in the gearbox
- ☐ **B** Faults in the engine
- ☐ **C** Faults in the suspension
- ☐ **D** Faults in the exhaust system

Uneven wear on your tyres can be caused by the condition of your vehicle. Having the vehicle serviced regularly will ensure that the brakes, steering, suspension and wheel alignment are maintained in good order.

91 Mark *one* answer
What is the main cause of brake fade?

- ☐ **A** The brakes overheating
- ☐ **B** Air in the brake fluid
- ☐ **C** Oil on the brakes
- ☐ **D** The brakes out of adjustment

Brakes can overheat and lose efficiency when they're used continually, such as on a long, steep, downhill stretch of road. Using a lower gear when you drive downhill can help prevent the vehicle from gaining speed.

92 Mark *one* answer
What should you do if your anti-lock brakes (ABS) warning light stays on?

- ☐ **A** Check the brake-fluid level
- ☐ **B** Check the footbrake free play
- ☐ **C** Check that the handbrake is released
- ☐ **D** Have the brakes checked immediately

Consult the vehicle handbook or a garage before driving the vehicle any further. Only drive to a garage if it's safe to do so. If you aren't sure, get expert help.

93 Mark *one* answer
What does it mean if this light comes on while you're driving?

- ☐ **A** A fault in the braking system
- ☐ **B** The engine oil is low
- ☐ **C** A rear light has failed
- ☐ **D** Your seat belt isn't fastened

If this light comes on, you should have the brake system checked immediately. A faulty braking system could have dangerous consequences.

94 Mark *one* answer
It's important to wear suitable shoes when you're driving. Why is this?

- ☐ **A** To prevent wear on the pedals
- ☐ **B** To maintain control of the pedals
- ☐ **C** To enable you to adjust your seat
- ☐ **D** To enable you to walk for assistance if you break down

When you're going to drive, make sure that you're wearing suitable clothing. Comfortable shoes will ensure that you have proper control of the foot pedals.

95 Mark *one* answer

What will reduce the risk of neck injury resulting from a collision?

☐ **A** An air-sprung seat
☐ **B** Anti-lock brakes
☐ **C** A collapsible steering wheel
☐ **D** A properly adjusted head restraint

If you're involved in a collision, head restraints will reduce the risk of neck injury. They must be properly adjusted. Make sure they aren't positioned too low: in a crash, this could cause damage to the neck.

96 Mark *one* answer

You're testing your suspension. You notice that your vehicle keeps bouncing when you press down on the front wing. What does this mean?

☐ **A** Worn tyres
☐ **B** Tyres under-inflated
☐ **C** Steering wheel not located centrally
☐ **D** Worn shock absorbers

If you find that your vehicle bounces as you drive around a corner or bend in the road, the shock absorbers might be worn. Press down on the front wing and, if the vehicle continues to bounce, take it to be checked by a qualified mechanic.

97 Mark *one* answer

How will a roof rack affect your car's performance?

☐ **A** There will be less wind noise
☐ **B** The engine will use more oil
☐ **C** The car will accelerate faster
☐ **D** Fuel consumption will increase

A roof rack increases your car's wind resistance. This will cause an increase in fuel consumption, so you should remove it when it isn't being used. An aerodynamically designed roof rack or box will help reduce wind resistance to a minimum, but the rack or box should still be removed when it isn't in use.

98 Mark *one* answer

Which of these makes your tyres illegal?

☐ **A** They were bought second-hand
☐ **B** They have a large, deep cut in the side wall
☐ **C** They're of different makes
☐ **D** They have different tread patterns

Your tyres may be of different treads and makes. They can even be second-hand, as long as they're in good condition. They must, however, be intact, without cuts or tears. When checking the side walls for cuts and bulges, don't forget to check the side of the tyre that's hidden from view, under the car.

99 Mark *one* answer

What is the legal minimum depth of tread for car tyres?

- ☐ **A** 1 mm
- ☐ **B** 1.6 mm
- ☐ **C** 2.5 mm
- ☐ **D** 4 mm

Car tyres must have sufficient depth of tread to give them a good grip on the road surface. The legal minimum for cars is 1.6 mm. This depth should be across the central three-quarters of the breadth of the tyre and around the entire circumference.

100 Mark *one* answer

You're carrying two 13-year-old children and their parents in your car. Who's responsible for seeing that the children wear seat belts?

- ☐ **A** The children's parents
- ☐ **B** You, the driver
- ☐ **C** The front-seat passenger
- ☐ **D** The children

Seat belts save lives and reduce the risk of injury. If you're carrying passengers under 14 years old, it's your responsibility as the driver to ensure that their seat belts are fastened or they're seated in an approved child restraint.

101 Mark *one* answer

How can drivers help the environment?

- ☐ **A** By accelerating harshly
- ☐ **B** By accelerating gently
- ☐ **C** By using leaded fuel
- ☐ **D** By driving faster

Rapid acceleration and heavy braking lead to increased:
- fuel consumption
- wear on your vehicle

Having your vehicle serviced regularly will maintain its efficiency, produce cleaner emissions and reduce the risk of a breakdown.

102 Mark *one* answer

How can you avoid wasting fuel?

- ☐ **A** By having your vehicle serviced regularly
- ☐ **B** By revving the engine in the lower gears
- ☐ **C** By keeping an empty roof rack on your vehicle
- ☐ **D** By driving at higher speeds where possible

If you don't have your vehicle serviced regularly, the engine will gradually become less efficient. This will cause increased fuel consumption and, in turn, an increase in the amount of harmful emissions it produces.

103 Mark *one* answer

What could you do to reduce the volume of traffic on the roads?

☐ **A** Drive in a bus lane
☐ **B** Use a car with a smaller engine
☐ **C** Walk or cycle on short journeys
☐ **D** Travel by car at all times

Try not to use your car as a matter of routine. For shorter journeys, consider walking or cycling instead – this is much better for both you and the environment.

104 Mark *one* answer

What is most likely to waste fuel?

☐ **A** Reducing your speed
☐ **B** Driving on motorways
☐ **C** Using different brands of fuel
☐ **D** Under-inflated tyres

Wasting fuel costs you money and also causes unnecessary pollution. Ensuring your tyres are correctly inflated, avoiding carrying unnecessary weight and removing a roof rack that's not in use will all help to reduce your fuel consumption.

105 Mark *one* answer

What does the law require you to keep in good condition?

☐ **A** Gears
☐ **B** Transmission
☐ **C** Door locks
☐ **D** Seat belts

Unless exempt, you and your passengers must wear a seat belt (or suitable child restraint). The seat belts in your car must be in good condition and working properly; they'll be checked during its MOT test.

106 Mark *one* answer

Up to how much more fuel will you use by driving at 70 mph, compared with driving at 50 mph?

☐ **A** 10%
☐ **B** 30%
☐ **C** 75%
☐ **D** 100%

Your vehicle will use less fuel if you avoid heavy acceleration. The higher the engine revs, the more fuel you'll use. Using the same gear, and covering the same distance, a vehicle travelling at 70 mph will use up to 30% more fuel than it would at 50 mph. However, don't travel so slowly that you inconvenience or endanger other road users.

107 Mark *one* answer

When you use the brakes, your vehicle pulls to one side. What should you do?

☐ **A** Increase the pressure in your tyres
☐ **B** Have the brakes checked as soon as possible
☐ **C** Change gear and pump the brake pedal
☐ **D** Use your parking brake at the same time

The brakes on your vehicle must be effective and properly adjusted. If your vehicle pulls to one side when braking, take it to be checked by a qualified mechanic as soon as you can.

108 Mark *one* answer
What will happen if your car's wheels are unbalanced?

- ☐ **A** The steering will pull to one side
- ☐ **B** The steering will vibrate
- ☐ **C** The brakes will fail
- ☐ **D** The tyres will deflate

If your wheels are out of balance, it will cause the steering to vibrate at certain speeds. This isn't a fault that will put itself right, so take your vehicle to a garage or tyre fitter to have the wheels rebalanced.

109 Mark *one* answer
Turning the steering wheel while stationary can cause damage to which part of your car?

- ☐ **A** Gearbox
- ☐ **B** Engine
- ☐ **C** Brakes
- ☐ **D** Tyres

Turning the steering wheel when the car isn't moving is known as dry steering. It can cause unnecessary wear to the tyres and steering mechanism.

110 Mark *one* answer
You have to leave valuables in your car. What would it be safest to do?

- ☐ **A** Put them in a carrier bag
- ☐ **B** Park near a school entrance
- ☐ **C** Lock them out of sight
- ☐ **D** Park near a bus stop

If you have to leave valuables in your car, lock them out of sight. This is the best way to deter an opportunist thief.

111 Mark *one* answer
Which of the following may help to deter a thief from stealing your car?

- ☐ **A** Always keeping the headlights on
- ☐ **B** Fitting reflective glass windows
- ☐ **C** Always keeping the interior light on
- ☐ **D** Etching the registration number on the windows

Having your car registration number etched on all your windows is a cheap and effective way to deter professional car thieves.

112 Mark *one* answer
Which of the following shouldn't be kept in your vehicle?

- ☐ **A** The car dealer's details
- ☐ **B** The owner's manual
- ☐ **C** The service record
- ☐ **D** The vehicle registration document

Never leave the vehicle registration document inside your car. This document would help a thief to dispose of your car more easily.

113 Mark *one* answer
What should you do when leaving your vehicle parked and unattended?

- ☐ **A** Park near a busy junction
- ☐ **B** Park in a housing estate
- ☐ **C** Lock it and remove the key
- ☐ **D** Leave the left indicator on

An unlocked car is an open invitation to thieves. Leaving the keys in the ignition not only makes your car easy to steal but could also invalidate your insurance.

114 Mark *one* answer
What will improve fuel consumption?

☐ **A** Reducing your speed
☐ **B** Rapid acceleration
☐ **C** Late and harsh braking
☐ **D** Driving in lower gears

Harsh braking, frequent gear changes and harsh acceleration increase fuel consumption. An engine uses less fuel when travelling at a constant low speed. You need to look well ahead so you're able to anticipate hazards early. Easing off the accelerator and timing your approach at junctions, for example, can reduce the fuel consumption of your vehicle.

115 Mark *one* answer
You service your own vehicle. How should you get rid of the old engine oil?

☐ **A** Take it to a local-authority site
☐ **B** Pour it down a drain
☐ **C** Tip it into a hole in the ground
☐ **D** Put it in your dustbin

It's illegal to pour engine oil down any drain. Oil is a pollutant and harmful to wildlife. Dispose of it safely at an authorised site.

116 Mark *one* answer
Why do MOT tests include a strict exhaust emission test?

☐ **A** To recover the cost of expensive garage equipment
☐ **B** To help protect the environment against pollution
☐ **C** To discover which fuel supplier is used the most
☐ **D** To make sure diesel and petrol engines emit the same fumes

Emission tests are carried out to make sure your vehicle's engine is operating efficiently. This ensures the pollution produced by the engine is kept to a minimum. If your vehicle isn't serviced regularly, it may fail the annual MOT test.

117 Mark *one* answer
How can you reduce the damage your vehicle causes to the environment?

☐ **A** Use narrow side streets
☐ **B** Brake heavily
☐ **C** Use busy routes
☐ **D** Anticipate well ahead

By looking well ahead and recognising hazards in good time, you can avoid late and heavy braking. Watch the traffic flow and look well ahead for potential hazards so you can control your speed in good time. Avoid over-revving the engine and accelerating harshly, as this increases wear to the engine and uses more fuel.

118 Mark *one* answer

What will be the result of having your vehicle properly serviced?

- ☐ **A** Reduced insurance premiums
- ☐ **B** Lower vehicle excise duty (road tax)
- ☐ **C** Better fuel economy
- ☐ **D** Slower journey times

All vehicles need to be serviced to keep working efficiently. An efficient engine uses less fuel and produces fewer harmful emissions than an engine that's running inefficiently. Keeping the vehicle serviced to the manufacturer's schedule should also make it more reliable and reduce the chance of it breaking down.

119 Mark *one* answer

You enter a road where there are road humps. What should you do?

- ☐ **A** Maintain a reduced speed throughout
- ☐ **B** Accelerate quickly between each one
- ☐ **C** Always keep to the maximum legal speed
- ☐ **D** Drive slowly at school times only

The humps are there for a reason – to protect vulnerable road users by reducing the speed of traffic. Don't accelerate harshly between the humps. Put the safety of others first and maintain a reduced speed throughout the zone.

120 Mark *one* answer

When should you especially check the engine oil level?

- ☐ **A** Before a long journey
- ☐ **B** When the engine is hot
- ☐ **C** Early in the morning
- ☐ **D** Every 6000 miles

An engine can use more oil during long journeys than on shorter trips. Insufficient engine oil is potentially dangerous: it can lead to excessive wear, mechanical breakdown and expensive repairs. Most cars have a dipstick to allow the oil level to be checked. If not, you should refer to the vehicle handbook.

121 Mark *one* answer

You're having difficulty finding a parking space in a busy town. You can see there's space on the zigzag lines of a zebra crossing. Can you park there?

- ☐ **A** No, not unless you stay with your car
- ☐ **B** Yes, in order to drop off a passenger
- ☐ **C** Yes, if you don't block people from crossing
- ☐ **D** No, not under any circumstances

It's an offence to park on the zigzag lines of a zebra crossing. You'll be causing an obstruction by obscuring the view of both pedestrians and drivers.

122 Mark *one* answer

What should you do when you leave your car unattended for a few minutes?

- ☐ **A** Leave the engine running
- ☐ **B** Switch the engine off but leave the key in
- ☐ **C** Lock it and remove the key
- ☐ **D** Park near a traffic warden

Always switch off the engine, remove the key and lock your car, even if you're only leaving it for a few minutes.

123 Mark *one* answer

When leaving your vehicle, where should you try to park?

- ☐ **A** Opposite a traffic island
- ☐ **B** In a secure car park
- ☐ **C** On a bend
- ☐ **D** At or near a taxi rank

Whenever possible, leave your car in a secure car park. This will help deter thieves.

124 Mark *one* answer

Where would parking your vehicle cause an obstruction?

- ☐ **A** Alongside a parking meter
- ☐ **B** In front of a property entrance
- ☐ **C** On your driveway
- ☐ **D** In a marked parking space

Don't park your vehicle where it may obstruct access to a business or property. Think carefully before you slow down and stop. Look at road markings and signs to ensure that you aren't parking illegally.

125 Mark *one* answer

What is the most important reason for having a properly adjusted head restraint?

- ☐ **A** To make you more comfortable
- ☐ **B** To help you avoid neck injury
- ☐ **C** To help you relax
- ☐ **D** To help you maintain your driving position

In a collision, rapid deceleration will violently throw vehicle occupants forward and then backwards as the vehicle stops. Seat belts and airbags protect occupants against the forward movement. Head restraints should be adjusted so they give maximum protection to the head and neck during the backward movement.

126 Mark *one* answer

What causes the most damage to the environment?

- ☐ **A** Choosing a fuel-efficient vehicle
- ☐ **B** Having your vehicle serviced regularly
- ☐ **C** Driving in as high a gear as possible
- ☐ **D** Making a lot of short journeys

Avoid using your car for short journeys. On a short journey, the engine is unlikely to warm up fully and will therefore be running less efficiently. This will result in the car using more fuel and producing higher levels of harmful emissions.

127 Mark *one* answer

What can people who live or work in towns and cities do to help reduce urban pollution levels?

☐ **A** Drive more quickly
☐ **B** Over-rev in a low gear
☐ **C** Walk or cycle
☐ **D** Drive short journeys

Using a vehicle for short journeys means the engine doesn't have time to reach its normal operating temperature. When an engine is running below its normal operating temperature, it produces increased amounts of pollution. Walking and cycling don't create pollution and have health benefits as well.

128 Mark *one* answer

How can you reduce the chances of your car being broken into when leaving it unattended?

☐ **A** Take all valuables with you
☐ **B** Park near a taxi rank
☐ **C** Place any valuables on the floor
☐ **D** Park near a fire station

When leaving your car, take all valuables with you if you can. Otherwise, lock them out of sight.

129 Mark *one* answer

How can you help to prevent your car radio being stolen?

☐ **A** Park in an unlit area
☐ **B** Leave the radio turned on
☐ **C** Park near a busy junction
☐ **D** Install a security-coded radio

A security-coded radio can deter thieves, as it's likely to be of little use when removed from the vehicle.

130 Mark *one* answer

How can you lessen the risk of your vehicle being broken into at night?

☐ **A** Leave it in a well-lit area
☐ **B** Park in a quiet side road
☐ **C** Don't engage the steering lock
☐ **D** Park in a poorly-lit area

Having your vehicle broken into or stolen can be very distressing and inconvenient. Avoid leaving your vehicle unattended in poorly-lit areas.

131 Mark *one* answer

Which of these will help you to keep your car secure?

☐ **A** Vehicle breakdown organisation
☐ **B** Vehicle watch scheme
☐ **C** Advanced driver's scheme
☐ **D** Car maintenance class

The vehicle watch scheme helps to reduce the risk of your car being stolen. By displaying high-visibility vehicle watch stickers in your car, you're inviting the police to stop your vehicle if it's seen in use between midnight and 5 am.

132   Mark *one* answer

On a vehicle, where would you find a catalytic converter?

☐ **A** In the fuel tank
☐ **B** In the air filter
☐ **C** On the cooling system
☐ **D** On the exhaust system

Although carbon dioxide is still produced, a catalytic converter fitted to the exhaust system reduces the toxic and polluting gases by up to 90%.

133   Mark *one* answer

What can driving smoothly achieve?

☐ **A** Reduction in journey times by about 15%
☐ **B** Increase in fuel consumption by about 15%
☐ **C** Reduction in fuel consumption by about 15%
☐ **D** Increase in journey times by about 15%

By driving smoothly, you'll not only save about 15% of your fuel but will also reduce the amount of wear and tear on your vehicle and the level of pollution it produces. You're also likely to feel more relaxed and have a more pleasant journey.

134   Mark *one* answer

Which driving technique can help you save fuel?

☐ **A** Using lower gears as often as possible
☐ **B** Accelerating sharply in each gear
☐ **C** Using each gear in turn
☐ **D** Missing out some gears

Missing out intermediate gears, when appropriate, helps to reduce the amount of time spent accelerating and decelerating – the times when your vehicle uses the most fuel.

135   Mark *one* answer

How can driving in an ecosafe manner help protect the environment?

☐ **A** Through the legal enforcement of speed regulations
☐ **B** By increasing the number of cars on the road
☐ **C** Through increased fuel bills
☐ **D** By reducing exhaust emissions

Ecosafe driving is all about becoming a more environmentally friendly driver. This will make your journeys more comfortable, as well as considerably reducing your fuel bills and reducing emissions that can damage the environment.

136 Mark *one* answer
What does ecosafe driving achieve?

- ☐ **A** Increased fuel consumption
- ☐ **B** Improved road safety
- ☐ **C** Damage to the environment
- ☐ **D** Increased exhaust emissions

The emphasis is on hazard awareness and planning ahead. By looking well ahead, you'll have plenty of time to deal with hazards safely and won't need to brake sharply. This will also reduce damage to the environment.

137 Mark *one* answer
You're checking your trailer tyres. What is the legal minimum tread depth over the central three-quarters of its breadth?

- ☐ **A** 1 mm
- ☐ **B** 1.6 mm
- ☐ **C** 2 mm
- ☐ **D** 2.6 mm

Trailers and caravans may be left in storage over the winter months, and tyres can deteriorate. It's important to check their tread depth and also their pressures and general condition. The legal tread depth of 1.6 mm applies to the central three-quarters of a tyre's breadth, over its entire circumference.

138 Mark *one* answer
Fuel consumption is at its highest when you're doing what?

- ☐ **A** Braking
- ☐ **B** Coasting
- ☐ **C** Accelerating
- ☐ **D** Steering

Accelerating uses a lot of fuel, so always try to use the accelerator smoothly. Taking your foot off the accelerator allows the momentum of the car to take you forward, especially when going downhill. This can save a considerable amount of fuel without any loss of control over the vehicle.

139 Mark *one* answer
When is it acceptable for a passenger to travel in a car without wearing wearing a seat belt?

- ☐ **A** When they're under 14 years old
- ☐ **B** When they're under 1.5 metres (5 feet) in height
- ☐ **C** When they're sitting in the rear seat
- ☐ **D** When they're exempt for medical reasons

If you have adult passengers, it's their responsibility to wear a seat belt, but you should still remind them to use one as they get in the car. It's your responsibility to make sure that all children in your car are secured with an appropriate restraint. Exemptions are allowed for those with a medical exemption certificate.

140   Mark *one* answer

You're driving a friend's children home from school. They're both under 14 years old. Who's responsible for making sure they wear a seat belt or approved child restraint where required?

☐ **A** An adult passenger
☐ **B** The children
☐ **C** You, the driver
☐ **D** Your friend

Passengers should always be secured and safe. Children should be encouraged to fasten their seat belts or approved restraints themselves from an early age, so that it becomes a matter of routine. As the driver, you must check that they're fastened securely. It's your responsibility.

141   Mark *one* answer

You have too much oil in your engine. What could this cause?

☐ **A** Low oil pressure
☐ **B** Engine overheating
☐ **C** Chain wear
☐ **D** Oil leaks

Too much oil in the engine will create excess pressure and could damage engine seals and cause oil leaks. Any excess oil should be drained off.

142   Mark *one* answer

You're carrying a five-year-old child in the back seat of your car. They're under 1.35 metres (4 feet 5 inches) tall. A correct child restraint isn't available. How should you seat them?

☐ **A** Behind the passenger seat
☐ **B** Using an adult seat belt
☐ **C** Sharing a belt with an adult
☐ **D** Between two other children

Usually, a correct child restraint must be used. In cases where one isn't available, an adult seat belt must be used instead. In a collision, unrestrained objects and people can cause serious injury or even death.

143   Mark *one* answer

You're carrying an 11-year-old child in the back seat of your car. They're under 1.35 metres (4 feet 5 inches) tall. What must you make sure of?

☐ **A** That they sit between two belted people
☐ **B** That they can fasten their own seat belt
☐ **C** That a suitable child restraint is available
☐ **D** That they can see clearly out of the front window

As the driver, it's your responsibility to make sure that children are secure and safe in your vehicle. Make yourself familiar with the rules. In a few very exceptional cases when a child restraint isn't available, an adult seat belt must be used.

144 Mark *one* answer

You're parked at the side of the road. You'll be waiting some time for a passenger. What should you do?

- ☐ **A** Switch off the engine
- ☐ **B** Apply the steering lock
- ☐ **C** Switch off the radio
- ☐ **D** Use your headlights

If your vehicle is stationary and is likely to remain so for some time, switch off the engine. We should all try to reduce global warming and pollution.

145 Mark *one* answer

You want to put a rear-facing baby seat on the front passenger seat, which is protected by a frontal airbag. What must you do before setting off?

- ☐ **A** Deactivate the airbag
- ☐ **B** Turn the seat to face sideways
- ☐ **C** Ask a passenger to hold the baby
- ☐ **D** Put the child in an adult seat belt

It's illegal to fit a rear-facing baby seat into a passenger seat protected by an active frontal airbag. If the airbag activates, it could cause serious injury or even death to the child. You must secure it in a different seat or deactivate the relevant airbag. Follow the manufacturer's advice when fitting a baby seat.

146 Mark *one* answer

You're leaving your vehicle parked on a road and unattended. When may you leave the engine running?

- ☐ **A** If you'll be parking for less than five minutes
- ☐ **B** If the battery keeps going flat
- ☐ **C** When parked in a 20 mph zone
- ☐ **D** Never if you're away from the vehicle

When you leave your vehicle parked on a road, switch off the engine and secure the vehicle. Make sure no valuables are visible, shut all the windows, lock the vehicle, and set the alarm the vehicle has one.

147 Mark *one* answer

By how much can stopping distances increase in icy conditions?

☐ **A** Two times
☐ **B** Three times
☐ **C** Five times
☐ **D** Ten times

Tyre grip is greatly reduced in icy conditions. For this reason, you need to allow up to ten times the stopping distance you would allow on dry roads.

148 Mark *one* answer

In windy conditions, which activity requires extra care?

☐ **A** Using the brakes
☐ **B** Moving off on a hill
☐ **C** Turning into a narrow road
☐ **D** Passing pedal cyclists

Always give cyclists plenty of room when overtaking them. You need to give them even more room when it's windy. A sudden gust could easily blow them off course and into your path.

149 Mark *one* answer

When approaching a right-hand bend, you should keep well to the left. Why is this?

☐ **A** To improve your view of the road
☐ **B** To overcome the effect of the road's slope
☐ **C** To let faster traffic from behind overtake
☐ **D** To be positioned safely if you skid

Doing this will give you an earlier view around the bend and enable you to see any hazards sooner. It also reduces the risk of collision with an oncoming vehicle that may have drifted over the centre line while taking the bend.

150 Mark *one* answer

You've just gone through deep water. What should you do to make sure your brakes are working properly?

☐ **A** Accelerate and keep to a high speed for a short time
☐ **B** Go slowly while gently applying the brakes
☐ **C** Avoid using the brakes at all for a few miles
☐ **D** Stop for at least an hour to allow them time to dry

Water on the brakes will act as a lubricant, causing them to work less efficiently. Using the brakes lightly as you go along will quickly dry them out.

151 Mark *one* answer

In very hot weather the road surface can become soft. What will this affect?

- ☐ **A** The suspension
- ☐ **B** The exhaust emissions
- ☐ **C** The fuel consumption
- ☐ **D** The tyre grip

If the road surface becomes very hot, it can soften. Tyres are unable to grip a soft surface as well as they can a firm dry one. Take care when cornering and braking.

152 Mark *one* answer

Where are you most likely to be affected by side winds?

- ☐ **A** On a narrow country lane
- ☐ **B** On an open stretch of road
- ☐ **C** On a busy stretch of road
- ☐ **D** On a long, straight road

In windy conditions, care must be taken on exposed roads. A strong gust of wind can blow you off course. Watch out for other road users who are particularly likely to be affected, such as cyclists, motorcyclists, high-sided lorries and vehicles towing trailers.

153 Mark *one* answer

In good conditions, what's the typical stopping distance at 70 mph?

- ☐ **A** 53 metres (175 feet)
- ☐ **B** 60 metres (197 feet)
- ☐ **C** 73 metres (240 feet)
- ☐ **D** 96 metres (315 feet)

Note that this is the typical stopping distance. It will take at least this distance to think, brake and stop in good conditions. In poor conditions, it will take much longer.

154 Mark *one* answer

What is the shortest overall stopping distance on a dry road at 60 mph?

- ☐ **A** 53 metres (175 feet)
- ☐ **B** 58 metres (190 feet)
- ☐ **C** 73 metres (240 feet)
- ☐ **D** 96 metres (315 feet)

This distance is the equivalent of 18 car lengths. Try pacing out 73 metres and then look back. It's probably further than you think.

155 Mark *one* answer

You're following a vehicle at a safe distance on a wet road. Another driver overtakes you and pulls into the gap you've left. What should you do?

- ☐ **A** Flash your headlights as a warning
- ☐ **B** Try to overtake safely as soon as you can
- ☐ **C** Drop back to regain a safe distance
- ☐ **D** Stay close to the other vehicle until it moves on

Wet weather will affect the time it takes for you to stop and can affect your control. Your speed should allow you to stop safely and in good time. If another vehicle pulls into the gap you've left, ease back until you've regained your stopping distance.

156 Mark *one* answer

You're travelling at 50 mph on a good, dry road. What is your typical overall stopping distance?

- ☐ **A** 36 metres (118 feet)
- ☐ **B** 53 metres (175 feet)
- ☐ **C** 75 metres (245 feet)
- ☐ **D** 96 metres (315 feet)

Even in good conditions, it will usually take you further than you think to stop. Don't just learn the figures; make sure you understand how far the distance is.

157 Mark *one* answer

You're on a good, dry road surface. Your brakes and tyres are good. What is the typical overall stopping distance at 40 mph?

- ☐ **A** 23 metres (75 feet)
- ☐ **B** 36 metres (118 feet)
- ☐ **C** 53 metres (175 feet)
- ☐ **D** 96 metres (315 feet)

Stopping distances are affected by a number of variables. These include the type, model and condition of your vehicle, the road and weather conditions, and your reaction time. Look well ahead for hazards and leave enough space between you and the vehicle in front. This should allow you to pull up safely if you have to, without braking sharply.

158 Mark *one* answer

What should you do when overtaking a motorcyclist in strong winds?

☐ **A** Pass closely
☐ **B** Pass very slowly
☐ **C** Pass wide
☐ **D** Pass immediately

In strong winds, riders of two-wheeled vehicles are particularly vulnerable. When you overtake them, allow plenty of room. Always check to the left as you pass.

---

159 Mark *one* answer

Overall stopping distance is made up of thinking distance and braking distance. You're on a good, dry road surface, with good brakes and tyres. What is the typical braking distance from 50 mph?

☐ **A** 14 metres (46 feet)
☐ **B** 24 metres (80 feet)
☐ **C** 38 metres (125 feet)
☐ **D** 55 metres (180 feet)

Be aware that this is just the braking distance. You need to add the thinking distance to this to give the overall stopping distance. At 50 mph, the typical thinking distance will be 15 metres (50 feet), plus a braking distance of 38 metres (125 feet), giving an overall stopping distance of 53 metres (175 feet). The stopping distance could be greater than this, depending on your attention and response to any hazards. These figures are a general guide.

160 Mark *one* answer

In heavy motorway traffic, the vehicle behind you is following too closely. How can you lower the risk of a collision?

☐ **A** Increase your distance from the vehicle in front
☐ **B** Brake sharply
☐ **C** Switch on your hazard warning lights
☐ **D** Move onto the hard shoulder and stop

On busy roads, traffic may still travel at high speeds despite being close together. Don't follow the vehicle in front too closely. If a driver behind seems to be 'pushing' you, gradually increase your distance from the vehicle in front by slowing down gently. This will give you more space in front if you have to brake, and will reduce the risk of a collision involving several vehicles.

161 Mark *one* answer

You're following other vehicles in fog. You have your lights on. What else can you do to reduce the chances of being in a collision?

☐ **A** Keep close to the vehicle in front
☐ **B** Use your main beam instead of dipped headlights
☐ **C** Keep up with the faster vehicles
☐ **D** Reduce your speed and increase the gap in front

When it's foggy, use dipped headlights. This will help you see and be seen by other road users. If visibility is seriously reduced, consider using front and rear fog lights if you have them. Keep to a sensible speed and don't follow the vehicle in front too closely. If the road is wet and slippery, you'll need to allow twice the normal stopping distance.

162 Mark *one* answer

You're using a contraflow system. What should you do?

☐ **A** Choose an appropriate lane in good time
☐ **B** Switch lanes at any time to make progress
☐ **C** Increase speed to pass through quickly
☐ **D** Follow other motorists closely to avoid long queues

In a contraflow system, you'll be travelling close to oncoming traffic and sometimes in narrow lanes. You should get into the correct lane in good time, obey any temporary speed-limit signs and keep a safe separation distance from the vehicle ahead.

163 Mark *one* answer

You're driving on an icy road. How can you avoid wheelspin?

☐ **A** Drive at a slow speed in as high a gear as possible
☐ **B** Use the handbrake if the wheels start to slip
☐ **C** Brake gently and repeatedly
☐ **D** Drive in a low gear at all times

If you're travelling on an icy road, extra caution will be required to avoid loss of control. Keeping your speed down and using the highest gear possible will reduce the risk of the tyres losing their grip on this slippery surface.

164 Mark *one* answer

What is the main cause of skidding?

☐ **A** The weather
☐ **B** The driver
☐ **C** The vehicle
☐ **D** The road

Skidding is usually caused by driver error. You should always adjust your driving to take account of the road and weather conditions.

165 Mark *one* answer

You're driving in freezing conditions. What should you do when approaching a sharp bend?

☐ **A** Coast into the bend
☐ **B** Gently apply your handbrake
☐ **C** Firmly use your footbrake
☐ **D** Slow down before you reach the bend

Harsh use of the accelerator, brakes or steering is likely to lead to skidding, especially on slippery surfaces. Avoid steering and braking at the same time. In icy conditions it's very important that you constantly assess what's ahead, so that you can take appropriate action in plenty of time.

166 Mark *one* answer

You're turning left on a slippery road. What should you do if the back of your vehicle slides to the right?

☐ **A** Brake firmly and don't turn the steering wheel
☐ **B** Steer carefully to the left
☐ **C** Steer carefully to the right
☐ **D** Brake firmly and steer to the left

To correct a skid, you need to steer into it. However, be careful not to overcorrect with too much steering, as this may cause a skid in the opposite direction. Skids don't just happen; they're caused – usually by the driver. Factors increasing the likelihood of a skid include the condition of the vehicle (especially its tyres) and the road and weather conditions.

167 Mark *one* answer

What should you clear of ice and snow before starting a journey in freezing weather?

☐ **A** The aerial
☐ **B** The windows
☐ **C** The bumper
☐ **D** The boot

Driving in bad weather increases your risk of having a collision. If you absolutely have to travel, clear your lights, mirrors, number plates and windows of any snow or ice, so that you can see and be seen.

168 Mark *one* answer

What will help when you're trying to move off on snow?

☐ **A** Use the car's lowest gear
☐ **B** Use a higher gear than normal
☐ **C** Use a high engine speed
☐ **D** Use the handbrake and footbrake together

If you attempt to move off in a low gear, there will be more torque (turning force) at the driven wheels than if you use a higher gear. More torque makes it easier for the tyres to lose grip and so spin the wheels.

169 Mark *one* answer

What should you do when you're driving in snowy conditions?

- ☐ **A** Brake firmly and quickly
- ☐ **B** Be ready to steer sharply
- ☐ **C** Use sidelights only
- ☐ **D** Brake gently in plenty of time

In snowy conditions, be careful with the steering, accelerator and brakes. Braking sharply while you're driving on snow is likely to make your car skid.

170 Mark *one* answer

What is the main benefit of driving a four-wheel-drive vehicle?

- ☐ **A** Improved grip on the road
- ☐ **B** Lower fuel consumption
- ☐ **C** Shorter stopping distances
- ☐ **D** Improved passenger comfort

By driving all four wheels, the vehicle has maximum grip on the road. This grip is especially helpful when travelling on slippery or uneven surfaces. However, having four-wheel drive doesn't replace the skills you need to drive safely.

171 Mark *one* answer

You're about to go down a steep hill. What should you do to control the speed of your vehicle?

- ☐ **A** Select a high gear and use the brakes carefully
- ☐ **B** Select a high gear and use the brakes firmly
- ☐ **C** Select a low gear and use the brakes carefully
- ☐ **D** Select a low gear and avoid using the brakes

When driving down a steep hill, gravity will cause your vehicle to speed up. This will make it more difficult for you to stop. To help keep your vehicle's speed under control, select a lower gear to give you more engine braking and make careful use of the brakes.

172 Mark *one* answer

What should you do when parking your vehicle facing downhill?

- ☐ **A** Turn the steering wheel towards the kerb
- ☐ **B** Park close to the bumper of another car
- ☐ **C** Park with two wheels on the kerb
- ☐ **D** Turn the steering wheel away from the kerb

Turning the wheels towards the kerb will allow them to act as a chock, preventing any forward movement of the vehicle. It will also help to leave your car in gear, or select 'Park' if you have an automatic.

173 Mark *one* answer

You're driving in a built-up area that has traffic-calming measures. What should you do when you approach a road hump?

☐ **A** Move across to the left-hand side of the road
☐ **B** Wait for any pedestrians to cross
☐ **C** Check your mirror and slow down
☐ **D** Stop and check both pavements

Many towns have road humps as part of traffic-calming measures, designed to slow down traffic. Reduce your speed when driving over them. If you go too fast, you could lose control or damage your car. Look out for pedestrians or cyclists while you're driving in these areas.

174 Mark *one* answer

Anti-lock brakes reduce the chances of skidding. When is this particularly important?

☐ **A** When you're driving down steep hills
☐ **B** When you're braking during normal driving
☐ **C** When you're braking in an emergency
☐ **D** When you're driving on good road surfaces

The anti-lock braking system (ABS) will operate when the brakes have been applied harshly and the wheels are about to lock, such as during an emergency. ABS will reduce the likelihood of your car skidding, but it isn't a substitute for safe and responsible driving.

175 Mark *one* answer

On what type of road surface may anti-lock brakes not work effectively?

☐ **A** Dry
☐ **B** Loose
☐ **C** Firm
☐ **D** Smooth

Poor contact with the road surface could cause one or more of the tyres to lose grip on the road. This is more likely to happen when braking in poor weather conditions and when the road has a loose, slippery or uneven surface.

176   Mark *one* answer
When are anti-lock brakes of most use to you?

☐ **A** When you're braking gently
☐ **B** When you're braking on rural roads
☐ **C** When you're braking harshly
☐ **D** When you're braking on a motorway

Anti-lock brakes won't be needed when you're braking normally. Looking well down the road and anticipating possible hazards could prevent you from having to brake late and harshly. Knowing that you have anti-lock brakes isn't an excuse to drive in a careless or reckless way.

177   Mark *one* answer
What does driving a vehicle with anti-lock brakes allow you to do?

☐ **A** Brake harder because it's impossible to skid
☐ **B** Drive at higher speeds
☐ **C** Steer and brake harshly at the same time
☐ **D** Pay less attention to the road ahead

If the wheels of your vehicle lock, they won't grip the road and you'll lose steering control. In good conditions, the anti-lock braking system (ABS) will prevent the wheels from locking and you'll keep control of your steering. In poor weather conditions or on loose surfaces, the ABS may be less effective.

178   Mark *one* answer
You're driving a vehicle that has anti-lock brakes. How should you apply the footbrake when you need to stop in an emergency?

☐ **A** Slowly and gently
☐ **B** Slowly but firmly
☐ **C** Rapidly and gently
☐ **D** Rapidly and firmly

You may have to stop in an emergency due to a misjudgement by another driver or a hazard arising suddenly, such as a child running out into the road. If your vehicle has anti-lock brakes, you should apply the brakes immediately and keep them firmly applied until you stop.

179   Mark *one* answer
In which conditions are your anti-lock brakes most unlikely to prevent skidding?

☐ **A** In foggy conditions
☐ **B** At night on unlit roads
☐ **C** On loose road surfaces
☐ **D** On dry tarmac

Anti-lock brakes may be ineffective on gravel or loose surfaces. They may also be ineffective in very wet weather, when water can build up between the tyre and the road surface; this is known as aquaplaning.

180 Mark *one* answer

You're driving along a country road. You see this sign. What should you do after dealing safely with the hazard?

☐ **A** Check your tyre pressures
☐ **B** Switch on your hazard warning lights
☐ **C** Accelerate briskly
☐ **D** Test your brakes

If your brakes have been thoroughly soaked, you should check that they're working properly before you build up speed again. Before you do this, remember to check your mirrors and consider what's behind you.

181 Mark *one* answer

What would suggest you're driving on ice?

☐ **A** There's less wind noise
☐ **B** There's less tyre noise
☐ **C** There's less transmission noise
☐ **D** There's less engine noise

Drive extremely carefully when the roads are icy. When travelling on ice, tyres make virtually no noise and the steering feels light and unresponsive. In icy conditions, be very gentle when braking, accelerating and steering.

182 Mark *one* answer

You're driving along a wet road. How can you tell if your vehicle's tyres are losing their grip on the surface?

☐ **A** The engine will stall
☐ **B** The steering will feel very heavy
☐ **C** The engine noise will increase
☐ **D** The steering will feel very light

If you drive at speed in very wet conditions, your steering may suddenly feel lighter than usual. This means that the tyres have lifted off the surface of the road and are skating on the surface of the water. This is known as aquaplaning. Reduce speed but don't brake until your steering returns to normal.

183 Mark *one* answer

In which conditions will your overall stopping distance increase?

☐ **A** In the rain
☐ **B** In fog
☐ **C** At night
☐ **D** In strong winds

Extra care should be taken in wet weather. On wet roads, your stopping distance could be double that in dry conditions.

184 Mark *one* answer

You're driving on an open road in dry weather. What should the distance be between you and the vehicle in front?

- ☐ **A** A two-second time gap
- ☐ **B** One car length
- ☐ **C** Two metres (6 feet 6 inches)
- ☐ **D** Two car lengths

One way of checking there's a safe distance between you and the vehicle in front is to use the two-second rule. To check for a two-second time gap, choose a stationary object ahead, such as a bridge or road sign. When the car in front passes the object, say 'Only a fool breaks the two-second rule'. If you reach the object before you finish saying the phrase, you're too close and need to increase the gap.

185 Mark *one* answer

How can you use your vehicle's engine as a brake?

- ☐ **A** By changing to a lower gear
- ☐ **B** By selecting reverse gear
- ☐ **C** By changing to a higher gear
- ☐ **D** By selecting neutral gear

When driving on downhill stretches of road, selecting a lower gear gives increased engine braking. This will prevent excessive use of the brakes, which become less effective if they overheat.

186 Mark *one* answer

When are anti-lock brakes (ABS) most effective?

- ☐ **A** When you keep pumping the foot brake to prevent skidding
- ☐ **B** When you brake normally but grip the steering wheel tightly
- ☐ **C** When you brake promptly and firmly until you've stopped
- ☐ **D** When you apply the handbrake to reduce the stopping distance

If you have ABS and need to stop in an emergency, keep your foot firmly on the brake pedal until the vehicle has stopped. When the ABS operates, you may hear a grating sound and feel vibration through the brake pedal. This is normal and you should maintain pressure on the brake pedal until the vehicle stops.

187 Mark *one* answer

When will anti-lock brakes take effect?

- ☐ **A** When you don't brake quickly enough
- ☐ **B** When the wheels are about to lock
- ☐ **C** When you haven't seen a hazard ahead
- ☐ **D** When you're speeding on a slippery road surface

If your car is fitted with anti-lock brakes, they'll only activate when they sense that the wheels are about to lock. By preventing the wheels from locking, you'll be able to steer to avoid the hazard, while maximum braking is also applied.

188 Mark *one* answer

You're driving on a wet motorway with surface spray. What lights should you use?

- ☐ **A** Hazard warning lights
- ☐ **B** Dipped headlights
- ☐ **C** Rear fog lights
- ☐ **D** Sidelights

When surface spray reduces visibility, switch on your dipped headlights. This will help other road users to see you.

189 Mark *one* answer

What can result when you travel for long distances in neutral (known as coasting)?

- ☐ **A** Improvement in control
- ☐ **B** Easier steering
- ☐ **C** Reduction in control
- ☐ **D** Increased fuel consumption

Coasting is the term used when the clutch is held down, or the gear lever is in neutral, and the vehicle is allowed to freewheel. This reduces the driver's control of the vehicle. When you coast, the engine can't drive the wheels to stabilise you through a corner, or give the assistance of engine braking to help slow the car.

190 Mark *one* answer

What should you do when driving in fog?

- ☐ **A** Use sidelights only
- ☐ **B** Position close to the centre line
- ☐ **C** Allow more time for your journey
- ☐ **D** Keep close to the car in front

Don't venture out if your journey isn't necessary. If you have to travel and someone is expecting you at the other end, let them know that you'll be taking longer than usual for your journey. This will stop them worrying if you don't turn up on time and will also take the pressure off you, so you don't feel you have to rush.

191 Mark *one* answer

Where would you expect to see these markers?

- ☐ **A** On a motorway sign
- ☐ **B** On a railway bridge
- ☐ **C** On a large goods vehicle
- ☐ **D** On a diversion sign

These markers must be fitted to vehicles over 13 metres long, large goods vehicles, and rubbish skips placed in the road. They're reflective to make them easier to see in the dark.

192 Mark *one* answer

What is the main hazard shown in this picture?

- ☐ **A** Vehicles turning right
- ☐ **B** Vehicles doing U-turns
- ☐ **C** The cyclist crossing the road
- ☐ **D** Parked cars around the corner

Look at the picture carefully and try to imagine you're there. The cyclist in this picture appears to be trying to cross the road. You must be able to deal with the unexpected, especially when you're approaching a hazardous junction. Look well ahead to give yourself time to deal with any hazards.

193 Mark *one* answer

Which road user has caused a hazard?

- ☐ **A** The parked car (A)
- ☐ **B** The pedestrian waiting to cross (B)
- ☐ **C** The moving car (C)
- ☐ **D** The car turning (D)

Car A is parked within the area marked by zigzag lines at the pedestrian crossing. Parking here is illegal. It also:
- blocks the view for pedestrians wishing to cross the road
- restricts the view of the crossing for approaching traffic

194 Mark *one* answer

What should the driver of the car approaching the crossing do?

- ☐ **A** Continue at the same speed
- ☐ **B** Sound the horn
- ☐ **C** Drive through quickly
- ☐ **D** Slow down and get ready to stop

Look well ahead to see whether any hazards are developing and give yourself time to deal with them. The man in the picture is clearly intending to cross the road. You should be travelling at a speed that allows you to check your mirror, slow down and stop in good time. You shouldn't have to brake harshly.

195 Mark *one* answer

What should the driver of the grey car (arrowed) be especially aware of?

- ☐ **A** The uneven road surface
- ☐ **B** Traffic following behind
- ☐ **C** Doors opening on parked cars
- ☐ **D** Empty parking spaces

When passing parked cars, there's a risk that a driver or passenger may not check before opening the door into the road. A defensive driver will drive slowly and be looking for people who may be about to get out of their car.

196 Mark *one* answer

You see this sign ahead. What should you expect?

- ☐ **A** The road will go steeply uphill
- ☐ **B** The road will go steeply downhill
- ☐ **C** The road will bend sharply to the left
- ☐ **D** The road will bend sharply to the right

This sign indicates that the road will bend sharply to the left. Slow down in plenty of time and select the correct gear before you start to turn. Braking hard and late, while also sharply changing direction, is likely to cause a skid.

197 Mark *one* answer

You're approaching this cyclist. What should you do?

- ☐ **A** Overtake before the cyclist gets to the junction
- ☐ **B** Flash your headlights at the cyclist
- ☐ **C** Slow down and allow the cyclist to turn
- ☐ **D** Overtake the cyclist on the left-hand side

Keep well back and give the cyclist time and room to turn safely. Don't intimidate them by getting too close or trying to squeeze past.

198 Mark *one* answer

Why must you take extra care when turning right at this junction?

- ☐ **A** The road surface is poor
- ☐ **B** The footpaths are narrow
- ☐ **C** The road markings are faint
- ☐ **D** The view is restricted

You may have to pull forward slowly until you can see up and down the road. Be aware that the traffic approaching the junction can't see you either. If you don't know that it's clear, don't go.

199 Mark *one* answer

Which type of vehicle should you be ready to give way to as you approach this bridge?

☐ **A** Bicycles
☐ **B** Buses
☐ **C** Motorcycles
☐ **D** Cars

A double-decker bus or high-sided lorry will have to take a position in the centre of the road to clear the bridge. There's normally a sign to show this. Look well ahead, past the bridge and be ready to stop and give way to large oncoming vehicles.

200 Mark *one* answer

What type of vehicle could you expect to meet in the middle of the road?

☐ **A** Lorry
☐ **B** Bicycle
☐ **C** Car
☐ **D** Motorcycle

The highest point of the bridge is in the centre, so a large vehicle might have to move to the centre of the road to have enough room to pass under the bridge.

201 Mark *one* answer

What must you do at this junction?

☐ **A** Stop behind the line, then edge forward to see clearly
☐ **B** Stop beyond the line, at a point where you can see clearly
☐ **C** Stop only if there's traffic on the main road
☐ **D** Stop only if you're turning right

The 'stop' sign has been put here because the view into the main road is poor. You must stop because it won't be possible to take proper observation while you're moving.

202 Mark *one* answer

A driver pulls out of a side road in front of you, causing you to brake hard. What should you do?

☐ **A** Ignore the error and stay calm
☐ **B** Flash your lights to show your annoyance
☐ **C** Sound your horn to show your annoyance
☐ **D** Overtake as soon as possible

Be tolerant if a vehicle emerges and you have to brake quickly. Anyone can make a mistake, so don't react aggressively. Be alert where there are side roads and be especially careful where there are parked vehicles, because these can make it difficult for emerging drivers to see you.

203 Mark *one* answer
How would age affect an elderly person's driving ability?

☐ **A** They won't be able to obtain car insurance
☐ **B** They'll need glasses to read road signs
☐ **C** They'll take longer to react to hazards
☐ **D** They won't signal at junctions

Be tolerant of older drivers. They may take longer to react to a hazard and they may be hesitant in some situations – for example, at a junction.

204 Mark *one* answer
You've just passed these warning lights. What hazard would you expect to see next?

☐ **A** A level crossing with no barrier
☐ **B** An ambulance station
☐ **C** A school crossing patrol
☐ **D** An opening bridge

These lights warn that children may be crossing the road to a nearby school. Slow down so that you're ready to stop if necessary.

205 Mark *one* answer
You're planning a long journey. Do you need to plan rest stops?

☐ **A** Yes, you should plan to stop every half an hour
☐ **B** Yes, regular stops help concentration
☐ **C** No, you'll be less tired if you get there as soon as possible
☐ **D** No, only fuel stops will be needed

Try to plan your journey so that you can take rest stops. It's recommended that you take a break of at least 15 minutes after every two hours of driving or riding. This should help to maintain your concentration.

206 Mark *one* answer
The red lights are flashing. What should you do when approaching this level crossing?

☐ **A** Go through quickly
☐ **B** Go through carefully
☐ **C** Stop before the barrier
☐ **D** Switch on hazard warning lights

At level crossings, the red lights flash before and while the barrier is down. At most crossings, an amber light will precede the red lights. You must stop behind the white line unless you've already crossed it when the amber light comes on. Never zigzag around half-barriers.

207 Mark *one* answer
You're approaching a crossroads. The traffic lights have failed. What should you do?

☐ **A** Brake and stop only for large vehicles
☐ **B** Brake sharply to a stop before looking
☐ **C** Be prepared to brake sharply to a stop
☐ **D** Be prepared to stop for any traffic

When approaching a junction where the traffic lights have failed, you should proceed with caution. Treat the situation as an unmarked junction and be prepared to stop.

208 Mark *one* answer
What should the driver of the red car (arrowed) do?

☐ **A** Wave towards the pedestrians who are waiting to cross
☐ **B** Wait for the pedestrian in the road to cross
☐ **C** Quickly drive behind the pedestrian in the road
☐ **D** Tell the pedestrian in the road she shouldn't have crossed

Some people might take a long time to cross the road. They may be older or have a disability. Be patient and don't hurry them by showing your impatience. If pedestrians are standing at the side of the road, don't signal or wave them to cross. Other road users might not have seen your signal and this could lead the pedestrians into a hazardous situation.

209 Mark *one* answer
You're following a slower-moving vehicle on a narrow country road. There's a junction just ahead on the right. What should you do?

☐ **A** Overtake after checking your mirrors and signalling
☐ **B** Only consider overtaking when you're past the junction
☐ **C** Accelerate quickly to pass before the junction
☐ **D** Slow down and prepare to overtake on the left

You should never overtake as you approach a junction. If a vehicle emerged from the junction while you were overtaking, a dangerous situation could develop very quickly.

210 Mark *one* answer
What should you do as you approach this overhead bridge?

☐ **A** Move out to the centre of the road before going through
☐ **B** Find another route; this one is only for high vehicles
☐ **C** Be prepared to give way to large vehicles in the middle of the road
☐ **D** Move across to the right-hand side before going through

Oncoming large vehicles may need to move to the middle of the road to pass safely under the bridge. There won't be enough room for you to continue, so you should be ready to stop and wait.

211 Mark *one* answer
Why are mirrors often slightly curved (convex)?

- ☐ **A** They give a wider field of vision
- ☐ **B** They totally cover blind spots
- ☐ **C** They make it easier to judge the speed of following traffic
- ☐ **D** They make following traffic look bigger

Although a convex mirror gives a wide view of the scene behind, you should be aware that it won't show you everything behind or to the side of your vehicle. Before you move off, you'll need to look over your shoulder to check for anything not visible in the mirrors.

212 Mark *one* answer
A slow-moving lorry showing this sign is travelling in the middle lane of a three-lane motorway. How should you pass it?

- ☐ **A** Cautiously approach the lorry, then pass on either side
- ☐ **B** Don't pass the lorry and leave the motorway at the next exit
- ☐ **C** Use the right-hand lane and pass the lorry normally
- ☐ **D** Approach with care and pass on the left of the lorry

This sign is found on slow-moving or stationary works vehicles. If you wish to overtake, do so on the left, as indicated. Be aware that there might be workmen in the area.

213 Mark *one* answer
You think the driver of the vehicle in front has forgotten to cancel their right indicator. What should you do?

- ☐ **A** Flash your lights to alert the driver
- ☐ **B** Sound your horn before overtaking
- ☐ **C** Overtake on the left if there's room
- ☐ **D** Stay behind and don't overtake

Be cautious and don't attempt to overtake. The driver may be unsure of the location of a junction and may turn suddenly.

214 Mark *one* answer
What is the main hazard the driver of the red car (arrowed) should be aware of?

- ☐ **A** Glare from the sun may affect the driver's vision
- ☐ **B** The black car may stop suddenly
- ☐ **C** The bus may move out into the road
- ☐ **D** Oncoming vehicles will assume the driver is turning right

If you can do so safely, give way to buses signalling to move off at bus stops. Try to anticipate the actions of other road users around you. The driver of the red car should be prepared for the bus pulling out. As you approach a bus stop, look to see how many passengers are waiting to board. If the last one has just got on, the bus is likely to move off.

215 Mark *one* answer

What type of vehicle displays this yellow sign?

- ☐ **A** A broken-down vehicle
- ☐ **B** A school bus
- ☐ **C** An ice-cream van
- ☐ **D** A private ambulance

Buses which carry children to and from school may stop at places other than scheduled bus stops. Be aware that they might pull over at any time to allow children to get on or off. This will normally be when traffic is heavy during rush hour.

216 Mark *one* answer

What hazard should you be aware of when travelling along this street?

- ☐ **A** Glare from the sun
- ☐ **B** Lack of road markings
- ☐ **C** Children running out between vehicles
- ☐ **D** Large goods vehicles

On roads where there are many parked vehicles, you might not be able to see children between parked cars and they may run out into the road without looking.

217 Mark *one* answer

What is the main hazard you should be aware of when following this cyclist?

- ☐ **A** The cyclist may move to the left and dismount
- ☐ **B** The cyclist may swerve into the road
- ☐ **C** The contents of the cyclist's carrier may fall onto the road
- ☐ **D** The cyclist may wish to turn right at the end of the road

When following a cyclist, be aware that they have to deal with the hazards around them. They may wobble or swerve to avoid a pothole in the road or see a potential hazard and change direction suddenly. Don't follow them too closely or rev your engine impatiently.

218 Mark *one* answer

A driver's behaviour has upset you. What can you do to safely get over this incident?

- ☐ **A** Stop and take a break
- ☐ **B** Shout abusive language
- ☐ **C** Gesture to them with your hand
- ☐ **D** Follow them, flashing your headlights

If you feel yourself becoming tense or upset, stop in a safe place and take a break. Tiredness can make things worse and may cause a different reaction to upsetting situations.

219 Mark *one* answer
How should you drive in areas with traffic-calming measures?

- ☐ **A** At a reduced speed
- ☐ **B** At the speed limit
- ☐ **C** In the centre of the road
- ☐ **D** With headlights on dipped beam

Traffic-calming measures such as road humps, chicanes and narrowings are intended to slow drivers down to protect vulnerable road users. Don't speed up until you reach the end of the traffic-calmed zone.

220 Mark *one* answer
When approaching this hazard, why should you slow down?

- ☐ **A** Because of the level crossing
- ☐ **B** Because it's hard to see to the right
- ☐ **C** Because of approaching traffic
- ☐ **D** Because of animals crossing

You should be slowing down and selecting the correct gear in case you have to stop at the level crossing. Look for the signals and be prepared to stop if necessary.

221 Mark *one* answer
Why are place names painted on the road surface?

- ☐ **A** To restrict the flow of traffic
- ☐ **B** To warn you of oncoming traffic
- ☐ **C** To enable you to change lanes early
- ☐ **D** To prevent you changing lanes

The names of towns and cities may be painted on the road at busy junctions and complex road systems. Their purpose is to let you move into the correct lane in good time, allowing traffic to flow more freely.

222 Mark *one* answer
Some two-way roads are divided into three lanes. Why are these particularly dangerous?

- ☐ **A** Traffic in both directions can use the middle lane to overtake
- ☐ **B** Traffic can travel faster in poor weather conditions
- ☐ **C** Traffic can overtake on the left
- ☐ **D** Traffic uses the middle lane for emergencies only

If you intend to overtake, you must consider that approaching traffic could be planning the same manoeuvre. When you've considered the situation and decided it's safe, indicate your intentions early. This will show the approaching traffic that you intend to pull out.

223　Mark *one* answer
You're on a dual carriageway. Ahead, you see a vehicle with an amber flashing light. What could this be?

☐ **A** An ambulance
☐ **B** A fire engine
☐ **C** A doctor on call
☐ **D** A disabled person's vehicle

An amber flashing light on a vehicle indicates that it's slow-moving. Battery-powered vehicles used by disabled people are limited to 8 mph. It isn't advisable for them to be used on dual carriageways where the speed limit exceeds 50 mph. If they are, then an amber flashing light must be used.

224　Mark *one* answer
What does this signal from a police officer mean to oncoming traffic?

☐ **A** Go ahead
☐ **B** Stop
☐ **C** Turn left
☐ **D** Turn right

Police officers may need to direct traffic; for example, at a junction where the traffic lights have broken down. Check your copy of *The Highway Code* for the signals that they use.

225　Mark *one* answer
Why should you be cautious when going past this stationary bus?

☐ **A** There is traffic approaching in the distance
☐ **B** The driver may open the door
☐ **C** People may cross the road in front of it
☐ **D** The road surface will be slippery

A stationary bus at a bus stop can hide pedestrians who might try to cross the road just in front of it. Drive at a speed that will enable you to respond safely if you have to.

226　Mark *one* answer
Where shouldn't you overtake?

☐ **A** On a single carriageway
☐ **B** On a one-way street
☐ **C** Approaching a junction
☐ **D** Travelling up a long hill

You should overtake only when it's really necessary and you can see it's clear ahead. Look out for road signs and markings that show it's illegal or would be unsafe to overtake; for example, approaching junctions or bends. In many cases, overtaking is unlikely to significantly improve your journey time.

227 Mark *one* answer
What is an effect of drinking alcohol?

- ☐ **A** Poor judgement of speed
- ☐ **B** A loss of confidence
- ☐ **C** Faster reactions
- ☐ **D** Greater awareness of danger

Alcohol will severely reduce your ability to drive or ride safely and there are serious consequences if you're caught over the drink-drive limit. It's known that alcohol can:
- affect your judgement
- cause overconfidence
- reduced coordination and control

228 Mark *one* answer
What does the solid white line at the side of the road indicate?

- ☐ **A** Traffic lights ahead
- ☐ **B** Edge of the carriageway
- ☐ **C** Footpath on the left
- ☐ **D** Cycle path

The continuous white line shows the edge of the carriageway. It can be especially useful when visibility is restricted, such as at night or in bad weather. It's discontinued in some places; for example, at junctions, lay-bys, entrances or other openings.

229 Mark *one* answer
You're driving towards this level crossing. What would be the first warning of an approaching train?

- ☐ **A** Both half-barriers down
- ☐ **B** A steady amber light
- ☐ **C** One half-barrier down
- ☐ **D** Twin flashing red lights

The steady amber light will be followed by twin flashing red lights that mean you must stop. An alarm will also sound to alert you to the fact that a train is approaching.

230 Mark *one* answer
You're behind this cyclist. When the traffic lights change, what should you do?

- ☐ **A** Try to move off before the cyclist
- ☐ **B** Allow the cyclist time and room
- ☐ **C** Turn right but give the cyclist room
- ☐ **D** Tap your horn and drive through first

Hold back and allow the cyclist to move off. Some junctions have special areas marked across the front of the traffic lane. These allow cyclists to wait for the lights to change and move off ahead of other traffic.

231 Mark *one* answer
What should the white car do when the traffic lights change to green?

- ☐ **A** Wait for the cyclist to pull away
- ☐ **B** Move off quickly and turn in front of the cyclist
- ☐ **C** Move up close to the cyclist to beat the lights
- ☐ **D** Sound their horn to warn the cyclist

If you're waiting at traffic lights, check all around you before you move away, as cyclists often filter through waiting traffic. Allow the cyclist to move off safely.

---

232 Mark *one* answer
You intend to turn left at the traffic lights. What should you do just before turning?

- ☐ **A** Check your right mirror
- ☐ **B** Move up close to the white car
- ☐ **C** Straddle the lanes
- ☐ **D** Check for bicycles on your left

Check your nearside for cyclists before moving away. This is especially important if you've been in a queue of traffic and are about to move off, as cyclists often filter past on the nearside of stationary vehicles.

233 Mark *one* answer
Why should you reduce your speed when driving along this road?

- ☐ **A** A staggered junction is ahead
- ☐ **B** A low bridge is ahead
- ☐ **C** The road surface changes ahead
- ☐ **D** The road narrows ahead

Traffic could be turning off or pulling out ahead of you, to the left or right. Vehicles turning left will be slowing down before the junction, and any vehicles turning right may have to stop to allow oncoming traffic to clear. Be prepared for this, as you might have to slow down or stop behind them.

---

234 Mark *one* answer
What might you expect to happen in this situation?

- ☐ **A** Traffic will move into the right-hand lane
- ☐ **B** Traffic speed will increase
- ☐ **C** Traffic will move into the left-hand lane
- ☐ **D** Traffic won't need to change position

Be courteous and allow the traffic to merge into the left-hand lane.

235 Mark *one* answer
You're driving on a road with several lanes. You see these signs above the lanes. What do they mean?

- ☐ **A** The two right lanes are open
- ☐ **B** The two left lanes are open
- ☐ **C** Traffic in the left lanes should stop
- ☐ **D** Traffic in the right lanes should stop

If you see a red cross above your lane, it means that there's an obstruction ahead. You'll have to move into one of the lanes that's showing a green light. If all the lanes are showing a red cross, then you must stop.

236 Mark *one* answer
You're invited to a pub lunch. You know that you'll have to drive in the evening. What is your best course of action?

- ☐ **A** Avoid mixing your alcoholic drinks
- ☐ **B** Don't drink any alcohol at all
- ☐ **C** Have some milk before drinking alcohol
- ☐ **D** Eat a hot meal with your alcoholic drinks

Alcohol will stay in your body for several hours and may make you unfit to drive later in the day. Drinking during the day will also affect your performance at work or study.

237 Mark *one* answer
You've been convicted of driving while unfit through drink or drugs. You'll find this is likely to cause the cost of one of the following to rise considerably. Which one?

- ☐ **A** Road fund licence
- ☐ **B** Insurance premiums
- ☐ **C** Vehicle test certificate
- ☐ **D** Driving licence

You've shown that you're a risk to yourself and others on the road. For this reason, insurance companies may charge you a higher premium.

238 Mark *one* answer
What advice should you give to a driver who has had a few alcoholic drinks at a party?

- ☐ **A** Have a strong cup of coffee and then drive home
- ☐ **B** Drive home carefully and slowly
- ☐ **C** Go home by public transport
- ☐ **D** Wait a short while and then drive home

Drinking black coffee or waiting a few hours won't make any difference. Alcohol takes time to leave the body. A driver who has been drinking should go home by public transport or taxi. They might even be unfit to drive the following morning.

239 Mark *one* answer

You've been taking medicine that causes drowsiness. You begin to feel better, but you still need to take the medicine. What should you do about driving?

□ **A** Only drive if your journey is necessary
□ **B** Drive on quiet roads
□ **C** Ask someone to come with you
□ **D** Avoid driving and check with your doctor

You aren't fit to drive if you're taking medicine that makes you drowsy. Check with your doctor if you're unsure. You mustn't put other road users, your passengers or yourself at risk.

240 Mark *one* answer

You're about to drive home from holiday when you become ill. A doctor prescribes drugs that are likely to affect your driving. What should you do?

□ **A** Only drive if someone is with you
□ **B** Avoid driving on motorways
□ **C** Get someone else to drive
□ **D** Never drive at more than 30 mph

You shouldn't drive if you're taking medicine that could cause you to feel drowsy at the wheel. Ask someone else to drive or, if that isn't possible, find another way to get home.

241 Mark *one* answer

During periods of illness, your ability to drive may be impaired. What must you do?

□ **A** See your doctor each time before you drive
□ **B** Take smaller doses of any medicines
□ **C** Make sure you're medically fit to drive
□ **D** Take all your medicines with you when you drive

Only drive if you're fit to do so. Driving when you're ill or taking some medicines can affect your concentration and judgement. It may also cause you to become drowsy or even fall asleep.

242 Mark *one* answer

What should you do if you begin to feel drowsy while you're driving?

□ **A** Stop and rest as soon as possible
□ **B** Turn the heater up to keep you warm and comfortable
□ **C** Close the car windows to help you concentrate
□ **D** Continue with your journey but drive more slowly

You'll be putting other road users at risk if you continue to drive when you're drowsy. Pull over and stop in a safe place for a rest. Caffeinated drinks and a short nap can temporarily help counter sleepiness. If you're driving a long distance, think about finding some accommodation so you can rest for longer before continuing your journey.

243 Mark *one* answer

What should you do if you become tired while you're driving on a motorway?

- ☐ **A** Pull up on the hard shoulder and change drivers
- ☐ **B** Leave the motorway at the next exit and rest
- ☐ **C** Increase your speed and turn up the radio volume
- ☐ **D** Close all your windows and set the heating to warm

If you feel yourself becoming tired or sleepy, you should leave the motorway at the next exit or services and stop for a rest. If you have to drive a long way, leave earlier and plan your journey to include rest stops. That way, you're less likely to become tired while driving and you'll still arrive in good time.

244 Mark *one* answer

You're about to drive home. You feel very tired and have a severe headache. What should you do?

- ☐ **A** Wait until you're fit and well before driving
- ☐ **B** Drive home, but take a tablet for headaches
- ☐ **C** Drive home if you can stay awake for the journey
- ☐ **D** Wait for a short time, then drive home slowly

All of your concentration should be on your driving. Any pain you feel will distract you, and you should avoid driving when drowsy. The safest course of action is to wait until you've rested and are feeling better before starting your journey.

245 Mark *one* answer

You're driving on a long journey. What can you do to help prevent tiredness?

- ☐ **A** Eat a large meal before driving
- ☐ **B** Take regular refreshment breaks
- ☐ **C** Play loud music in the car
- ☐ **D** Complete the journey without stopping

Long-distance driving can be boring. This, coupled with a stuffy, warm vehicle, can make you feel tired and sleepy. Make sure you take rest breaks to help you stay awake and alert. Stop in a safe place before you get to the stage of fighting sleep.

246 Mark *one* answer

You take some cough medicine given to you by a friend. What should you do before driving?

- ☐ **A** Ask your friend if taking the medicine affected their driving
- ☐ **B** Drink some strong coffee one hour before driving
- ☐ **C** Check the label to see if the medicine will affect your driving
- ☐ **D** Drive a short distance to see if the medicine is affecting your driving

If you've taken medicine, never drive without first checking what the side effects might be; they might affect your judgement and perception, and therefore endanger lives.

247 Mark *one* answer

You take the wrong route and find you're on a one-way street. What should you do?

☐ **A** Reverse out of the road
☐ **B** Turn around in a side road
☐ **C** Continue to the end of the road
☐ **D** Reverse into a driveway

Never reverse or turn your vehicle around in a one-way street. It's illegal and could even cause a collision. If you've taken a wrong turn, carry on along the one-way street and find another route, checking the direction signs as you drive. Stop in a safe place if you need to check a map.

248 Mark *one* answer

What will be a serious distraction from driving?

☐ **A** Looking at road maps
☐ **B** Switching on your demister
☐ **C** Using your windscreen washers
☐ **D** Looking in your door mirror

Looking at road maps while driving is very dangerous. If you aren't sure of your route, stop in a safe place and check the map. You must not allow anything to take your attention away from the road while you're driving.

249 Mark *one* answer

You're driving along this road. The driver on the left is reversing from a driveway. What should you do?

☐ **A** Move to the opposite side of the road
☐ **B** Drive through as you have priority
☐ **C** Sound your horn and be prepared to stop
☐ **D** Speed up and drive through quickly

White lights at the rear of a car show that the driver has selected reverse gear. Sound your horn to warn the other driver of your presence, and reduce your speed as a precaution.

250 Mark *one* answer

You've been involved in an argument that has made you feel angry. What should you do before starting your journey?

☐ **A** Open a window
☐ **B** Turn on your radio
☐ **C** Have an alcoholic drink
☐ **D** Calm down

If you're feeling upset or angry, you'll find it much more difficult to concentrate on your driving. You should wait until you've calmed down before starting a journey.

251 Mark *one* answer

You're driving on this dual carriageway. Why may you need to slow down?

- ☐ **A** There's a broken white line in the centre
- ☐ **B** There are solid white lines on either side
- ☐ **C** There are roadworks ahead of you
- ☐ **D** There are no footpaths

Look well ahead and read any road signs as you drive. They're there to inform you of what's ahead. In this case, you may need to slow down and change direction. Check your mirrors so you know what's happening around you before you change speed or direction.

252 Mark *one* answer

You've just been overtaken by this motorcyclist, who has cut in sharply. What should you do?

- ☐ **A** Sound the horn
- ☐ **B** Brake firmly
- ☐ **C** Keep a safe gap
- ☐ **D** Flash your lights

If another vehicle cuts in sharply, ease off the accelerator and drop back to allow a safe separation distance. Try not to overreact by braking sharply or swerving, as you could lose control. If vehicles behind you are too close or unprepared, it could lead to a crash.

253 Mark *one* answer

You're about to drive home. You can't find the glasses you need to wear. What should you do?

- ☐ **A** Drive home slowly, keeping to quiet roads
- ☐ **B** Borrow a friend's glasses and use those
- ☐ **C** Drive home at night, so that the lights will help you
- ☐ **D** Find a way of getting home without driving

If you need to wear glasses for driving, it's illegal to drive without them. You must be able to see clearly when you're driving.

254 Mark *one* answer
What is a common effect of drinking alcohol?

☐ **A** Colour blindness
☐ **B** Increased confidence
☐ **C** Faster reactions
☐ **D** Increased concentration

Alcohol can increase confidence to a point where a driver's behaviour might become 'out of character'. Someone who normally behaves sensibly might suddenly enjoy taking risks. Never let yourself or your friends get into this situation.

255 Mark *one* answer
Your doctor has given you a course of medicine. Why should you ask how it will affect you?

☐ **A** Drugs make you a better driver by quickening your reactions
☐ **B** You'll have to let your insurance company know about the medicine
☐ **C** Some types of medicine can cause your reactions to slow down
☐ **D** The medicine you take may affect your hearing

Always check the label or information leaflet for any medication you take. The medicine might affect your driving. If you aren't sure, ask your doctor or pharmacist.

256 Mark *one* answer
You find that you need glasses to read vehicle number plates at the required distance. When must you wear them?

☐ **A** Only in bad weather conditions
☐ **B** At all times when driving
☐ **C** Only when you think it's necessary
☐ **D** Only in bad light or at night time

Have your eyesight tested before you start your practical training. Then, throughout your driving life, have checks periodically, as your vision may change.

257 Mark *one* answer
Which of the following types of glasses shouldn't be worn when driving at night?

☐ **A** Half-moon
☐ **B** Round
☐ **C** Bifocal
☐ **D** Tinted

If you're driving at night or in poor visibility, tinted lenses will reduce the efficiency of your vision by reducing the amount of light reaching your eyes.

258 Mark *one* answer

What can seriously affect your ability to concentrate?

- ☐ **A** Drugs
- ☐ **B** Busy roads
- ☐ **C** Tinted windows
- ☐ **D** Contact lenses

Both recreational drugs and prescribed medicine can affect your concentration. It's also now an offence to drive with certain drugs in your body and a positive test could lead to a conviction.

259 Mark *one* answer

You find that your eyesight has become very poor and your optician cannot help you. By law, who should you tell?

- ☐ **A** The driver licensing authority
- ☐ **B** Your own doctor
- ☐ **C** The local police
- ☐ **D** Another optician

Having very poor eyesight will have a serious effect on your ability to drive safely. If you can't meet the driver's eyesight requirements, you must tell DVLA (or DVA in Northern Ireland).

260 Mark *one* answer

When should you use hazard warning lights?

- ☐ **A** When you're double-parked on a two-way road
- ☐ **B** When your direction indicators aren't working
- ☐ **C** When warning oncoming traffic that you intend to stop
- ☐ **D** When your vehicle has broken down and is causing an obstruction

Hazard warning lights are an important safety feature and should be used if you've broken down and are causing an obstruction. Don't use them as an excuse to park illegally. You may also use them on motorways to warn traffic behind you of danger ahead.

261 Mark *one* answer

You want to turn left at this junction. Your view of the main road is restricted. What should you do?

- ☐ **A** Stay well back and wait to see if anything comes
- ☐ **B** Build up your speed so that you can emerge quickly
- ☐ **C** Stop and apply the handbrake even if the road is clear
- ☐ **D** Approach slowly and edge out until you can see more clearly

You should slow right down, and stop if necessary, at any junction where your view is restricted. Edge forward until you can see properly. Only then can you decide whether it's safe to go.

262 Mark *one* answer

When driving a car fitted with automatic transmission, what would you use 'kick down' for?

- ☐ **A** Cruise control
- ☐ **B** Quick acceleration
- ☐ **C** Slow braking
- ☐ **D** Fuel economy

'Kick down' selects a lower gear, enabling the vehicle to accelerate faster.

263 Mark *one* answer

You're driving along this motorway. It's raining. What should you do when following this lorry?

- ☐ **A** Allow at least a two-second gap
- ☐ **B** Move left and drive on the hard shoulder
- ☐ **C** Move right and stay in the right-hand lane
- ☐ **D** Be aware of spray reducing your vision

The usual two-second time gap increases to four seconds when the roads are wet. If you stay well back, you'll:
- be able to see past the vehicle
- be out of the spray thrown up by the lorry's tyres
- give yourself more time to stop if the need arises
- increase your chances of being seen by the lorry driver

264 Mark *one* answer
You're driving towards this left-hand bend. What dangers should you be aware of?

- ☐ **A** A vehicle overtaking you
- ☐ **B** No white lines in the centre of the road
- ☐ **C** No sign to warn you of the bend
- ☐ **D** Pedestrians walking towards you

Pedestrians walking on a road with no pavement should walk against the direction of the traffic. You can't see around this bend: there may be hidden dangers. Always keep this in mind and give yourself time to react if a hazard does appear.

265 Mark *one* answer
Ahead of you, traffic in the left-hand lane is slowing. What should you do?

- ☐ **A** Slow down, keeping a safe separation distance
- ☐ **B** Accelerate past the vehicles in the left-hand lane
- ☐ **C** Pull up on the left-hand verge
- ☐ **D** Move across and continue in the right-hand lane

Allow the traffic to merge into the left-hand lane. Leave enough room so that you can maintain a safe separation distance, even if vehicles pull in ahead of you.

266 Mark *one* answer
In what way are provisional car licence holders restricted?

- ☐ **A** They can't drive at more than 40 mph
- ☐ **B** They can't carry passengers in the rear seats
- ☐ **C** They can't drive on the motorway
- ☐ **D** They can't drive between 11.30 pm and 7.00 am

It's illegal for you to drive on the motorway before you pass your practical test. After you've passed, it's recommended that you have instruction on motorway driving before you drive there on your own. Ask your instructor about this.

267 Mark *one* answer
In which circumstances may you use hazard warning lights?

- ☐ **A** When driving on a motorway to warn traffic behind of a hazard ahead
- ☐ **B** When you're double-parked on a two-way road
- ☐ **C** When your direction indicators aren't working
- ☐ **D** When warning oncoming traffic that you intend to stop

Hazard warning lights are an important safety feature. Use them when driving on a motorway to warn traffic behind you of danger ahead. You should also use them if your vehicle has broken down and is causing an obstruction.

268 Mark *one* answer

You're waiting to emerge at a junction. Your view is restricted by parked vehicles. What can help you to see traffic on the road you're joining?

☐ **A** Looking for traffic behind you
☐ **B** Reflections of traffic in shop windows
☐ **C** Making eye contact with other road users
☐ **D** Checking for traffic in your interior mirror

You must be completely sure it's safe to emerge. Try to look for traffic through the windows of the parked cars or in the reflections in shop windows. Keep looking in all directions as you slowly edge forwards until you can see it's safe.

269 Mark *one* answer

After passing your driving test, you suffer from ill health. This affects your driving. What must you do?

☐ **A** Inform your local police
☐ **B** Avoid using motorways
☐ **C** Always drive accompanied
☐ **D** Inform the licensing authority

You must tell DVLA (or DVA in Northern Ireland) if your health is likely to affect your ability to drive. The licensing authority will investigate your situation and then make a decision on whether or not to take away your licence.

270 Mark *one* answer

Why should the junction on the left be kept clear?

☐ **A** To allow vehicles to enter and emerge
☐ **B** To allow the bus to reverse
☐ **C** To allow vehicles to make a U-turn
☐ **D** To allow vehicles to park

You should always try to keep junctions clear. If you're in queuing traffic, make sure that when you stop you leave enough space for traffic to flow into and out of the junction.

271 Mark *one* answer

Your motorway journey is boring and you feel drowsy. What should you do?

☐ **A** Stop on the hard shoulder for a sleep
☐ **B** Open a window and stop as soon as it's safe and legal
☐ **C** Speed up to arrive at your destination sooner
☐ **D** Slow down and let other drivers overtake

Never stop on the hard shoulder to rest. If there's no service area for several miles, leave the motorway at the next exit and find somewhere safe and legal to pull over.

272 Mark *one* answer
Which sign means that there may be people walking along the road?

☐ A   ☐ B

☐ C   ☐ D

Always check the road signs. Triangular signs are warning signs: they inform you about hazards ahead and help you to anticipate any problems. There are a number of different signs showing pedestrians. Learn the meaning of each one.

273 Mark *one* answer
You're turning left at a junction where pedestrians have started to cross. What should you do?

☐ **A** Go around them, leaving plenty of room
☐ **B** Stop and wave at them to cross
☐ **C** Sound your horn and proceed
☐ **D** Give way to them

When you're turning into a side road, pedestrians who are crossing have priority. You should wait to allow them to finish crossing safely. Be patient if they're slow or unsteady. Don't try to rush them by sounding your horn, flashing your lights, revving your engine or giving any other inappropriate signal.

274 Mark *one* answer
You're turning left into a side road. What hazard should you be especially aware of?

☐ **A** One-way street
☐ **B** Pedestrians
☐ **C** Traffic congestion
☐ **D** Parked vehicles

Make sure that you've reduced your speed and are in the correct gear for the turn. Look into the road before you turn and always give way to any pedestrians who are crossing.

275 Mark *one* answer
You intend to turn right into a side road. Why should you check for motorcyclists just before turning?

☐ **A** They may be overtaking on your left
☐ **B** They may be following you closely
☐ **C** They may be emerging from the side road
☐ **D** They may be overtaking on your right

Never attempt to change direction to the right without first checking your right-hand mirror and blind spot. A motorcyclist might not have seen your signal and could be hidden by other traffic. This observation should become a matter of routine.

276 Mark *one* answer
Why is a toucan crossing different from other crossings?

☐ **A** Moped riders can use it
☐ **B** It's controlled by a traffic warden
☐ **C** It's controlled by two flashing lights
☐ **D** Cyclists can use it

Toucan crossings are shared by pedestrians and cyclists, who are permitted to cycle across. They're shown the green light together. The signals are push-button-operated and there's no flashing amber phase.

277 Mark *one* answer
How will a school crossing patrol signal you to stop?

☐ **A** By pointing to children on the opposite pavement
☐ **B** By displaying a red light
☐ **C** By displaying a 'stop' sign
☐ **D** By giving you an arm signal

If a school crossing patrol steps out into the road with a 'stop' sign, you must stop. Don't wave anyone across the road and don't get impatient or rev your engine.

278 Mark *one* answer
Where would you see this sign?

☐ **A** In the window of a car taking children to school
☐ **B** At the side of the road
☐ **C** At playground areas
☐ **D** On the rear of a school bus or coach

Vehicles that are used to carry children to and from school will be travelling at busy times of the day. If you're following a vehicle with this sign, be prepared for it to make frequent stops. It might pick up or set down passengers in places other than normal bus stops.

279 Mark *one* answer
What does this sign mean?

☐ **A** No route for pedestrians and cyclists
☐ **B** A route for pedestrians only
☐ **C** A route for cyclists only
☐ **D** A route for pedestrians and cyclists

This sign shows a shared route for pedestrians and cyclists: when it ends, the cyclists will be rejoining the main road.

280 Mark *one* answer

You see a pedestrian carrying a white stick with a red band. What does this tell you?

- ☐ **A** They have limited mobility
- ☐ **B** They're deaf
- ☐ **C** They're blind
- ☐ **D** They're deaf and blind

When someone is deaf as well as blind, they may carry a white stick with a red reflective band. They may not be aware that you're approaching and they may not be able to hear anything; so, for example, your horn would be ineffective as a warning to them.

281 Mark *one* answer

What action would you take when elderly people are crossing the road?

- ☐ **A** Wave them across so they know that you've seen them
- ☐ **B** Be patient and allow them to cross in their own time
- ☐ **C** Rev the engine to let them know that you're waiting
- ☐ **D** Tap the horn in case they're hard of hearing

Be aware that older people might take a long time to cross the road. They might also be hard of hearing and not hear you approaching. Don't hurry older people across the road by getting too close to them or revving your engine.

282 Mark *one* answer

What should you do when you see two elderly pedestrians about to cross the road ahead?

- ☐ **A** Expect them to wait for you to pass
- ☐ **B** Speed up to get past them quickly
- ☐ **C** Stop and wave them across the road
- ☐ **D** Be careful; they may misjudge your speed

Older people may have impaired hearing, vision, concentration and judgement. They may also walk slowly and so could take a long time to cross the road.

283 Mark *one* answer

You're coming up to a roundabout. A cyclist is signalling to turn right. What should you do?

- ☐ **A** Overtake on the right
- ☐ **B** Give a warning with your horn
- ☐ **C** Signal the cyclist to move across
- ☐ **D** Give the cyclist plenty of room

If you're following a cyclist who's signalling to turn right at a roundabout, leave plenty of room. Give them space and time to get into the correct lane.

284 Mark *one* answer
Which of these should you allow extra room when overtaking?

☐ **A** Lorry
☐ **B** Tractor
☐ **C** Bicycle
☐ **D** Road-sweeping vehicle

Don't pass cyclists too closely, as they may:
- need to veer around a pothole or other obstacle
- be buffeted by side wind
- be made unsteady by your vehicle

Always leave as much room as you would for a car, and don't cut in front of them.

285 Mark *one* answer
Why should you look particularly for motorcyclists and cyclists at junctions?

☐ **A** They may want to turn into the side road
☐ **B** They may slow down to let you turn
☐ **C** They're harder to see
☐ **D** They might not see you turn

Cyclists and motorcyclists are smaller than other vehicles and so are more difficult to see. They can easily be hidden from your view by cars parked near a junction.

286 Mark *one* answer
You're waiting to come out of a side road. Why should you look carefully for motorcycles?

☐ **A** Motorcycles are usually faster than cars
☐ **B** Police patrols often use motorcycles
☐ **C** Motorcycles can easily be hidden behind obstructions
☐ **D** Motorcycles have right of way

If you're waiting to emerge from a side road, look carefully for motorcycles: they can be difficult to see. Be especially careful if there are parked vehicles or other obstructions restricting your view.

287 Mark *one* answer
In daylight, an approaching motorcyclist is using dipped headlights. Why?

☐ **A** So that the rider can be seen more easily
☐ **B** To stop the battery overcharging
☐ **C** To improve the rider's vision
☐ **D** The rider is inviting you to proceed

A motorcycle can be lost from sight behind another vehicle. The use of the headlights helps to make it more conspicuous and therefore more easily seen.

288 Mark *one* answer

Why should motorcyclists wear bright clothing?

☐ **A** They must do so by law
☐ **B** It helps keep them cool in summer
☐ **C** The colours are popular
☐ **D** Drivers often do not see them

Motorcycles and scooters are generally smaller than other vehicles and can be difficult to see. Wearing bright clothing makes it easier for other road users to see a motorcyclist approaching, especially at junctions.

289 Mark *one* answer

You're unsure what a slow-moving motorcyclist ahead of you is going to do. What should you do?

☐ **A** Pass on the left
☐ **B** Pass on the right
☐ **C** Stay behind
☐ **D** Move closer

When a motorcyclist is travelling slowly, it's likely that they're looking for a turning or entrance. Be patient and stay behind them in case they stop or change direction suddenly.

290 Mark *one* answer

Why will a motorcyclist look round over their right shoulder just before turning right?

☐ **A** To listen for following traffic
☐ **B** Motorcycles don't have mirrors
☐ **C** It helps them balance as they turn
☐ **D** To check for traffic in their blind area

When you see a motorcyclist take a glance over their shoulder, they're probably about to change direction. Recognising a clue like this helps you to anticipate their next action. This can improve road safety for you and others.

291 Mark *one* answer

Which is the most vulnerable road user at road junctions?

☐ **A** Car driver
☐ **B** Tractor driver
☐ **C** Lorry driver
☐ **D** Motorcyclist

Pedestrians and riders on two wheels can be harder to see than other road users. Make sure you look for them, especially at junctions. Effective observation, coupled with appropriate action, can save lives.

292 Mark *one* answer

You're approaching a roundabout. There are horses just ahead of you. What should you do?

- ☐ **A** sound your horn as a warning
- ☐ **B** treat them like any other vehicle
- ☐ **C** give them plenty of room
- ☐ **D** accelerate past as quickly as possible

Horse riders often keep to the outside of the roundabout even if they're turning right. Give them plenty of room and remember that they may have to cross lanes of traffic.

293 Mark *one* answer

As you approach a pelican crossing, the lights change to green. What should you do if elderly people are halfway across?

- ☐ **A** Wave them to cross as quickly as they can
- ☐ **B** Rev your engine to make them hurry
- ☐ **C** Flash your lights in case they haven't noticed you
- ☐ **D** Wait patiently because they'll probably take longer to cross

If the lights turn to green, wait for any pedestrians to clear the crossing. Allow them to finish crossing the road in their own time, and don't try to hurry them by revving your engine.

294 Mark *one* answer

There are flashing amber lights under a school warning sign. What action should you take?

- ☐ **A** Reduce speed until you're clear of the area
- ☐ **B** Keep up your speed and sound the horn
- ☐ **C** Increase your speed to clear the area quickly
- ☐ **D** Wait at the lights until they change to green

The flashing amber lights are switched on to warn you that children may be crossing near a school. Slow down and take extra care, as you may have to stop.

295 Mark *one* answer

Why must these road markings be kept clear?

- ☐ **A** To allow schoolchildren to be dropped off
- ☐ **B** To allow teachers to park
- ☐ **C** To allow schoolchildren to be picked up
- ☐ **D** To allow a clear view of the crossing area

The markings are there to show that the area must be kept clear. This is to allow an unrestricted view for:
- approaching drivers and riders
- children wanting to cross the road

296 Mark *one* answer
Where would you see this sign?

- ☐ **A** Near a school crossing
- ☐ **B** At a playground entrance
- ☐ **C** On a school bus
- ☐ **D** At a 'pedestrians only' area

Watch out for children crossing the road from the other side of the bus.

297 Mark *one* answer
You're following two cyclists. They approach a roundabout in the left-hand lane. In which direction should you expect the cyclists to go?

- ☐ **A** Left
- ☐ **B** Right
- ☐ **C** Any direction
- ☐ **D** Straight ahead

Cyclists approaching a roundabout in the left-hand lane may be turning right but may not have been able to get into the correct lane due to heavy traffic. They may also feel safer keeping to the left all the way around the roundabout. Be aware of them and give them plenty of room.

298 Mark *one* answer
You're travelling behind a moped. What should you do when you want to turn left just ahead?

- ☐ **A** Overtake the moped before the junction
- ☐ **B** Pull alongside the moped and stay level until just before the junction
- ☐ **C** Sound your horn as a warning and pull in front of the moped
- ☐ **D** Stay behind until the moped has passed the junction

Passing the moped and turning into the junction could mean that you cut across the front of the rider. This might force them to slow down, stop or even lose control. Stay behind the moped until it has passed the junction and then you can turn without affecting the rider.

299 Mark *one* answer

You see a horse rider as you approach a roundabout. What should you do if they're signalling right but keeping well to the left?

☐ **A** Proceed as normal
☐ **B** Keep close to them
☐ **C** Cut in front of them
☐ **D** Stay well back

Allow the horse rider to enter and exit the roundabout in their own time. They may feel safer keeping to the left all the way around the roundabout. Don't get up close behind or alongside them, because that would probably upset the horse and create a dangerous situation.

300 Mark *one* answer

How would you react to drivers who appear to be inexperienced?

☐ **A** Sound your horn to warn them of your presence
☐ **B** Be patient and prepare for them to react more slowly
☐ **C** Flash your headlights to indicate that it's safe for them to proceed
☐ **D** Overtake them as soon as possible

Learners might not have confidence when they first start to drive. Allow them plenty of room and don't react adversely to their hesitation. We all learn from experience, but new drivers will have had less practice in dealing with all the situations that might occur.

301 Mark *one* answer

What should you do when you're following a learner driver who stalls at a junction?

☐ **A** Be patient, as you expect them to make mistakes
☐ **B** Stay very close behind and flash your headlights
☐ **C** Start to rev your engine if they take too long to restart
☐ **D** Immediately steer around them and drive on

Learning to drive is a process of practice and experience. Try to understand this and tolerate those who make mistakes while they're learning.

302 Mark *one* answer

You're on a country road. What should you expect to see coming towards you on your side of the road?

☐ **A** Motorcycles
☐ **B** Bicycles
☐ **C** Pedestrians
☐ **D** Horse riders

On a quiet country road, always be aware that there may be a hazard just around the next bend, such as a slow-moving vehicle or pedestrians. Pedestrians are advised to walk on the right-hand side of the road if there's no pavement, so they may be walking towards you on your side of the road.

303 Mark *one* answer

What should you do when following a car driven by an elderly driver?

☐ **A** Expect the driver to drive badly
☐ **B** Flash your lights and overtake
☐ **C** Be aware that their reactions may be slower than yours
☐ **D** Stay very close behind but be careful

You must show consideration to other road users. The reactions of older drivers may be slower and they might need more time to deal with a situation. Be tolerant and don't lose patience or show annoyance.

304 Mark *one* answer

You're following a cyclist. What should you do when you wish to turn left just ahead?

☐ **A** Overtake the cyclist before you reach the junction
☐ **B** Pull alongside the cyclist and stay level until after the junction
☐ **C** Hold back until the cyclist has passed the junction
☐ **D** Go around the cyclist on the junction

Make allowances for cyclists, and give them plenty of room. Don't overtake and then immediately turn left. Be patient and turn behind them when they've passed the junction.

305 Mark *one* answer

A horse rider is in the left-hand lane approaching a roundabout. Where should you expect the rider to go?

☐ **A** In any direction
☐ **B** To the right
☐ **C** To the left
☐ **D** Straight ahead

Horses and their riders move more slowly than other road users. They might not have time to cut across heavy traffic to take up a position in the right-hand lane. For this reason, a horse and rider may approach a roundabout in the left-hand lane even though they're turning right.

306 Mark *one* answer
Powered vehicles used by disabled people are small and hard to see. How do they give early warning when on a dual carriageway?

- ☐ **A** They'll have a flashing red light
- ☐ **B** They'll have a flashing green light
- ☐ **C** They'll have a flashing blue light
- ☐ **D** They'll have a flashing amber light

Powered vehicles used by disabled people are small, low, hard to see and travel very slowly. On a dual carriageway, a flashing amber light will warn other road users.

307 Mark *one* answer
Where should you never overtake a cyclist?

- ☐ **A** Just before you turn left
- ☐ **B** On a left-hand bend
- ☐ **C** On a one-way street
- ☐ **D** On a dual carriageway

If you want to turn left and there's a cyclist in front of you, hold back. Wait until the cyclist has passed the junction and then turn left behind them. Don't try to intimidate them by driving too closely.

308 Mark *one* answer
What does a flashing amber beacon mean when it's on a moving vehicle?

- ☐ **A** The vehicle is slow moving
- ☐ **B** The vehicle has broken down
- ☐ **C** The vehicle is a doctor's car
- ☐ **D** The vehicle belongs to a school crossing patrol

Different coloured beacons warn of different types of vehicle needing special attention. Blue beacons are used on emergency vehicles that need priority. Green beacons are found on doctors' cars. Amber beacons generally denote slower moving vehicles, which are often large. These vehicles are usually involved in road maintenance or local amenities and make frequent stops.

309 Mark *one* answer
What does this sign mean?

- ☐ **A** Contraflow cycle lane
- ☐ **B** With-flow cycle lane
- ☐ **C** Cycles and buses only
- ☐ **D** No cycles or buses

Usually, a picture of a cycle will also be painted on the road, and sometimes the lane will have a different coloured surface. Leave these areas clear for cyclists and don't pass too closely when you overtake.

310 Mark *one* answer

You notice horse riders in front. What should you do first?

- ☐ **A** Pull out to the middle of the road
- ☐ **B** Slow down and be ready to stop
- ☐ **C** Accelerate around them
- ☐ **D** Signal right

Be particularly careful when approaching horse riders – slow down and be prepared to stop. Always pass wide and slowly, and look out for signals given by the riders. Horses are unpredictable: always treat them as potential hazards and take great care when passing them.

311 Mark *one* answer

What is the purpose of these road markings?

- ☐ **A** To ensure children have a clear view from the crossing area
- ☐ **B** To enable teachers to have clear access to the school
- ☐ **C** To ensure delivery vehicles have easy access to the school
- ☐ **D** To enable parents to pick up or drop off children safely

These markings are found on the road outside schools. Don't stop or park on them, even to set down or pick up children. The markings are there to ensure that drivers, riders, children and other pedestrians have a clear view of the road in all directions.

312 Mark *one* answer

The left-hand pavement is closed due to street repairs. What should you do?

- ☐ **A** Watch out for pedestrians walking in the road
- ☐ **B** Use your right-hand mirror more often
- ☐ **C** Speed up to get past the roadworks more quickly
- ☐ **D** Position close to the left-hand kerb

Where street repairs have closed off pavements, proceed carefully and slowly, as pedestrians might have to walk in the road.

313 Mark *one* answer

What should you do when you're following a motorcyclist along a road that has a poor surface?

☐ **A** Drive closely so they can see you in their mirrors

☐ **B** Overtake immediately to avoid delays

☐ **C** Allow extra room in case they swerve to avoid potholes

☐ **D** Allow the same room as normal to avoid wasting road space

To avoid being unbalanced, a motorcyclist might swerve to avoid potholes and bumps in the road. Be prepared for this and allow them extra space.

314 Mark *one* answer

What does this sign tell you?

☐ **A** No cycling

☐ **B** Cycle route ahead

☐ **C** Cycle parking only

☐ **D** End of cycle route

With people's concern today for the environment, cycle routes are being extended in our towns and cities. Respect the presence of cyclists on the road and give them plenty of room if you need to pass.

315 Mark *one* answer

You're approaching this roundabout and see the cyclist signal right. Why is the cyclist keeping to the left?

☐ **A** It's a quicker route for the cyclist

☐ **B** The cyclist is going to turn left instead

☐ **C** The cyclist thinks *The Highway Code* doesn't apply to bicycles

☐ **D** The cyclist is slower and more vulnerable

Cycling in today's heavy traffic can be hazardous. Some cyclists may not feel happy about crossing the path of traffic to take up a position in an outside lane. Be aware of this and understand that, although they're in the left-hand lane, the cyclist might be turning right.

316 Mark *one* answer

What should you do when approaching this crossing?

☐ **A** Prepare to slow down and stop

☐ **B** Stop and wave the pedestrians across

☐ **C** Speed up and pass by quickly

☐ **D** Continue unless the pedestrians step out

Be courteous and prepare to stop. Don't wave people across, because this could be dangerous if another vehicle is approaching the crossing.

317 Mark *one* answer
You see a pedestrian with a dog wearing a yellow or burgundy coat. What does this indicate?

☐ **A** The pedestrian is elderly
☐ **B** The pedestrian is a dog trainer
☐ **C** The pedestrian is colour-blind
☐ **D** The pedestrian is deaf

Dogs trained to help deaf people have a yellow or burgundy coat. If you see one, you should take extra care, as the pedestrian may not be aware of vehicles approaching.

318 Mark *one* answer
Who may use toucan crossings?

☐ **A** Motorcyclists and cyclists
☐ **B** Motorcyclists and pedestrians
☐ **C** Only cyclists
☐ **D** Cyclists and pedestrians

There are some crossings where cycle routes lead cyclists to cross at the same place as pedestrians. These are called toucan crossings. Always look out for cyclists, as they're likely to be approaching faster than pedestrians.

319 Mark *one* answer
Some junctions controlled by traffic lights have a marked area between two stop lines. What is this for?

☐ **A** To allow taxis to position in front of other traffic
☐ **B** To allow people with disabilities to cross the road
☐ **C** To allow cyclists and pedestrians to cross the road together
☐ **D** To allow cyclists to position in front of other traffic

These are known as advanced stop lines. When the lights are red (or about to become red), you should stop at the first white line. However, if you've crossed that line as the lights change, you must stop at the second line even if it means you're in the area reserved for cyclists.

320 Mark *one* answer
When you're overtaking a cyclist, you should leave as much room as you would give to a car. What is the main reason for this?

☐ **A** The cyclist might speed up
☐ **B** The cyclist might get off their bike
☐ **C** The cyclist might swerve
☐ **D** The cyclist might have to make a left turn

Before overtaking, assess the situation. Look well ahead to see whether the cyclist will need to change direction. Be especially aware of a cyclist approaching parked vehicles, as they'll need to alter course. Don't pass too closely or cut in sharply.

321 Mark *one* answer

What should you do when passing sheep on a road?

- ☐ **A** Briefly sound your horn
- ☐ **B** Go very slowly
- ☐ **C** Pass quickly but quietly
- ☐ **D** Herd them to the side of the road

Slow down and be ready to stop if you see animals in the road ahead. Animals are easily frightened by noise and vehicles passing too close to them. Stop if signalled to do so by the person in charge.

322 Mark *one* answer

At night, you see a pedestrian wearing reflective clothing and carrying a bright red light. What does this mean?

- ☐ **A** You're approaching roadworks
- ☐ **B** You're approaching an organised walk
- ☐ **C** You're approaching a slow-moving vehicle
- ☐ **D** You're approaching a traffic danger spot

The people on the walk should be keeping to the left, but don't assume this. Pass carefully, making sure you have time to do so safely. Be aware that the pedestrians have their backs to you and may not know that you're there.

323 Mark *one* answer

You've just passed your test. How can you reduce your risk of being involved in a collision?

- ☐ **A** By always staying close to the vehicle in front
- ☐ **B** By never going over 40 mph
- ☐ **C** By staying in the left-hand lane on all roads
- ☐ **D** By taking further training

New drivers and riders are often involved in a collision or incident early in their driving career. Due to a lack of experience, they may not react to hazards appropriately. Approved training courses are offered by driver and rider training schools for people who have passed their test but want extra training.

324 Mark *one* answer

You want to reverse into a side road, but you aren't sure that the area behind your car is clear. What should you do?

- ☐ **A** Look through the rear window only
- ☐ **B** Get out and check
- ☐ **C** Check the mirrors only
- ☐ **D** Carry on, assuming it's clear

If you can't tell whether there's anything behind you, it's always safest to check before reversing. There may be a small child or a low obstruction close behind your car.

325 Mark *one* answer

You're about to reverse into a side road. A pedestrian is waiting to cross behind you. What should you do?

☐ **A** Wave to the pedestrian to stop
☐ **B** Give way to the pedestrian
☐ **C** Sound your horn to warn the pedestrian
☐ **D** Reverse before the pedestrian starts to cross

If you need to reverse into a side road, try to find a place that's free from traffic and pedestrians. Look all around before and during the manoeuvre. Stop and give way to any pedestrians who want to cross behind you. Avoid waving them across, sounding the horn, flashing your lights or giving any signals that could mislead them and create a dangerous situation.

326 Mark *one* answer

Who's especially in danger of not being seen as you reverse your car?

☐ **A** Motorcyclists
☐ **B** Car drivers
☐ **C** Cyclists
☐ **D** Children

It may not be possible to see a small child through the rear windscreen of your vehicle. Be aware of this before you reverse. If there are children about, get out and check that it's clear before reversing.

327 Mark *one* answer

You want to turn right from a junction but your view is restricted by parked vehicles. What should you do?

☐ **A** Move out quickly, but be prepared to stop
☐ **B** Sound your horn and pull out if there's no reply
☐ **C** Stop, then move forward slowly until you have a clear view
☐ **D** Stop, get out and look along the main road to check

If you want to turn right from a junction and your view is restricted, stop. Ease forward until you can see – something might be approaching. If you don't know, don't go.

328 Mark *one* answer

You're at the front of a queue of traffic waiting to turn right into a side road. Why is it important to check your right mirror just before turning?

☐ **A** To look for pedestrians about to cross
☐ **B** To check for overtaking vehicles
☐ **C** To make sure the side road is clear
☐ **D** To check for emerging traffic

A motorcyclist could be riding along the outside of the queue. Always check your mirror before turning, as situations behind you can change in the time you've been waiting to turn.

329 Mark *one* answer

What must a driver do at a pelican crossing when the amber light is flashing?

- ☐ **A** Signal the pedestrian to cross
- ☐ **B** Always wait for the green light before proceeding
- ☐ **C** Give way to any pedestrians on the crossing
- ☐ **D** Wait for the red-and-amber light before proceeding

The flashing amber light allows pedestrians already on the crossing to get to the other side before a green light shows to the traffic. Be aware that some pedestrians, such as elderly people and young children, need longer to cross. Let them do this at their own pace.

330 Mark *one* answer

You've stopped at a pelican crossing. A disabled person is crossing slowly in front of you when the lights change to green. What should you do?

- ☐ **A** Wait for them to finish crossing
- ☐ **B** Drive in front of them
- ☐ **C** Edge forward slowly
- ☐ **D** Sound your horn

At a pelican crossing, the green light means you may proceed as long as the crossing is clear. If someone hasn't finished crossing, be patient and wait for them, whether they're disabled or not.

331 Mark *one* answer

You're driving past a line of parked cars. You notice a ball bouncing out into the road ahead. What should you do?

- ☐ **A** Continue driving at the same speed and sound your horn
- ☐ **B** Continue driving at the same speed and flash your headlights
- ☐ **C** Slow down and be prepared to stop for children
- ☐ **D** Stop and wave the children across to fetch their ball

Beware of children playing in the street and running out into the road. If a ball bounces out from the pavement, slow down and be prepared to stop. Don't encourage anyone to retrieve it. Other road users may not see your signal and you might lead a child into a dangerous situation.

332 Mark *one* answer

You want to turn right from a main road into a side road. What should you do just before turning?

☐ **A** Cancel your right-turn signal
☐ **B** Select first gear
☐ **C** Check for traffic overtaking on your right
☐ **D** Stop and set the handbrake

In some circumstances, your indicators may be difficult to see and another road user may not realise you're about to turn. A final check in your mirror and blind spot can help you to see an overtaking vehicle, so that you can avoid turning across their path.

333 Mark *one* answer

You're driving in a slow-moving queue of traffic. Just before changing lane, what should you do?

☐ **A** Sound the horn and flash your lights
☐ **B** Look for motorcyclists filtering through the traffic
☐ **C** Give a 'slowing down' arm signal
☐ **D** Change down to first gear

In queuing traffic, motorcyclists could be passing you on either side. Use your mirrors and check your blind area before changing lanes or changing direction.

334 Mark *one* answer

You're driving in town. There's a bus at the bus stop on the other side of the road. Why should you be careful?

☐ **A** The bus might have broken down
☐ **B** Pedestrians might come from behind the bus
☐ **C** The bus might move off suddenly
☐ **D** The bus might remain stationary

If you see a bus ahead, watch out for pedestrians. They might not be able to see you if they're crossing from behind the bus.

335 Mark *one* answer

How should you overtake horse riders?

☐ **A** Drive up close and overtake as soon as possible
☐ **B** Speed isn't important but allow plenty of room
☐ **C** Use your horn just once to warn them
☐ **D** Drive slowly and leave plenty of room

When you decide to overtake a horse rider, make sure you can do so safely before you move out. Leave them plenty of room and pass slowly. Passing too closely at speed could startle the horse and unseat the rider.

336 Mark *one* answer
Why should you allow extra room when overtaking a motorcyclist on a windy day?

- ☐ **A** The rider may turn off suddenly to get out of the wind
- ☐ **B** The rider may be blown across in front of you
- ☐ **C** The rider may stop suddenly
- ☐ **D** The rider may be travelling faster than normal

If you're driving in high winds, be aware that the conditions might force a motorcyclist or cyclist to swerve or wobble. Take this into consideration if you're following or wish to overtake a two-wheeled vehicle.

337 Mark *one* answer
Where should you take particular care to look for motorcyclists and cyclists?

- ☐ **A** On dual carriageways
- ☐ **B** At junctions
- ☐ **C** At zebra crossings
- ☐ **D** On one-way streets

Motorcyclists and cyclists are often more difficult to see at junctions. They're easily hidden from view and you may not be able to see them approaching a junction if your view is partially blocked; for example, by other traffic.

338 Mark *one* answer
The road outside this school is marked with yellow zigzag lines. What do these lines mean?

- ☐ **A** You may park on the lines when dropping off schoolchildren
- ☐ **B** You may park on the lines when picking up schoolchildren
- ☐ **C** You mustn't wait or park your vehicle here at all
- ☐ **D** You must stay with your vehicle if you park here

Parking here would block other road users' view of the school entrance and would endanger the lives of children on their way to and from school.

339 Mark *one* answer

You're driving past parked cars. You notice a bicycle wheel sticking out between them. What should you do?

☐ **A** Accelerate past quickly and sound your horn
☐ **B** Slow down and wave the cyclist across
☐ **C** Brake sharply and flash your headlights
☐ **D** Slow down and be prepared to stop for a cyclist

Scan the road as you drive. Try to anticipate hazards by being aware of the places where they're likely to occur. You'll then be able to react in good time.

340 Mark *one* answer

You're dazzled at night by a vehicle behind you. What should you do?

☐ **A** Set your mirror to the anti-dazzle position
☐ **B** Set your mirror to dazzle the other driver
☐ **C** Brake sharply to a stop
☐ **D** Switch your rear lights on and off

The interior mirror of most vehicles can be set to an anti-dazzle position. You'll still be able to see the lights of the traffic behind you, but the dazzle will be greatly reduced.

341 Mark *one* answer

You're driving towards a zebra crossing. A person in a wheelchair is waiting to cross. What should you do?

☐ **A** Continue on your way
☐ **B** Wave to the person to cross
☐ **C** Wave to the person to wait
☐ **D** Be prepared to stop

You should slow down and be prepared to stop, as you would for an able-bodied person. Don't wave them across, as other traffic may not stop.

342 Mark *one* answer

You're about to overtake a slow-moving motorcyclist. Which one of these signs would make you take special care?

☐ A ☐ B

☐ C ☐ D

In windy weather, watch out for motorcyclists and also cyclists, as they can be blown sideways into your path. When you pass them, leave plenty of room and check their position in your mirror before pulling back in.

---

343 Mark *one* answer

You're waiting to emerge left from a minor road. A large vehicle is approaching from the right. You have time to turn, but you should wait. Why?

☐ **A** The large vehicle can easily hide an overtaking vehicle

☐ **B** The large vehicle can turn suddenly

☐ **C** The large vehicle is difficult to steer in a straight line

☐ **D** The large vehicle can easily hide vehicles from the left

Large vehicles can hide other vehicles that are overtaking – especially motorcycles, which may be filtering past queuing traffic. You need to be aware of the possibility of hidden vehicles and not assume that it's safe to emerge.

344 Mark *one* answer

You're following a long vehicle. As it approaches a crossroads, it signals left but moves out to the right. What should you do?

☐ **A** Get closer in order to pass it quickly

☐ **B** Stay well back and give it room

☐ **C** Assume the signal is wrong and that it's turning right

☐ **D** Overtake it as it starts to slow down

A long vehicle may need to swing out in the opposite direction as it approaches a turn, to allow the rear wheels to clear the kerb. Don't try to filter through if you see a gap; as the lorry turns, the gap will close.

345 Mark *one* answer

You're following a long vehicle approaching a crossroads. The driver signals right but moves close to the left-hand kerb. What should you do?

- ☐ **A** Warn the driver about the wrong signal
- ☐ **B** Wait behind the long vehicle
- ☐ **C** Report the driver to the police
- ☐ **D** Overtake on the right-hand side

When a long vehicle is going to turn right, it may need to keep close to the left-hand kerb. This is to prevent the rear end of the trailer cutting the corner. You need to be aware of how long vehicles behave in such situations. Don't overtake the lorry, because it could turn as you're alongside. Stay behind and wait for it to turn.

346 Mark *one* answer

You're approaching a mini-roundabout. What should you do when you see the long vehicle in front signalling left but positioned over to the right?

- ☐ **A** Sound your horn
- ☐ **B** Overtake on the left
- ☐ **C** Follow the same course as the lorry
- ☐ **D** Keep well back

At mini-roundabouts, there isn't much room for a long vehicle to manoeuvre. It will have to swing out wide so that it can complete the turn safely. Keep well back and don't try to move up alongside it.

347 Mark *one* answer

Before overtaking a large vehicle, you should keep well back. Why is this?

- ☐ **A** To give acceleration space to overtake quickly on blind bends
- ☐ **B** To get the best view of the road ahead
- ☐ **C** To leave a gap in case the vehicle stops and rolls back
- ☐ **D** To offer other drivers a safe gap if they want to overtake you

When following a large vehicle, keep well back. If you're too close, you won't be able to see the road ahead and the driver of the long vehicle might not be able to see you in their mirrors.

348 Mark *one* answer

You're travelling behind a bus that pulls up at a bus stop. What should you do?

- ☐ **A** Accelerate past the bus
- ☐ **B** Watch carefully for pedestrians
- ☐ **C** Sound your horn
- ☐ **D** Pull in closely behind the bus

There might be pedestrians crossing from in front of the bus. Look out for them if you intend to pass. Consider how many people are waiting to get on the bus - check the queue if you can. The bus might move off straight away if no-one is waiting to get on. If a bus is signalling to pull out, give it priority if it's safe to do so.

349 Mark *one* answer

You're following a lorry on a wet road. What should you do when spray makes it difficult to see the road ahead?

- ☐ **A** Drop back until you can see better
- ☐ **B** Put your headlights on full beam
- ☐ **C** Keep close to the lorry, away from the spray
- ☐ **D** Speed up and overtake quickly

Large vehicles throw up a lot of spray when it's wet. This makes it difficult for following drivers to see the road ahead. You'll be able to see more by dropping back further, out of the spray. This will also increase your separation distance, giving you more room to stop if you have to.

350 Mark *one* answer

You keep well back while waiting to overtake a large vehicle. What should you do if a car moves into the gap?

- ☐ **A** Sound your horn
- ☐ **B** Drop back further
- ☐ **C** Flash your headlights
- ☐ **D** Start to overtake

Sometimes your separation distance is shortened by a driver moving into the gap you've allowed. When this happens, react positively, stay calm and drop further back to re-establish a safe following distance.

351 Mark *one* answer

What should you do when you're approaching a bus that's signalling to move away from a bus stop?

- ☐ **A** Get past before it moves
- ☐ **B** Allow it to pull away, if it's safe to do so
- ☐ **C** Flash your headlights as you approach
- ☐ **D** Signal left and wave the bus on

Try to give way to buses if you can do so safely, especially when the driver signals to pull away from a bus stop. Look out for people getting off the bus or running to catch it, because they may cross the road without looking. Don't accelerate to get past the bus, and don't flash your lights, as this could mislead other road users.

352 Mark *one* answer

How should you overtake a long, slow-moving vehicle on a busy road?

- ☐ **A** Follow it closely and keep moving out to see the road ahead
- ☐ **B** Flash your headlights for the oncoming traffic to give way
- ☐ **C** Stay behind until the driver waves you past
- ☐ **D** Keep well back until you can see that it's clear

When you're following a long vehicle, stay well back so that you can get a better view of the road ahead. The closer you get, the less you'll be able to see of the road. Be patient and don't take a gamble. Only overtake when you're certain that you can complete the manoeuvre safely.

353 Mark *one* answer

Which of these is least likely to be affected by side winds?

- ☐ **A** Cyclists
- ☐ **B** Motorcyclists
- ☐ **C** High-sided vehicles
- ☐ **D** Cars

Although cars are the least likely to be affected, side winds can take anyone by surprise. This is most likely to happen after overtaking a large vehicle, when passing gaps between hedges or buildings, and on exposed sections of road.

354 Mark *one* answer
What should you do as you approach this lorry?

☐ **A** Slow down and be prepared to wait
☐ **B** Make the lorry wait for you
☐ **C** Flash your lights at the lorry
☐ **D** Move to the right-hand side of the road

When turning, long vehicles need much more room on the road than other vehicles. At junctions, they may take up the whole of the road space, so be patient and allow them the room they need.

355 Mark *one* answer
You're following a large vehicle approaching a crossroads. The driver signals to turn left. What should you do?

☐ **A** Overtake if you can leave plenty of room
☐ **B** Overtake only if there are no oncoming vehicles
☐ **C** Don't overtake until the vehicle begins to turn
☐ **D** Don't overtake as you approach or at the junction

Hold back and wait until the vehicle has turned before proceeding. Don't overtake, because the vehicle turning left could hide a vehicle emerging from the same junction.

356 Mark *one* answer
What is the maximum speed of powered wheelchairs or scooters used by disabled people?

☐ **A** 8 mph
☐ **B** 12 mph
☐ **C** 16 mph
☐ **D** 20 mph

Some powered wheelchairs and mobility scooters are designed for use on the pavement only and cannot exceed 4 mph (6 km/h). Others can go on the road as well, and this category cannot exceed 8 mph (12 km/h). Take great care around these vehicles. They're extremely vulnerable because of their low speed and small size.

357 Mark *one* answer
Why is it more difficult to overtake a large vehicle than a car?

☐ **A** It will take longer to pass one
☐ **B** It will be fitted with a speed limiter
☐ **C** It will have air brakes
☐ **D** It will be slow climbing hills

Depending on relative speed, it will usually take you longer to pass a lorry than other vehicles. Hazards to watch for include oncoming traffic, junctions ahead, bends or dips that could restrict your view, and signs or road markings that prohibit overtaking. Make sure you can see that it's safe to complete the manoeuvre before you start to overtake.

358 Mark *one* answer

It's very windy. You're behind a motorcyclist who's overtaking a high-sided vehicle. What should you do?

- ☐ **A** Overtake the motorcyclist immediately
- ☐ **B** Keep well back
- ☐ **C** Stay level with the motorcyclist
- ☐ **D** Keep close to the motorcyclist

Windy weather affects motorcyclists more than other vehicles. In windy conditions, high-sided vehicles cause air turbulence. You should keep well back, as the motorcyclist could be blown off course.

359 Mark *one* answer

You're driving in town. Ahead of you a bus is at a bus stop. Which of the following should you do?

- ☐ **A** Flash your lights to warn the driver of your presence
- ☐ **B** Continue at the same speed but sound your horn as a warning
- ☐ **C** Watch carefully for the sudden appearance of pedestrians
- ☐ **D** Pass the bus as quickly as you possibly can

As you approach, look out for any signal the driver might make. If you pass the vehicle, watch out for pedestrians attempting to cross the road from behind the bus. They'll be hidden from view until the last moment.

360 Mark *one* answer

You're driving along this road. What should you be prepared to do?

- ☐ **A** Sound your horn and continue
- ☐ **B** Slow down and give way
- ☐ **C** Report the driver to the police
- ☐ **D** Squeeze through the gap

Sometimes, large vehicles may need more space than other road users. If a vehicle needs more time and space to turn, be prepared to stop and wait.

361 Mark *one* answer

As a driver, why should you be more careful where trams operate?

- ☐ **A** Because they don't have a horn
- ☐ **B** Because they can't stop for cars
- ☐ **C** Because they don't have lights
- ☐ **D** Because they can't steer to avoid you

You should take extra care when you first encounter trams. You'll have to get used to dealing with a different traffic system. Be aware that trams can accelerate and travel very quickly, and they can't change direction to avoid obstructions.

362 Mark *one* answer

You're towing a caravan. Which is the safest type of rear-view mirror to use?

☐ **A** Interior wide-angle mirror
☐ **B** Extended-arm side mirrors
☐ **C** Ordinary door mirrors
☐ **D** Ordinary interior mirror

Towing a large trailer or caravan can greatly reduce your view of the road behind. You may need to fit extended-arm side mirrors so that you can see clearly behind and down both sides of the caravan or trailer.

363 Mark *one* answer

You're driving in heavy traffic on a wet road. Spray makes it difficult to be seen. What lights should you use?

☐ **A** Full-beam headlights
☐ **B** Sidelights only
☐ **C** Rear fog lights if visibility is more than 100 metres (328 feet)
☐ **D** Dipped headlights

You must make sure that other road users can see you, but you don't want to dazzle them. Use your dipped headlights during the day if visibility is poor. If visibility falls below 100 metres (328 feet), you may use your rear fog lights, but don't forget to turn them off when the visibility improves.

364 Mark *one* answer

It's a very windy day and you're about to overtake a cyclist. What should you do?

☐ **A** Overtake very slowly
☐ **B** Keep close as you pass
☐ **C** Sound your horn repeatedly
☐ **D** Allow extra room

Cyclists, and motorcyclists, are very vulnerable in high winds. They can easily be blown well off course and veer into your path. Always allow plenty of room when overtaking them. Passing too close could cause a draught and unbalance the rider.

365 Mark *one* answer

When may you overtake another vehicle on the left?

- ☐ **A** When you're in a one-way street
- ☐ **B** When approaching a motorway slip road where you'll be turning off
- ☐ **C** When the vehicle in front is signalling to turn left
- ☐ **D** When a slower vehicle is travelling in the right-hand lane of a dual carriageway

You may pass slower vehicles on their left while travelling along a one-way street. Be aware of drivers who may need to change lanes and may not expect faster traffic passing on their left.

366 Mark *one* answer

You're travelling in very heavy rain. How is this likely to affect your overall stopping distance?

- ☐ **A** It will be doubled
- ☐ **B** It will be halved
- ☐ **C** It will be ten times greater
- ☐ **D** It will be no different

The road will be very wet and spray from other vehicles will reduce your visibility. Tyre grip will also be reduced, increasing your stopping distance. You should at least double your separation distance.

367 Mark *one* answer

What should you do when you're overtaking at night?

- ☐ **A** Wait until a bend so that you can see oncoming headlights
- ☐ **B** Sound your horn twice before moving out
- ☐ **C** Put your headlights on full beam
- ☐ **D** Beware of bends in the road ahead

Don't overtake if there's a possibility of a road junction, bend or brow of a bridge or hill ahead. There are many hazards that are difficult to see in the dark. Only overtake if you're certain that the road ahead is clear. Don't take a chance.

368 Mark *one* answer

When may you wait in a box junction?

- ☐ **A** When you're stationary in a queue of traffic
- ☐ **B** When approaching a pelican crossing
- ☐ **C** When approaching a zebra crossing
- ☐ **D** When oncoming traffic prevents you turning right

The purpose of a box junction is to keep the junction clear by preventing vehicles from stopping in the path of crossing traffic. You mustn't enter a box junction unless your exit is clear. However, you may enter the box and wait if you want to turn right and are only prevented from doing so by oncoming traffic.

369 Mark *one* answer

Which of these plates normally appears with this road sign?

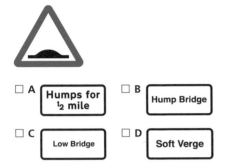

☐ **A** Humps for ¹⁄₂ mile

☐ **B** Hump Bridge

☐ **C** Low Bridge

☐ **D** Soft Verge

Road humps are used to slow down traffic. They're found in places where there are often pedestrians, such as:

• shopping areas
• near schools
• residential areas

Watch out for people close to the kerb or crossing the road.

370 Mark *one* answer

What do traffic-calming measures do?

☐ **A** Stop road rage
☐ **B** Make overtaking easier
☐ **C** Slow traffic down
☐ **D** Make parking easier

Traffic-calming measures make the roads safer for vulnerable road users, such as cyclists, pedestrians and children. These can be designed as chicanes, road humps or other obstacles that encourage drivers and riders to slow down.

371 Mark *one* answer

You're on a motorway in fog. The left-hand edge of the motorway can be identified by reflective studs. What colour are they?

☐ **A** Green
☐ **B** Amber
☐ **C** Red
☐ **D** White

Be especially careful if you're on a motorway in fog. Reflective studs are there to help you in poor visibility. Different colours are used so that you'll know which lane you're in. These are:

• red on the left-hand edge of the carriageway
• white between lanes
• amber on the right-hand edge of the carriageway
• green between the carriageway and slip roads

372 Mark *one* answer
What is a rumble device designed to do?

- ☐ **A** Give directions
- ☐ **B** Prevent cattle escaping
- ☐ **C** Alert you to low tyre pressure
- ☐ **D** Alert you to a hazard

A rumble device consists of raised markings or strips across the road, designed to give drivers an audible, visual and tactile warning. These devices are used in various locations, including in the line separating the hard shoulder and the left-hand lane on the motorway and on the approach to some hazards, to alert drivers to the need to slow down.

373 Mark *one* answer
What should you do when making a journey in foggy conditions?

- ☐ **A** Follow other vehicles' tail lights closely
- ☐ **B** Avoid using dipped headlights
- ☐ **C** Leave plenty of time for your journey
- ☐ **D** Keep two seconds behind the vehicle ahead

If you're planning to make a journey when it's foggy, listen to the weather reports. If visibility is very poor, avoid making unnecessary journeys. If you do travel, leave plenty of time – and if someone is waiting for you to arrive, let them know that your journey will take longer than normal. This will also take off any pressure you may feel to rush.

374 Mark *one* answer
What must you do when overtaking a car at night?

- ☐ **A** Flash your headlights before overtaking
- ☐ **B** Select a higher gear
- ☐ **C** Switch your lights to full beam before overtaking
- ☐ **D** Make sure you don't dazzle other road users

To prevent your lights from dazzling the driver of the car in front, wait until you've passed them before switching to full beam.

375 Mark *one* answer
You're travelling on a road that has speed humps. What should you do when the driver in front is travelling more slowly than you?

- ☐ **A** Sound your horn
- ☐ **B** Overtake as soon as you can
- ☐ **C** Flash your headlights
- ☐ **D** Slow down and stay behind

Be patient and stay behind the car in front. You shouldn't normally overtake other vehicles in areas subject to traffic calming. If you overtake here, you may easily exceed the speed limit, defeating the purpose of the traffic-calming measures.

376 Mark *one* answer

You see these markings on the road. Why are they there?

- ☐ **A** To show a safe distance between vehicles
- ☐ **B** To keep the area clear of traffic
- ☐ **C** To make you aware of your speed
- ☐ **D** To warn you to change direction

These lines may be painted on the road on the approach to a roundabout, a village or a particular hazard. The lines are raised and painted yellow, and their purpose is to make you aware of your speed. Reduce your speed in good time so that you avoid having to brake harshly over the last few metres before reaching the junction.

377 Mark *one* answer

How would you identify a section of road used by trams?

- ☐ **A** There would be metal studs around it
- ☐ **B** There would be zigzag markings alongside it
- ☐ **C** There would be a different surface texture
- ☐ **D** There would be yellow hatch markings around it

Trams may run on roads used by other vehicles and pedestrians. The section of road used by trams is known as the reserved area and should be kept clear. It usually has a different surface, edged with white lane markings.

378 Mark *one* answer

What should you do when you meet an oncoming vehicle on a single-track road?

- ☐ **A** Reverse back to the main road
- ☐ **B** Carry out an emergency stop
- ☐ **C** Stop at a passing place
- ☐ **D** Switch on your hazard warning lights

Take care when using single-track roads. It can be difficult to see around bends, because of hedges or fences, so expect to meet oncoming vehicles. Drive carefully and be ready to pull into or stop opposite a passing place, where you can pass each other safely.

379 Mark *one* answer

The road is wet. Why might a motorcyclist steer round drain covers on a bend?

- ☐ **A** To avoid puncturing the tyres on the edge of the drain covers
- ☐ **B** To prevent the motorcycle sliding on the metal drain covers
- ☐ **C** To help judge the bend using the drain covers as marker points
- ☐ **D** To avoid splashing pedestrians on the pavement

Other drivers or riders may have to change course due to the size or characteristics of their vehicle. Understanding this will help you to anticipate their actions. Motorcyclists and cyclists will be checking the road ahead for uneven or slippery surfaces, especially in wet weather. They may need to move across their lane to avoid surface hazards such as potholes and drain covers.

380 Mark *one* answer

After this hazard you should test your brakes. Why is this?

- ☐ **A** You'll be on a slippery road
- ☐ **B** Your brakes will be soaking wet
- ☐ **C** You'll be going down a long hill
- ☐ **D** You'll have just crossed a long bridge

A ford is a crossing over a stream that's shallow enough to drive or ride through. After you've gone through a ford or deep puddle, your brakes will be wet and they won't work as well as usual. To dry them out, apply a light brake pressure while moving slowly. Don't travel at normal speeds until you're sure your brakes are working properly again.

381 Mark *one* answer

Why should you always reduce your speed when travelling in fog?

- ☐ **A** The brakes don't work as well
- ☐ **B** You'll be dazzled by other headlights
- ☐ **C** The engine will take longer to warm up
- ☐ **D** It's more difficult to see what's ahead

You won't be able to see as far ahead in fog as you can on a clear day. You'll need to reduce your speed so that, if a hazard looms out of the fog, you have the time and space to take avoiding action.Travelling in fog is hazardous. If you can, try to delay your journey until it has cleared.

382 Mark *one* answer

How will your vehicle be affected when you drive up steep hills?

- ☐ **A** The higher gears will pull better
- ☐ **B** The steering will feel heavier
- ☐ **C** Overtaking will be easier
- ☐ **D** The engine will work harder

The engine will need more power to pull the vehicle up the hill. When approaching a steep hill you should select a lower gear to help maintain your speed. You should do this without hesitation, so that you don't lose too much speed before engaging the lower gear.

383 Mark *one* answer

You're driving on the motorway in windy conditions. What should you do as you pass a high-sided vehicle?

- ☐ **A** Increase your speed
- ☐ **B** Be wary of a sudden gust
- ☐ **C** Drive alongside very closely
- ☐ **D** Expect normal conditions

The draught caused by other vehicles – particularly those with high sides – could be strong enough to push you out of your lane. Be prepared for a sudden gust of wind as you pass large vehicles. Keep both hands on the steering wheel to help you keep full control.

384 Mark *one* answer
What should you do to correct a rear-wheel skid?

☐ **A** Not steer at all
☐ **B** Steer away from it
☐ **C** Steer into it
☐ **D** Apply your handbrake

If your car skids and the rear wheels slide to the right, you need to steer into the skid (ie to the right), until the front and rear wheels are brought into line. Don't oversteer or you'll cause a skid in the opposite direction and this will make the situation worse.

385 Mark *one* answer
You're driving in fog. Why should you keep well back from the vehicle in front?

☐ **A** In case it changes direction suddenly
☐ **B** In case its fog lights dazzle you
☐ **C** In case it stops suddenly
☐ **D** In case its brake lights dazzle you

If you're following another road user in fog, stay well back. The driver in front won't be able to see hazards until they're close and might need to brake suddenly. Also, the road surface is likely to be wet and could be slippery.

386 Mark *one* answer
What should you do if you park on the road when it's foggy?

☐ **A** Leave sidelights switched on
☐ **B** Leave dipped headlights and fog lights switched on
☐ **C** Leave dipped headlights switched on
☐ **D** Leave main-beam headlights switched on

If you have to park your vehicle in foggy conditions, try to find a place to park off the road. If this isn't possible, park on the road facing in the same direction as the traffic. Leave your sidelights switched on and make sure they're clean.

387 Mark *one* answer
You're driving at night and are dazzled by vehicle headlights coming towards you. What should you do?

☐ **A** Pull down your sun visor
☐ **B** Slow down or stop
☐ **C** Flash your main-beam headlights
☐ **D** Shade your eyes with your hand

If the headlights of an oncoming vehicle dazzle you, slow down or, if necessary, stop. Don't close your eyes or swerve, as you'll increase your chances of having a collision. Don't flash your headlights either, as this could dazzle other drivers and make the situation worse.

388 Mark *one* answer
When may front fog lights be used?

☐ **A** When visibility is seriously reduced
☐ **B** When they're fitted above the bumper
☐ **C** When they aren't as bright as the headlights
☐ **D** When an audible warning device is used

Your fog lights must only be used when visibility is reduced to 100 metres (328 feet) or less. You need to be familiar with the layout of your dashboard so you're aware if your fog lights have been switched on in error, or you've forgotten to switch them off.

389 Mark *one* answer
You're driving with your front fog lights switched on. Earlier fog has now cleared. What should you do?

☐ **A** Leave them on if other drivers have their lights on
☐ **B** Switch them off as long as visibility remains good
☐ **C** Flash them to warn oncoming traffic that it's foggy
☐ **D** Drive with them on instead of your headlights

Switch off your fog lights if the weather improves, but be prepared to use them again if visibility reduces to less than 100 metres (328 feet).

390 Mark *one* answer
Why should you switch off your rear fog lights when the fog has cleared?

☐ **A** To allow your headlights to work
☐ **B** To stop draining the battery
☐ **C** To stop the engine losing power
☐ **D** To prevent dazzling following drivers

Don't forget to switch off your fog lights when the weather improves. You could be prosecuted for driving with them on in good visibility. The high intensity of rear fog lights can dazzle following drivers and make your brake lights difficult to notice.

391 Mark *one* answer
What will happen if you use rear fog lights in good conditions?

☐ **A** They'll make it safer when towing a trailer
☐ **B** They'll protect you from larger vehicles
☐ **C** They'll dazzle other drivers
☐ **D** They'll make following drivers keep back

Rear fog lights shine more brightly than normal rear lights, so that they show up in reduced visibility. When the visibility improves, you must switch them off; this stops them dazzling the driver behind.

392 Mark *one* answer

What can fitting chains to your wheels help to prevent?

☐ **A** Damage to the road surface
☐ **B** Wear to the tyres
☐ **C** Skidding in deep snow
☐ **D** The brakes locking

Chains can be fitted to your wheels in snowy conditions. They can help you to move off without wheelspin, or to keep moving in deep snow. You'll still need to adjust your driving to suit these conditions.

393 Mark *one* answer

How can you use your vehicle's engine to control your speed?

☐ **A** By changing to a lower gear
☐ **B** By selecting reverse gear
☐ **C** By changing to a higher gear
☐ **D** By selecting neutral

You should brake and slow down before selecting a lower gear. The gear can then be used to keep the speed low and help you control the vehicle. This is particularly helpful on long downhill stretches, where brake fade can occur if the brakes overheat.

394 Mark *one* answer

Why could it be dangerous to keep the clutch down, or select neutral, for long periods of time while you're driving?

☐ **A** Fuel spillage will occur
☐ **B** Engine damage may be caused
☐ **C** You'll have less steering and braking control
☐ **D** It will wear tyres out more quickly

Letting your vehicle roll or coast in neutral reduces your control over steering and braking. This can be dangerous on downhill slopes, where your vehicle could pick up speed very quickly.

395 Mark *one* answer

You're driving on an icy road. What distance from the car in front should you drive?

☐ **A** Four times the normal distance
☐ **B** Six times the normal distance
☐ **C** Eight times the normal distance
☐ **D** Ten times the normal distance

Don't travel in icy or snowy weather unless your journey is essential. Drive extremely carefully when roads are or may be icy. Stopping distances can be ten times greater than on dry roads.

396 Mark *one* answer

You're driving on a well-lit motorway on a clear night. What must you do?

☐ **A** Use only your sidelights
☐ **B** Use your headlights
☐ **C** Use rear fog lights
☐ **D** Use front fog lights

If you're driving on a motorway at night or in poor visibility, you must always use your headlights, even if the road is well lit. Other road users must be able to see you, but you should avoid causing dazzle.

397 Mark *one* answer

You're on a motorway at night, with other vehicles just ahead of you. Which lights should you have on?

☐ **A** Front fog lights
☐ **B** Main-beam headlights
☐ **C** Sidelights only
☐ **D** Dipped headlights

If you're driving behind other traffic on the motorway at night, use dipped headlights. Main-beam headlights will dazzle the other drivers. Your headlights' dipped beam should fall short of the vehicle in front.

398 Mark *one* answer

What will affect your vehicle's stopping distance?

☐ **A** The speed limit
☐ **B** The street lighting
☐ **C** The time of day
☐ **D** The condition of the tyres

Having tyres correctly inflated and in good condition will ensure they have maximum grip on the road; how well your tyres grip the road has a significant effect on your car's stopping distance.

399 Mark *one* answer

You're driving on a motorway at night. When may you switch off your headlights?

☐ **A** When there are vehicles close in front of you
☐ **B** When you're travelling below 50 mph
☐ **C** When the motorway is lit
☐ **D** When your vehicle is broken down on the hard shoulder

Always use your headlights at night on a motorway unless you've had to stop on the hard shoulder. If you break down and have to use the hard shoulder, switch off your headlights but leave your sidelights on, so that other road users can see your vehicle.

400 Mark *one* answer

When will you feel the effects of engine braking?

☐ **A** When you only use the handbrake
☐ **B** When you're in neutral
☐ **C** When you change to a lower gear
☐ **D** When you change to a higher gear

When you take your foot off the accelerator, engines have a natural resistance to turn, caused mainly by the cylinder compression. Changing to a lower gear requires the engine to turn faster and so it will have greater resistance than when it's made to turn more slowly. When going downhill, changing to a lower gear will therefore help to keep the vehicle's speed in check.

401 Mark *one* answer

Daytime visibility is poor but not seriously reduced. Which lights should you switch on?

☐ **A** Headlights and fog lights
☐ **B** Front fog lights
☐ **C** Dipped headlights
☐ **D** Rear fog lights

Only use your fog lights when visibility is seriously reduced. Use dipped headlights in poor conditions because this helps other road users to see you without the risk of causing dazzle.

402 Mark *one* answer

Why are vehicles fitted with rear fog lights?

☐ **A** To make them more visible when driving at high speed
☐ **B** To show when they've broken down in a dangerous position
☐ **C** To make them more visible in thick fog
☐ **D** To warn drivers following closely to drop back

Rear fog lights make it easier to spot a vehicle ahead in foggy conditions. Avoid the temptation to use other vehicles' lights as a guide, as they may give you a false sense of security.

403 Mark *one* answer

While you're driving in fog, it becomes necessary to use front fog lights. What should you remember?

☐ **A** Only use them in heavy traffic conditions
☐ **B** Don't use them on motorways
☐ **C** Only use them on dual carriageways
☐ **D** Switch them off when visibility improves

It's illegal to use your fog lights in conditions other than when visibility is seriously reduced; that is, less than 100 metres (328 feet). Fog lights are very bright and, if you use them when visibility has improved, you could dazzle other drivers.

404 Mark *one* answer

What should you do when there's been a heavy fall of snow?

☐ **A** Drive with your hazard warning lights on
☐ **B** Don't drive unless you have a mobile phone
☐ **C** Only drive when your journey is short
☐ **D** Don't drive unless it's essential

Consider whether the increased risk is worth it. If the weather conditions are bad and your journey isn't essential, then don't drive.

405 Mark *one* answer

You're driving down a long, steep hill. You suddenly notice that your brakes aren't working as well as normal. What is the usual cause of this?

☐ **A** The brakes overheating
☐ **B** Air in the brake fluid
☐ **C** Oil on the brakes
☐ **D** Badly adjusted brakes

This is more likely to happen on vehicles fitted with drum brakes, but it can apply to disc brakes as well. Using a lower gear will assist the braking and help you to keep control of your vehicle.

406 Mark *one* answer

You have to make a journey in fog. What should you do before you set out?

☐ **A** Top up the radiator with anti-freeze
☐ **B** Make sure that you have a warning triangle in the vehicle
☐ **C** Make sure that the windows are clean
☐ **D** Check the battery

If you have to drive in fog, switch your dipped-beam headlights on and keep your windscreen clear. You should always be able to pull up within the distance you can see ahead.

407 Mark *one* answer

You've just driven out of fog. What must you do now that visibility has improved?

☐ **A** Switch off your fog lights
☐ **B** Keep your rear fog lights switched on
☐ **C** Keep your front fog lights switched on
☐ **D** Leave your fog lights switched on in case the fog returns

You must turn off your fog lights if visibility is more than 100 metres (328 feet). Be prepared for the fact that the fog may be patchy and you may need to turn them on again if the fog returns.

408 Mark *one* answer

Why is it dangerous to leave rear fog lights on when they're not needed?

☐ **A** They may be confused with brake lights
☐ **B** The bulbs would fail
☐ **C** Electrical systems could be overloaded
☐ **D** Direction indicators may not work properly

If your rear fog lights are left on when it isn't foggy, the glare they cause makes it difficult for road users behind to know whether you're braking or you've just forgotten to turn off your rear fog lights. This can be a particular problem on wet roads and on motorways. If you leave your rear fog lights on at night, road users behind you are likely to be dazzled and this could put them at risk.

409 Mark *one* answer

What will happen if you hold the clutch pedal down or roll in neutral for too long?

☐ **A** It will use more fuel
☐ **B** It will cause the engine to overheat
☐ **C** It will reduce your control
☐ **D** It will improve tyre wear

Holding the clutch down or staying in neutral for too long will cause your vehicle to freewheel. This is known as 'coasting' and it's dangerous because it reduces your control of the vehicle.

410 Mark *one* answer

You're driving down a steep hill. Why could it be dangerous to keep the clutch down or roll in neutral for too long?

☐ **A** Fuel consumption will be higher
☐ **B** Your vehicle will pick up speed
☐ **C** It will damage the engine
☐ **D** It will wear tyres out more quickly

Driving in neutral or with the clutch down for long periods is known as 'coasting'. There will be no engine braking and your vehicle will pick up speed on downhill slopes. Coasting can be very dangerous because it reduces steering and braking control.

411 Mark *one* answer

Why is it bad technique to coast when driving downhill?

☐ **A** The fuel consumption will increase
☐ **B** The engine will overheat
☐ **C** The tyres will wear more quickly
☐ **D** The vehicle will gain speed

Coasting is when you allow the vehicle to freewheel in neutral or with the clutch pedal depressed. Speed will increase as you lose the benefits of engine braking and have less control. You shouldn't coast, especially when approaching hazards such as junctions or bends and when travelling downhill.

412 Mark *one* answer

What should you do when dealing with this hazard?

- ☐ **A** Switch on your hazard warning lights
- ☐ **B** Use a low gear and drive slowly
- ☐ **C** Use a high gear to prevent wheelspin
- ☐ **D** Switch on your windscreen wipers

In normal conditions, a ford can be crossed quite safely by driving through it slowly. The water may affect your brakes, so when you're clear of the ford, test them before you resume normal driving.

413 Mark *one* answer

Why is travelling in neutral for long distances (known as coasting) wrong?

- ☐ **A** It will cause the car to skid
- ☐ **B** It will make the engine stall
- ☐ **C** The engine will run faster
- ☐ **D** There won't be any engine braking

Try to look ahead and read the road. Plan your approach to junctions and select the correct gear in good time. This will give you the control you need to deal with any hazards that occur. You'll coast a little every time you change gear. This can't be avoided, but it should be kept to a minimum.

414 Mark *one* answer

When must you use dipped headlights during the day?

- ☐ **A** All the time
- ☐ **B** On narrow streets
- ☐ **C** In poor visibility
- ☐ **D** When parking

You must use dipped headlights when daytime visibility is seriously reduced, generally to 100 metres (328 feet) or less. You may also use front or rear fog lights, but they must be switched off when visibility improves.

415 Mark *one* answer

You're braking on a wet road. Your vehicle begins to skid. It doesn't have anti-lock brakes. What is the first thing you should do?

- ☐ **A** Quickly pull up the handbrake
- ☐ **B** Release the footbrake
- ☐ **C** Push harder on the brake pedal
- ☐ **D** Gently use the accelerator

If the skid has been caused by braking too hard for the conditions, release the brake. You may then need to reapply and release the brake again. You may need to do this a number of times. This will allow the wheels to turn and so some steering should also be possible.

416 Mark *one* answer
What should you do when you're joining a motorway?

☐ **A** Use the hard shoulder
☐ **B** Stop at the end of the acceleration lane
☐ **C** Slow to a stop before joining the motorway
☐ **D** Give way to traffic already on the motorway

You should give way to traffic already on the motorway. Where possible, traffic may move over to let you in, but don't force your way into the traffic stream. Traffic could be travelling at high speed, so try to match your speed to filter in without affecting the traffic flow.

417 Mark *one* answer
What is the national speed limit on motorways for cars and motorcycles?

☐ **A** 30 mph
☐ **B** 50 mph
☐ **C** 60 mph
☐ **D** 70 mph

Travelling at the national speed limit doesn't allow you to hog the right-hand lane. Always use the left-hand lane whenever possible. When leaving a motorway, get into the left-hand lane well before your exit. Reduce your speed on the slip road and look out for sharp bends or curves and traffic queuing at roundabouts.

418 Mark *one* answer
Which vehicles should use the left-hand lane on a three-lane motorway?

☐ **A** Any vehicle
☐ **B** Large vehicles only
☐ **C** Emergency vehicles only
☐ **D** Slow vehicles only

On a motorway, all traffic should use the left-hand lane unless overtaking. When overtaking a number of slower vehicles, move back to the left-hand lane when you're safely past. Check your mirrors frequently and don't stay in the middle or right-hand lane if the left-hand lane is free.

419 Mark *one* answer
Which of these isn't allowed to travel in the right-hand lane of a three-lane motorway?

☐ **A** A small delivery van
☐ **B** A motorcycle
☐ **C** A vehicle towing a trailer
☐ **D** A motorcycle and sidecar

A vehicle with a trailer is restricted to 60 mph. For this reason, it isn't allowed in the right-hand lane, as it might hold up faster-moving traffic that wishes to overtake in that lane.

420 Mark *one* answer

You break down on a motorway. You need to call for help. Why may it be better to use an emergency roadside telephone rather than a mobile phone?

- [ ] **A** It connects you to a local garage
- [ ] **B** Using a mobile phone will distract other drivers
- [ ] **C** It allows easy location by the emergency services
- [ ] **D** Mobile phones don't work on motorways

On a motorway, it's best to use a roadside emergency telephone so that the emergency services are able to find you easily. The location of the nearest telephone is shown by an arrow on marker posts at the edge of the hard shoulder. If you use a mobile, the operator will need to know your exact location. Before you call, find out the number on the nearest marker post. This number will identify your exact location.

421 Mark *one* answer

You've had a breakdown on the hard shoulder of a motorway. When the problem has been fixed, how should you rejoin the main carriageway?

- [ ] **A** Move out onto the carriageway, then build up your speed
- [ ] **B** Move out onto the carriageway using your hazard warning lights
- [ ] **C** Gain speed on the hard shoulder before moving out onto the carriageway
- [ ] **D** Wait on the hard shoulder until someone flashes their headlights at you

Signal your intention and build up sufficient speed on the hard shoulder so that you can filter into a safe gap in the traffic. Don't push your way in, causing other traffic to alter speed or direction.

422 Mark *one* answer

You're travelling along a motorway. Where would you find a crawler or climbing lane?

- [ ] **A** On a steep gradient
- [ ] **B** Before a service area
- [ ] **C** Before a junction
- [ ] **D** Along the hard shoulder

Large, slow-moving vehicles can hinder the progress of other traffic. On a steep gradient, an extra crawler lane may be provided for slow-moving vehicles to allow faster-moving traffic to flow more easily.

423 Mark *one* answer

What do these motorway signs show?

- [ ] **A** They're countdown markers to a bridge
- [ ] **B** They're distance markers to the next telephone
- [ ] **C** They're countdown markers to the next exit
- [ ] **D** They warn of a police control ahead

The exit from a motorway is indicated by countdown markers. These are positioned 90 metres (100 yards) apart, the first being 270 metres (300 yards) from the start of the slip road. Move into the left-hand lane well before you reach the start of the slip road.

424 Mark *one* answer
On which part of a motorway are amber reflective studs found?

☐ **A** Between the hard shoulder and the carriageway
☐ **B** Between the acceleration lane and the carriageway
☐ **C** Between the central reservation and the carriageway
☐ **D** Between each pair of lanes

On motorways, reflective studs of various colours are fixed in the road between the lanes. These help you to identify which lane you're in when it's dark or in poor visibility. Amber-coloured studs are found on the right-hand edge of the main carriageway, next to the central reservation.

425 Mark *one* answer
What colour are the reflective studs between the lanes on a motorway?

☐ **A** Green
☐ **B** Amber
☐ **C** White
☐ **D** Red

White studs are found between the lanes on motorways. They reflect back the light from your headlights. This is especially useful in bad weather, when visibility is restricted.

426 Mark *one* answer
What colour are the reflective studs between a motorway and its slip road?

☐ **A** Amber
☐ **B** White
☐ **C** Green
☐ **D** Red

The studs between the carriageway and the hard shoulder are normally red. These change to green where there's a slip road, helping you to identify slip roads when visibility is poor or when it's dark.

427 Mark *one* answer
You've broken down on a motorway. In which direction should you walk to find the nearest emergency telephone?

☐ **A** With the traffic flow
☐ **B** Facing oncoming traffic
☐ **C** In the direction shown on the marker posts
☐ **D** In the direction of the nearest exit

Along the hard shoulder there are marker posts at 100-metre intervals. These will direct you to the nearest emergency telephone.

428 Mark *one* answer

You are joining a motorway. Why is it important to make full use of the slip road?

☐ **A** Because there is space available to turn round if you need to
☐ **B** To allow you direct access to the overtaking lanes
☐ **C** To build up a speed similar to traffic on the motorway
☐ **D** Because you can continue on the hard shoulder

Try to join the motorway without affecting the progress of the traffic already travelling on it. Always give way to traffic already on the motorway. At busy times you may have to slow down to merge into slow-moving traffic.

429 Mark *one* answer

How should you use the emergency telephone on a motorway?

☐ **A** Stay close to the carriageway
☐ **B** Face the oncoming traffic
☐ **C** Keep your back to the traffic
☐ **D** Stand on the hard shoulder

Traffic is passing you at speed. If the draught from a large lorry catches you by surprise, it could blow you off balance and even onto the carriageway. By facing the oncoming traffic, you can see approaching lorries and so be prepared for their draught. You'll also be in a position to see other hazards approaching.

430 Mark *one* answer

You're on a motorway. What colour are the reflective studs on the left of the carriageway?

☐ **A** Green
☐ **B** Red
☐ **C** White
☐ **D** Amber

Red studs are placed between the edge of the carriageway and the hard shoulder. Where slip roads leave or join the motorway, the studs are green.

431 Mark *one* answer

On a three-lane motorway, which lane should you normally use?

☐ **A** Left
☐ **B** Right
☐ **C** Centre
☐ **D** Either the right or centre

On a three-lane motorway, you should travel in the left-hand lane unless you're overtaking. This applies regardless of the speed at which you're travelling.

432 Mark *one* answer

What should you do when going through a contraflow system on a motorway?

- ☐ **A** Ensure that you don't exceed 30 mph
- ☐ **B** Keep a good distance from the vehicle ahead
- ☐ **C** Switch lanes to keep the traffic flowing
- ☐ **D** Stay close to the vehicle ahead to reduce queues

At roadworks, and especially where a contraflow system is operating, a speed restriction is likely to be in place. Keep to the lower speed limit and don't:

- switch lanes
- get too close to the vehicle in front of you

Be aware that there will be no permanent barrier between you and the oncoming traffic.

433 Mark *one* answer

You're on a three-lane motorway. There are red reflective studs on your left and white ones to your right. Which lane are you in?

- ☐ **A** In the right-hand lane
- ☐ **B** In the middle lane
- ☐ **C** On the hard shoulder
- ☐ **D** In the left-hand lane

The colours of the reflective studs on the motorway and their locations are:

- red – between the hard shoulder and the carriageway
- white – between lanes
- amber – between the carriageway and the central reservation
- green – along slip-road exits and entrances
- bright green/yellow – at roadworks and contraflow systems

434 Mark *one* answer

You're approaching roadworks on a motorway. What should you do?

- ☐ **A** Speed up to clear the area quickly
- ☐ **B** Always use the hard shoulder
- ☐ **C** Obey all speed limits
- ☐ **D** Stay very close to the vehicle in front

Collisions often happen at roadworks. Be aware of the speed limits, slow down in good time and keep your distance from the vehicle in front.

435 Mark *one* answer
Which of these mustn't use motorways?

- ☐ **A** Cars driven by learner drivers
- ☐ **B** Motorcycles over 50 cc
- ☐ **C** Double-deck buses
- ☐ **D** Cars with automatic transmission

Motorways mustn't be used by learner drivers, pedestrians, cyclists, motorcycles under 50 cc, certain slow-moving vehicles without permission, and invalid carriages weighing less than 254 kg (560 lbs).

436 Mark *one* answer
What should you do when driving or riding along a motorway?

- ☐ **A** Look much further ahead than you would on other roads
- ☐ **B** Travel much faster than you would on other roads
- ☐ **C** Maintain a shorter separation distance than you would on other roads
- ☐ **D** Concentrate more than you would on other roads

Traffic on motorways usually travels faster than on other roads. You need to be looking further ahead to give yourself more time to react to any hazard that may develop.

437 Mark *one* answer
What should you do immediately after joining a motorway?

- ☐ **A** Try to overtake
- ☐ **B** Re-adjust your mirrors
- ☐ **C** Position your vehicle in the centre lane
- ☐ **D** Keep in the left-hand lane

Stay in the left-hand lane long enough to get used to the higher speeds of motorway traffic before considering overtaking.

438 Mark *one* answer
What is the right-hand lane used for on a three-lane motorway?

- ☐ **A** Emergency vehicles only
- ☐ **B** Overtaking
- ☐ **C** Vehicles towing trailers
- ☐ **D** Coaches only

You should keep to the left and only use the right-hand lane if you're passing slower-moving traffic.

439 Mark *one* answer
What should you use the hard shoulder of a motorway for?

- ☐ **A** Stopping in an emergency
- ☐ **B** Leaving the motorway
- ☐ **C** Stopping when you're tired
- ☐ **D** Joining the motorway

Don't use the hard shoulder for stopping unless it's an emergency. If you want to stop for any other reason, go to the next exit or service station.

440 Mark *one* answer
You're in the right-hand lane of a three-lane motorway. What do these overhead signs mean?

- ☐ **A** Move to the left and reduce your speed to 50 mph
- ☐ **B** There are roadworks 50 metres (55 yards) ahead
- ☐ **C** Use the hard shoulder until you've passed the hazard
- ☐ **D** Leave the motorway at the next exit

You must obey these signs even if there appear to be no problems ahead. There could be queuing traffic or another hazard which you can't yet see.

441 Mark *one* answer
When are you allowed to stop on a motorway?

- ☐ **A** When you need to walk and get fresh air
- ☐ **B** When you wish to pick up hitchhikers
- ☐ **C** When you're signalled to do so by flashing red lights
- ☐ **D** When you need to use a mobile telephone

You must stop if overhead gantry signs show flashing red lights above every lane on the motorway. If any of the other lanes doesn't show flashing red lights or a red cross, you may move into that lane and continue if it's safe to do so.

442 Mark *one* answer
You're travelling in the left-hand lane of a three-lane motorway. How should you react to traffic joining from a slip road?

- ☐ **A** Race the other vehicles
- ☐ **B** Move to another lane
- ☐ **C** Maintain a steady speed
- ☐ **D** Switch on your hazard warning lights

Plan well ahead when approaching a slip road. If you see traffic joining the motorway, move to another lane if it's safe to do so. This can help the flow of traffic joining the motorway, especially at peak times.

443 Mark *one* answer
What basic rule applies when you're using a motorway?

- ☐ **A** Use the lane that has the least traffic
- ☐ **B** Keep to the left-hand lane unless overtaking
- ☐ **C** Overtake on the side that's clearest
- ☐ **D** Try to keep above 50 mph to prevent congestion

You should normally travel in the left-hand lane unless you're overtaking a slower-moving vehicle. When you've finished overtaking, move back into the left-hand lane, but don't cut across in front of the vehicle that you've overtaken.

444 Mark *one* answer
You're travelling along a motorway. When are you allowed to overtake on the left?

- ☐ **A** When you can see well ahead that the hard shoulder is clear
- ☐ **B** When the traffic in the right-hand lane is signalling right
- ☐ **C** When you warn drivers behind by signalling left
- ☐ **D** When in queues and traffic to your right is moving more slowly than you are

Never overtake on the left, unless the traffic is moving in queues and the queue on your right is moving more slowly than the one you're in.

445 Mark *one* answer
On a motorway, what's an emergency refuge area used for?

- ☐ **A** In cases of emergency or breakdown
- ☐ **B** If you think you'll be involved in a road rage incident
- ☐ **C** For a police patrol to park and watch traffic
- ☐ **D** For construction and road workers to store emergency equipment

Emergency refuge areas are built at the side of the hard shoulder. If you break down, try to get your vehicle into the refuge, where there's an emergency telephone. The phone connects directly to a control centre. Remember to take care when rejoining the motorway, especially if the hard shoulder is being used as a running lane.

446 Mark *one* answer
Traffic officers operate on motorways and some primary routes in England. What are they authorised to do?

- ☐ **A** Stop and arrest drivers who break the law
- ☐ **B** Repair broken-down vehicles on the motorway
- ☐ **C** Issue fixed penalty notices
- ☐ **D** Stop and direct anyone on a motorway

Traffic officers don't have enforcement powers but are able to stop and direct people on motorways and some 'A' class roads. They only operate in England and work in partnership with the police at incidents, providing a highly trained and visible service. They're recognised by an orange-and-yellow jacket and their vehicle has yellow-and-black markings.

447 Mark *one* answer

You're on a motorway. A red cross is displayed above the hard shoulder. What does this mean?

- ☐ **A** Pull up in this lane to answer your mobile phone
- ☐ **B** Use this lane as a running lane
- ☐ **C** This lane can be used if you need a rest
- ☐ **D** You shouldn't travel in this lane

Active traffic management operates on some motorways. Within these areas, at certain times, the hard shoulder will be used as a running lane. A red cross above the hard shoulder shows that this lane should only be used for emergencies and breakdowns.

448 Mark *one* answer

You're on a smart motorway. A mandatory speed limit is displayed above the hard shoulder. What does this mean?

- ☐ **A** You shouldn't travel in this lane
- ☐ **B** The hard shoulder can be used as a running lane
- ☐ **C** You can park on the hard shoulder if you feel tired
- ☐ **D** You can pull up in this lane to answer a mobile phone

A mandatory speed-limit sign above the hard shoulder shows that this part of the road can be used as a running lane between junctions. You must stay within the speed limit. Look out for vehicles that may have broken down and could be blocking the hard shoulder.

449 Mark *one* answer

What is the aim of a smart motorway?

- ☐ **A** To prevent overtaking
- ☐ **B** To reduce rest stops
- ☐ **C** To prevent tailgating
- ☐ **D** To reduce congestion

Smart motorway schemes are intended to reduce congestion and make journey times more reliable. In these areas, the hard shoulder may be used as a running lane to ease congestion at peak times or in the event of an incident. Variable speed limits are used to help keep the traffic moving and to avoid bunching.

450 Mark *one* answer
You're using a smart motorway. What happens when it's operating?

- ☐ **A** Speed limits above lanes are advisory
- ☐ **B** The national speed limit will apply
- ☐ **C** The speed limit is always 30 mph
- ☐ **D** You must obey the speed limits shown

When a smart motorway is operating, you must follow the mandatory signs on the gantries above each lane, including the hard shoulder. Variable speed limits help keep the traffic moving and also help to prevent bunching.

451 Mark *one* answer
Why can it be an advantage for traffic speed to stay constant over a longer distance?

- ☐ **A** You'll do more stop–start driving
- ☐ **B** You'll use far more fuel
- ☐ **C** You'll be able to use more direct routes
- ☐ **D** Your overall journey time will normally improve

When traffic travels at a constant speed over a longer distance, journey times normally improve. You may feel that you could travel faster for short periods, but this generally leads to bunching and increased overall journey time.

452 Mark *one* answer
You shouldn't normally travel on the hard shoulder of a motorway. When can you use it?

- ☐ **A** When taking the next exit
- ☐ **B** When traffic is stopped
- ☐ **C** When signs direct you to
- ☐ **D** When traffic is slow moving

Normally, you should only use the hard shoulder for emergencies and breakdowns, and at roadworks when signs direct you to do so. Smart motorways use active traffic management to ease traffic congestion. In these areas, the hard shoulder may be used as a running lane when speed-limit signs are shown directly above.

453 Mark *one* answer
What is used to reduce traffic bunching on a motorway?

- ☐ **A** Variable speed limits
- ☐ **B** Contraflow systems
- ☐ **C** National speed limits
- ☐ **D** Lane closures

Congestion can be reduced by keeping traffic at a constant speed. At busy times, maximum speed limits are displayed on overhead gantries. These can be varied quickly, depending on the amount of traffic. By keeping to a constant speed on busy sections of motorway, overall journey times are normally improved.

454 Mark *one* answer
When may you stop on a motorway?

- ☐ **A** If you have to read a map
- ☐ **B** When you're tired and need a rest
- ☐ **C** If your mobile phone rings
- ☐ **D** In an emergency or breakdown

You shouldn't normally stop on a motorway, but there may be occasions when you need to do so. If you're unfortunate enough to break down, make every effort to pull up on the hard shoulder.

455 Mark *one* answer
Unless signs show otherwise, what's the national speed limit for a car or motorcycle on a motorway?

- ☐ **A** 50 mph
- ☐ **B** 60 mph
- ☐ **C** 70 mph
- ☐ **D** 80 mph

The national speed limit for a car or motorcycle on a motorway is 70 mph. Lower speed limits may be in force; for example, at roadworks. Variable speed limits also operate in some areas when the motorway is very busy. Cars or motorcycles towing trailers are subject to a lower speed limit.

456 Mark *one* answer
You're on a motorway and there are red flashing lights above every lane. What must you do?

- ☐ **A** Pull onto the hard shoulder
- ☐ **B** Slow down and watch for further signals
- ☐ **C** Leave at the next exit
- ☐ **D** Stop and wait

Red flashing lights above all lanes mean you must stop and wait. You'll also see a red cross lit up. Don't change lanes, don't continue and don't pull onto the hard shoulder (unless in an emergency).

457 Mark *one* answer
You're on a three-lane motorway. A red cross is showing above the hard shoulder and mandatory speed limits above all other lanes. What does this mean?

- ☐ **A** The hard shoulder can be used as a rest area if you feel tired
- ☐ **B** The hard shoulder is for emergency or breakdown use only
- ☐ **C** The hard shoulder can be used as a normal running lane
- ☐ **D** The hard shoulder has a speed limit of 50 mph

A red cross above the hard shoulder shows that it's closed as a running lane and should only be used for emergencies or breakdowns. On a smart motorway, the hard shoulder may be used as a running lane at busy times. This will be shown by a mandatory speed limit on the gantry above the hard shoulder.

458 Mark *one* answer
On a three-lane motorway, what does this sign mean?

☐ **A** Use any lane except the hard shoulder
☐ **B** Use the hard shoulder only
☐ **C** Use the three right-hand lanes only
☐ **D** Use all the lanes, including the hard shoulder

You must obey mandatory speed-limit signs above motorway lanes, including the hard shoulder. In this case, you can use the hard shoulder as a running lane but you should look for any vehicles that may have broken down and may be blocking the hard shoulder.

459 Mark *one* answer
You're travelling along a motorway and feel tired. Where should you stop to rest?

☐ **A** On the hard shoulder
☐ **B** At the nearest service area
☐ **C** On a slip road
☐ **D** On the central reservation

If you feel tired, stop at the nearest service area. If that's too far away, leave the motorway at the next exit and find a safe place to stop. You mustn't stop on the carriageway or hard shoulder of a motorway except in an emergency, when in a traffic queue, or when signalled to do so by a police officer, a traffic officer or traffic signals. Plan your journey so that you have regular rest stops.

460 Mark *one* answer
You're towing a trailer on a motorway. What is the speed limit for a car towing a trailer on this road?

☐ **A** 40 mph
☐ **B** 50 mph
☐ **C** 60 mph
☐ **D** 70 mph

Don't forget that you're towing a trailer. If you're towing a small, light trailer, it won't reduce your vehicle's performance by very much. However, strong winds or buffeting from large vehicles might cause the trailer to snake from side to side. Be aware of your speed and don't exceed the reduced speed limit imposed on vehicles towing trailers.

461 Mark *one* answer
What should the left-hand lane of a motorway be used for?

☐ **A** Breakdowns and emergencies only
☐ **B** Overtaking slower traffic in the other lanes
☐ **C** Slow vehicles only
☐ **D** Normal driving

You should drive in the left-hand lane whenever possible. Only use the other lanes for overtaking or when directed to do so by signals. Using other lanes when the left-hand lane is empty can frustrate drivers behind you.

462 Mark *one* answer

You're driving on a motorway and have to slow down quickly due to a hazard ahead. How can you warn drivers behind of the hazard?

☐ **A** Switch on your hazard warning lights
☐ **B** Switch on your headlights
☐ **C** Sound your horn
☐ **D** Flash your headlights

Using your hazard warning lights, as well as your brake lights, will give following traffic an extra warning of the problem ahead. Only use them for long enough for your warning to be seen.

463 Mark *one* answer

Your car gets a puncture while you're driving on the motorway. You get it onto the hard shoulder. What should you do?

☐ **A** Carefully change the wheel yourself
☐ **B** Use an emergency telephone and call for help
☐ **C** Try to wave down another vehicle for help
☐ **D** Only change the wheel if you have a passenger to help you

Park as far to the left as you can and leave the vehicle by the nearside door. Don't attempt even simple repairs. Instead, walk to an emergency telephone on your side of the road and phone for help. While waiting for help to arrive, stay by your car, keeping well away from the carriageway and hard shoulder.

464 Mark *one* answer

You're driving on a motorway. By mistake, you go past the exit that you wanted to take. What should you do?

☐ **A** Carefully reverse on the hard shoulder
☐ **B** Carry on to the next exit
☐ **C** Carefully reverse in the left-hand lane
☐ **D** Make a U-turn at a gap in the central reservation

It's illegal to reverse, cross the central reservation or drive against the traffic flow on a motorway. If you miss your exit, carry on until you reach the next one. Ask yourself why you missed your exit – if you think that your concentration is fading, take a break before completing your journey.

465 Mark *one* answer

Your vehicle has broken down on a motorway. You aren't able to stop on the hard shoulder. What should you do?

☐ **A** Switch on your hazard warning lights
☐ **B** Stop following traffic and ask for help
☐ **C** Attempt to repair your vehicle quickly
☐ **D** Stand behind your vehicle to warn others

If you can't get your vehicle onto the hard shoulder, use your hazard warning lights to warn others. Leave your vehicle only when you can safely get clear of the carriageway. Don't try to repair the vehicle or attempt to place any warning device on the carriageway.

466 Mark *one* answer

Why is it particularly important to carry out a check on your vehicle before making a long motorway journey?

- ☐ **A** You'll have to do more harsh braking on motorways
- ☐ **B** Motorway service stations don't deal with breakdowns
- ☐ **C** The road surface will wear down the tyres faster
- ☐ **D** Continuous high speeds increase the risk of your vehicle breaking down

Before you start your journey, make sure that your vehicle can cope with the demands of high-speed driving. You should check a number of things, the main ones being oil, water and tyres. You also need to plan rest stops if you're making a long journey.

467 Mark *one* answer

You're driving on a motorway. The car in front shows its hazard warning lights for a short time. What does this tell you?

- ☐ **A** The driver wants you to overtake
- ☐ **B** The other car is going to change lanes
- ☐ **C** Traffic ahead is slowing or stopping suddenly
- ☐ **D** There's a police speed check ahead

If the vehicle in front shows its hazard warning lights, there may be an incident, stopped traffic or queuing traffic ahead. By keeping a safe distance from the vehicle in front, you're able to look beyond it and see any hazards well ahead.

468 Mark *one* answer

You're driving on the motorway. Well before you reach your intended exit, where should you position your vehicle?

- ☐ **A** In the middle lane
- ☐ **B** In the left-hand lane
- ☐ **C** On the hard shoulder
- ☐ **D** In any lane

You'll see the first advance direction sign one mile from a motorway exit. If you're travelling at 60 mph in the right-hand lane, you'll only have about 50 seconds before you reach the countdown markers. There'll be another sign at the half-mile point. Move to the left-hand lane in good time. Don't cut across traffic at the last moment and don't risk missing your exit.

469 Mark *one* answer

What restrictions apply to new drivers holding a provisional driving licence?

- ☐ **A** They can't drive over 30 mph
- ☐ **B** They can't drive at night
- ☐ **C** They can't drive on the motorway
- ☐ **D** They can't drive with more than one passenger

You won't be able to drive on the motorway until you've passed your practical driving test. When you've passed, it's a good idea to ask your instructor to take you for a lesson on the motorway. Alternatively, you could take part in the Pass Plus scheme. This has been created for new drivers and includes motorway driving. Ask your instructor for details.

470 Mark *one* answer

Your vehicle breaks down on the hard shoulder of a motorway. You need to use your mobile phone to call for help. What should you do?

- ☐ **A** Stand at the rear of the vehicle while making the call
- ☐ **B** Phone a friend and ask them to come and collect you
- ☐ **C** Open the bonnet to help the emergency services know you've broken down
- ☐ **D** Check your location from the marker posts on the left

You should use an emergency telephone when you break down on the motorway; only use your mobile if this isn't possible. The emergency services need to know your exact location so they can reach you as quickly as possible. Look for a number on the nearest marker post beside the hard shoulder. Give this number when you call the emergency services.

471 Mark *one* answer

You're towing a trailer along a three-lane motorway. When may you use the right-hand lane?

- ☐ **A** When there are lane closures
- ☐ **B** When there's slow-moving traffic
- ☐ **C** When you can maintain a high speed
- ☐ **D** When large vehicles are in the left and centre lanes

If you're towing a caravan or trailer, you mustn't use the right-hand lane of a motorway with three or more lanes except in certain specified circumstances, such as when lanes are closed.

472 Mark *one* answer

You're on a motorway. There's a contraflow system ahead. What would you expect to find?

- ☐ **A** Temporary traffic lights
- ☐ **B** Lower speed limits
- ☐ **C** Wider lanes than normal
- ☐ **D** Speed humps

When approaching a contraflow system, reduce speed in good time and obey all speed limits. You may be travelling in a narrower lane than normal, with no permanent barrier between you and the oncoming traffic. Be aware that the hard shoulder may be used for traffic and the road ahead could be obstructed by slow-moving or broken-down vehicles.

473 Mark *one* answer

When may you stop on the hard shoulder of a motorway?

- ☐ **A** In an emergency
- ☐ **B** If you feel tired and need to rest
- ☐ **C** If you miss the exit that you wanted
- ☐ **D** To pick up a hitchhiker

You should only stop on the hard shoulder in a genuine emergency. Don't stop there to have a rest or picnic, pick up hitchhikers, answer a mobile phone or check a map. If you miss your intended exit, carry on to the next. Never reverse along the hard shoulder.

474 Mark *one* answer
What is the meaning of this sign?

- ☐ **A** Local speed limit applies
- ☐ **B** No waiting on the carriageway
- ☐ **C** National speed limit applies
- ☐ **D** No entry for vehicles

This sign doesn't tell you the speed limit in figures. You should know the speed limit for the type of road that you're on and the type of vehicle that you're driving. Study your copy of *The Highway Code*.

475 Mark *one* answer
What is the national speed limit for cars and motorcycles on a dual carriageway?

- ☐ **A** 30 mph
- ☐ **B** 50 mph
- ☐ **C** 60 mph
- ☐ **D** 70 mph

Make sure that you know the speed limit for the road that you're on. The speed limit on a dual carriageway or motorway is 70 mph for cars and motorcycles, unless signs indicate otherwise. The speed limits for different types of vehicle are listed in *The Highway Code*.

476 Mark *one* answer
There are no speed-limit signs on the road. How is a 30 mph limit indicated?

- ☐ **A** By hazard warning lines
- ☐ **B** By street lighting
- ☐ **C** By pedestrian islands
- ☐ **D** By double or single yellow lines

There's a 30 mph speed limit where there are street lights unless signs show another limit.

477 Mark *one* answer
You see street lights but no speed-limit signs. What will the speed limit usually be?

- ☐ **A** 30 mph
- ☐ **B** 40 mph
- ☐ **C** 50 mph
- ☐ **D** 60 mph

The presence of street lights generally indicates that there's a 30 mph speed limit, unless signs tell you otherwise.

478 Mark *one* answer
What does this sign mean?

- ☐ **A** Minimum speed 30 mph
- ☐ **B** End of maximum speed
- ☐ **C** End of minimum speed
- ☐ **D** Maximum speed 30 mph

The red slash through the sign indicates that the restriction has ended. In this case, the restriction was a minimum speed limit of 30 mph.

479 Mark *one* answer
There's a tractor ahead. You want to overtake but you aren't sure whether it's safe. What should you do?

- ☐ **A** Follow another vehicle as it overtakes the tractor
- ☐ **B** Sound your horn to make the tractor pull over
- ☐ **C** Speed past, flashing your lights at oncoming traffic
- ☐ **D** Stay behind the tractor if you're in any doubt

Following a tractor can be frustrating, but never overtake if you're unsure whether it's safe. Ask yourself: 'Can I see far enough down the road to ensure that I can complete the manoeuvre safely?' It's better to be delayed for a minute or two than to take a chance that may cause a collision.

480 Mark *one* answer
Which vehicle is most likely to take an unusual course at a roundabout?

- ☐ **A** Estate car
- ☐ **B** Milk float
- ☐ **C** Delivery van
- ☐ **D** Long lorry

Long vehicles might have to take a slightly different position when approaching the roundabout or going around it. This is to stop the rear of the vehicle cutting in and mounting the kerb.

481 Mark *one* answer
When mustn't you stop on a clearway?

- ☐ **A** At any time
- ☐ **B** When it's busy
- ☐ **C** In the rush hour
- ☐ **D** During daylight hours

Clearways are in place so that traffic can flow without the obstruction of parked vehicles. Just one parked vehicle can cause an obstruction for all other traffic. You mustn't stop where a clearway is in force, not even to pick up or set down passengers.

482 Mark *one* answer
What is the meaning of this sign?

☐ **A** No entry
☐ **B** Waiting restrictions
☐ **C** National speed limit
☐ **D** School crossing patrol

This sign indicates that there are waiting restrictions. It's normally accompanied by details of when the restrictions are in force. Details of most signs in common use are shown in *The Highway Code*. For a more comprehensive coverage, see *Know Your Traffic Signs*.

---

483 Mark *one* answer
When can you park on the right-hand side of a road at night?

☐ **A** When you're in a one-way street
☐ **B** When you have your sidelights on
☐ **C** When you're more than 10 metres (32 feet) from a junction
☐ **D** When you're under a lamppost

Red rear reflectors show up when headlights shine on them. These are useful when you're parked at night, but they'll only reflect if you park in the same direction as the traffic flow. Normally you should park on the left, but in a one-way street you may also park on the right-hand side.

484 Mark *one* answer
On a three-lane dual carriageway, what can the right-hand lane be used for?

☐ **A** Overtaking only, never turning right
☐ **B** Overtaking or turning right
☐ **C** Fast-moving traffic only
☐ **D** Turning right only, never overtaking

You should normally use the left-hand lane on any dual carriageway unless you're overtaking or turning right. When overtaking on a dual carriageway, look for vehicles ahead that are turning right. They may be slowing or stopped. You need to see them in good time so that you can take appropriate action.

---

485 Mark *one* answer
You're approaching a busy junction. What should you do when, at the last moment, you realise you're in the wrong lane?

☐ **A** Continue in that lane
☐ **B** Force your way across
☐ **C** Stop until the area has cleared
☐ **D** Use clear arm signals to cut across

There are times when road markings are obscured by queuing traffic, or you're unsure which lane to use. If, at the last moment, you find you're in the wrong lane, don't cut across or bully other drivers to let you in. Follow the lane you're in and find somewhere safe to turn around and rejoin your route.

486 Mark *one* answer
Where may you overtake on a one-way street?

☐ **A** Only on the left-hand side
☐ **B** Overtaking isn't allowed
☐ **C** Only on the right-hand side
☐ **D** On either the right or the left

You can overtake other traffic on either side when travelling in a one-way street. Make full use of your mirrors and ensure it's clear all around before you attempt to overtake. Look for signs and road markings, and use the most suitable lane for your destination.

487 Mark *one* answer
How should you signal when going straight ahead at a roundabout?

☐ **A** Indicate left before leaving the roundabout
☐ **B** Don't indicate at any time
☐ **C** Indicate right when approaching the roundabout
☐ **D** Indicate left when approaching the roundabout

When going straight ahead at a roundabout, don't signal as you approach it. Indicate left just after passing the exit before the one you wish to take.

488 Mark *one* answer
Which vehicle might have to take a different course from normal at roundabouts?

☐ **A** Sports car
☐ **B** Van
☐ **C** Estate car
☐ **D** Long vehicle

A long vehicle may have to straddle lanes either on or approaching a roundabout so that the rear wheels don't hit the kerb. If you're following a long vehicle, stay well back and give it plenty of room.

489 Mark *one* answer
On which occasion may you enter a box junction?

☐ **A** When there are fewer than two vehicles ahead
☐ **B** When signalled by another road user
☐ **C** When your exit road is clear
☐ **D** When traffic signs direct you

Yellow box junctions are marked on the road to prevent the road becoming blocked. Don't enter the box unless your exit road is clear. You may wait in the box if you want to turn right and your exit road is clear but oncoming traffic or other vehicles waiting to turn right are preventing you from making the turn.

490 Mark *one* answer
When may you stop and wait in a box junction?

☐ **A** When oncoming traffic prevents you from turning right
☐ **B** When you're in a queue of traffic turning left
☐ **C** When you're in a queue of traffic going ahead
☐ **D** When you're on a roundabout

The purpose of yellow box markings is to keep junctions clear of queuing traffic. You may only wait in the marked area when you're turning right and your exit lane is clear but you can't complete the turn because of oncoming traffic or other traffic waiting to turning right.

491 Mark *one* answer
Which person's signal to stop must you obey?

☐ **A** A motorcyclist
☐ **B** A pedestrian
☐ **C** A police officer
☐ **D** A bus driver

You must obey signals to stop given by police and traffic officers, traffic wardens and school crossing patrols. Failure to do so is an offence and could lead to prosecution.

492 Mark *one* answer
You see a pedestrian waiting at a zebra crossing. What should you normally do?

☐ **A** Go on quickly before they step onto the crossing
☐ **B** Stop before you reach the zigzag lines and let them cross
☐ **C** Stop to let them cross and wait patiently
☐ **D** Ignore them as they're still on the pavement

By standing on the pavement, the pedestrian is showing an intention to cross. By looking well ahead, you'll give yourself time to see the pedestrian, check your mirrors and respond safely.

493 Mark *one* answer
Who can use a toucan crossing?

☐ **A** Cars and motorcycles
☐ **B** Cyclists and pedestrians
☐ **C** Buses and lorries
☐ **D** Trams and trains

Toucan crossings are similar to pelican crossings but there's no flashing amber phase. Cyclists share the crossing with pedestrians and are allowed to cycle across when the green cycle symbol is shown.

494 Mark *one* answer

You're waiting at a pelican crossing. What does it mean when the red light changes to flashing amber?

- ☐ **A** Wait for pedestrians on the crossing to clear
- ☐ **B** Move off immediately without any hesitation
- ☐ **C** Wait for the green light before moving off
- ☐ **D** Get ready and go when the continuous amber light shows

This light allows pedestrians already on the crossing to get to the other side in their own time, without being rushed. Don't rev your engine or start to move off while they're still crossing.

495 Mark *one* answer

When can you park on the left opposite these road markings?

- ☐ **A** If the line nearest to you is broken
- ☐ **B** When there are no yellow lines
- ☐ **C** To pick up or set down passengers
- ☐ **D** During daylight hours only

You mustn't park or stop on a road marked with double white lines (even where one of the lines is broken) except to pick up or set down passengers.

496 Mark *one* answer

You're turning right at a crossroads. An oncoming driver is also turning right. How should you normally deal with this?

- ☐ **A** Keep the other vehicle to your right and turn behind it (offside to offside)
- ☐ **B** Keep the other vehicle to your left and turn in front of it (nearside to nearside)
- ☐ **C** Carry on and turn at the next junction instead
- ☐ **D** Hold back and wait for the other driver to turn first

At crossroads, traffic normally turns offside to offside. This is the safest way to turn, but sometimes the layout or road markings indicate drivers should pass nearside to nearside. Take extra care at these crossroads because, as you turn, your view ahead will be obscured by the oncoming vehicle crossing in front of you.

497 Mark *one* answer

You're travelling along a street with parked vehicles on the left-hand side. Why should you keep your speed down?

- ☐ **A** So that oncoming traffic can see you more clearly
- ☐ **B** You may set off car alarms
- ☐ **C** There may be delivery lorries on the street
- ☐ **D** Children may run out from between the vehicles

Travel slowly and carefully near parked vehicles. Beware of:
- vehicles pulling out, especially bicycles and motorcycles
- pedestrians, especially children, who may run out from between cars
- drivers opening their doors

498 Mark *one* answer

What should you do when you meet an obstruction on your side of the road?

- ☐ **A** Carry on, as you have priority
- ☐ **B** Give way to oncoming traffic
- ☐ **C** Wave oncoming vehicles through
- ☐ **D** Accelerate to get past first

Take care if you have to pass a parked vehicle on your side of the road. Give way to oncoming traffic if there isn't enough room for you both to continue safely.

499 Mark *one* answer

You're on a two-lane dual carriageway. Why would you use the right-hand lane?

- ☐ **A** To overtake slower traffic
- ☐ **B** For normal progress
- ☐ **C** When staying at the minimum allowed speed
- ☐ **D** To keep driving at a constant high speed

Normally you should travel in the left-hand lane and only use the right-hand lane for overtaking or turning right. Move back into the left lane as soon as it's safe but don't cut in across the path of the vehicle you've just passed.

500 Mark *one* answer

Who has priority at an unmarked crossroads?

- ☐ **A** The larger vehicle
- ☐ **B** No-one has priority
- ☐ **C** The faster vehicle
- ☐ **D** The smaller vehicle

Practise good observation in all directions before you emerge or make a turn. Proceed only when you're sure it's safe to do so.

501 Mark *one* answer **NI**

What is the nearest you may park to a junction?

- ☐ **A** 10 metres (32 feet)
- ☐ **B** 12 metres (39 feet)
- ☐ **C** 15 metres (49 feet)
- ☐ **D** 20 metres (66 feet)

Don't park within 10 metres (32 feet) of a junction (unless in an authorised parking place). This is to allow drivers emerging from, or turning into, the junction a clear view of the road they're joining. It also allows them to see hazards such as pedestrians or cyclists at the junction.

502 Mark *one* answer NI
Where shouldn't you park?

- ☐ **A** On a road with a 40 mph speed limit
- ☐ **B** At or near a bus stop
- ☐ **C** Where there's no pavement
- ☐ **D** Within 20 metres (65 feet) of a junction

It may be tempting to park where you shouldn't while you run a quick errand. Careless parking is a selfish act and could endanger other road users. It's important not to park at or near a bus stop, as this could inconvenience passengers and may put them at risk as they get on or off the bus.

503 Mark *one* answer
You're waiting at a level crossing. A train passes but the lights keep flashing. What must you do?

- ☐ **A** Carry on waiting
- ☐ **B** Phone the signal operator
- ☐ **C** Edge over the stop line and look for trains
- ☐ **D** Park and investigate

If the lights at a level crossing keep flashing after a train has passed, you should continue to wait, because another train might be coming. Time seems to pass slowly when you're held up in a queue. Be patient and wait until the lights stop flashing.

504 Mark *one* answer
What does this sign tell you?

- ☐ **A** No through road
- ☐ **B** End of traffic-calming zone
- ☐ **C** Free-parking zone ends
- ☐ **D** No-waiting zone ends

The blue-and-red circular sign on its own means that waiting restrictions are in force. This sign shows that you're leaving the controlled zone and waiting restrictions no longer apply.

505 Mark *one* answer
What must you do when entering roadworks where a temporary speed limit is displayed?

- ☐ **A** Obey the speed limit
- ☐ **B** Obey the limit, but only during rush hour
- ☐ **C** Ignore the displayed limit
- ☐ **D** Use your own judgment; the limit is only advisory

Where there are extra hazards, such as at roadworks, it's often necessary to slow traffic down by imposing a lower speed limit. These speed limits aren't advisory; they must be obeyed.

506 Mark *one* answer
You're on a well-lit road at night, in a built-up area. How will using dipped headlights help?

☐ **A** You can see further along the road
☐ **B** You can go at a much faster speed
☐ **C** You can switch to main beam quickly
☐ **D** You can be easily seen by others

You may be difficult to see when you're travelling at night, even on a well-lit road. If you use dipped headlights rather than sidelights, other road users should be able to see you more easily.

507 Mark *one* answer
The dual carriageway you're turning right onto has a very narrow central reservation. What should you do?

☐ **A** Proceed to the central reservation and wait
☐ **B** Wait until the road is clear in both directions
☐ **C** Stop in the first lane so that other vehicles give way
☐ **D** Emerge slightly to show your intentions

When the central reservation is narrow, you should treat a dual carriageway as one road. Wait until the road is clear in both directions before emerging to turn right. If you try to treat it as two separate roads and wait in the middle, you're likely to cause an obstruction and possibly a collision.

508 Mark *one* answer
What is the national speed limit on a single carriageway road for cars and motorcycles?

☐ **A** 30 mph
☐ **B** 50 mph
☐ **C** 60 mph
☐ **D** 70 mph

Exceeding the speed limit is dangerous and can result in you receiving penalty points on your licence. It isn't worth it. You should know the speed limit for the road that you're on by observing the road signs. Different speed limits apply if you're towing a trailer.

509 Mark *one* answer
You park at night on a road with a 40 mph speed limit. What should you do?

☐ **A** Park facing the traffic
☐ **B** Park with parking lights on
☐ **C** Park with dipped headlights on
☐ **D** Park near a street light

You must use parking lights when parking at night on a road or in a lay-by on a road with a speed limit greater than 30 mph. You must also park in the direction of the traffic flow and not close to a junction.

510 Mark *one* answer
Where will you see these red and white markers?

- ☐ **A** Approaching the end of a motorway
- ☐ **B** Approaching a concealed level crossing
- ☐ **C** Approaching a concealed speed-limit sign
- ☐ **D** Approaching the end of a dual carriageway

If there's a bend just before a level crossing, you may not be able to see the level-crossing barriers or waiting traffic. These signs give you an early warning that you may find these hazards just around the bend.

511 Mark *one* answer
You're travelling on a motorway in England. You must stop when signalled to do so by which of these?

- ☐ **A** Flashing amber lights above your lane
- ☐ **B** A traffic officer
- ☐ **C** Pedestrians on the hard shoulder
- ☐ **D** A driver who has broken down

You'll find traffic officers on England's motorways. They work in partnership with the police, helping to keep traffic moving and helping to make your journey as safe as possible. It's an offence not to comply with the directions given by a traffic officer.

512 Mark *one* answer
You're going straight ahead at a roundabout. How should you signal?

- ☐ **A** Signal right on the approach and then left to leave the roundabout
- ☐ **B** Signal left after you leave the roundabout and enter the new road
- ☐ **C** Signal right on the approach to the roundabout and keep the signal on
- ☐ **D** Signal left just after you pass the exit before the one you're going to take

To go straight ahead at a roundabout, you should normally approach in the left-hand lane, but check the road markings. At some roundabouts, the left lane on approach is marked 'left turn only', so make sure you use the correct lane to go ahead. You won't normally need to signal as you approach, but signal before you leave the roundabout, as other road users need to know your intentions.

513 Mark *one* answer
When may you drive over a footpath?

- ☐ **A** To overtake slow-moving traffic
- ☐ **B** When the pavement is very wide
- ☐ **C** If there are no pedestrians nearby
- ☐ **D** To get onto a property

It's illegal to drive on or over a footpath, except to gain access to a property. If you need to cross a pavement, give priority to pedestrians.

514 Mark *one* answer

A single carriageway road has this sign. What is the maximum permitted speed for a car towing a trailer?

- ☐ **A** 30 mph
- ☐ **B** 40 mph
- ☐ **C** 50 mph
- ☐ **D** 60 mph

When you're towing a trailer, a reduced speed limit also applies on dual carriageways and motorways. These lower speed limits apply to vehicles pulling all sorts of trailers, including caravans and horse boxes.

515 Mark *one* answer

What is the speed limit for a car towing a small caravan along a dual carriageway?

- ☐ **A** 50 mph
- ☐ **B** 40 mph
- ☐ **C** 70 mph
- ☐ **D** 60 mph

The speed limit for cars towing caravans or trailers on dual carriageways or motorways is 60 mph. Due to the increased weight and size of the combination, you should plan further ahead. Take care in windy weather, as a strong side wind can make a caravan or large trailer unstable.

516 Mark *one* answer

You want to park and you see this sign. What should you do on the days and times shown?

- ☐ **A** Park in a bay and not pay
- ☐ **B** Park on yellow lines and pay
- ☐ **C** Park on yellow lines and not pay
- ☐ **D** Park in a bay and pay

Parking restrictions apply in a variety of places and situations. Make sure you know the rules and understand where and when restrictions apply. Controlled parking areas will be indicated by signs and road markings. Parking in the wrong place could cause an obstruction and danger to other traffic. It can also result in a fine.

517 Mark *one* answer

A cycle lane, marked by a solid white line, is in operation. What does this mean for car drivers?

- ☐ **A** The lane may be used for parking your car
- ☐ **B** You may drive in the lane at any time
- ☐ **C** The lane may be used when necessary
- ☐ **D** You mustn't drive in that lane

Leave the lane free for cyclists. At other times, when the lane isn't in operation, you should still be aware that there may be cyclists about. Give them plenty of room as you pass and allow for their movement from side to side, especially in windy weather or on a bumpy road.

518 Mark *one* answer

You intend to turn left from a main road into a minor road. What should you do as you approach it?

- ☐ **A** Keep just left of the middle of the road
- ☐ **B** Keep in the middle of the road
- ☐ **C** Swing out to the right just before turning
- ☐ **D** Keep well to the left of the road

Your road position can help other road users to anticipate your actions. Keep to the left as you approach a left turn and don't swing out into the centre of the road in order to make the turn easier. This could endanger oncoming traffic and may cause other road users to misunderstand your intentions.

519 Mark *one* answer

You're waiting at a level crossing. The red warning lights continue to flash after a train has passed by. What should you do?

- ☐ **A** Get out and investigate
- ☐ **B** Telephone the signal operator
- ☐ **C** Continue to wait
- ☐ **D** Drive across carefully

At a level crossing, flashing red lights mean you must stop. If the train passes but the lights keep flashing, wait. Another train may be coming.

520 Mark *one* answer

You're driving over a level crossing. The warning lights come on and a bell rings. What should you do?

- ☐ **A** Get everyone out of the vehicle immediately
- ☐ **B** Stop and reverse back to clear the crossing
- ☐ **C** Keep going and clear the crossing
- ☐ **D** Stop immediately and use your hazard warning lights

Keep going; don't stop on the crossing. If the amber warning lights come on as you're approaching the crossing, you must stop unless it's unsafe to do so. Red flashing lights together with an audible signal mean you must stop.

521 Mark *one* answer

You're on a busy main road and find that you're travelling in the wrong direction. What should you do?

- ☐ **A** Turn into a side road on the right and reverse into the main road
- ☐ **B** Make a U-turn in the main road
- ☐ **C** Make a 'three-point' turn in the main road
- ☐ **D** Turn around in a side road

Don't turn around in a busy street or reverse from a side road into a main road. Find a quiet side road and choose a place where you won't obstruct an entrance or exit. Look out for pedestrians and cyclists as well as other traffic.

522 Mark *one* answer
During which manoeuvre may you remove your seat belt?

☐ **A** Reversing
☐ **B** Hill start
☐ **C** Emergency stop
☐ **D** Driving slowly

You may remove your seat belt while you're carrying out a manoeuvre that includes reversing. However, you must remember to put it back on again before you resume driving.

523 Mark *one* answer
Over what distance are you allowed to reverse?

☐ **A** No further than is necessary
☐ **B** No more than a car's length
☐ **C** As far as it takes to reverse around a corner
☐ **D** The length of a residential street

You mustn't reverse further than is necessary. You may decide to turn your vehicle around by reversing into an opening or side road. When you reverse, always look all around you, and watch for pedestrians. Don't reverse from a side road into a main road.

524 Mark *one* answer
What should you do when you're unsure whether it's safe to reverse your vehicle?

☐ **A** Sound your horn
☐ **B** Rev your engine
☐ **C** Get out and check
☐ **D** Reverse slowly

A small child could be hidden directly behind you, so, if you can't see all around your vehicle, get out and have a look. You could also ask someone reliable outside the vehicle to guide you.

525 Mark *one* answer
When may you reverse from a side road into a main road?

☐ **A** Only if both roads are clear of traffic
☐ **B** Not at any time
☐ **C** At any time
☐ **D** Only if the main road is clear of traffic

Don't reverse into a main road from a side road. The main road is likely to be busy and the traffic on it moving quickly.

526 Mark *one* answer

You want to turn right at a box junction. There's oncoming traffic. What should you do?

☐ **A** Wait in the box junction if your exit is clear
☐ **B** Wait before the junction until it's clear of all traffic
☐ **C** Drive on; you can't turn right at a box junction
☐ **D** Drive slowly into the box junction when signalled by oncoming traffic

You can wait in the box junction as long as your exit is clear. At some point there'll be a gap in the oncoming traffic, or the traffic lights will change, allowing you to proceed.

527 Mark *one* answer

You're reversing your vehicle into a side road. When would the greatest hazard to passing traffic occur?

☐ **A** After you've completed the manoeuvre
☐ **B** Just before you actually begin to manoeuvre
☐ **C** After you've entered the side road
☐ **D** When the front of your vehicle swings out

Always check in all directions before reversing into a side road. Keep a good lookout throughout the manoeuvre. Act on what you see and wait if necessary.

528 Mark *one* answer

Where's the safest place to park your vehicle at night?

☐ **A** In a garage
☐ **B** On a busy road
☐ **C** In a quiet car park
☐ **D** Near a red route

If you have a garage, use it. Your vehicle is less likely to be a victim of car crime if it's in a garage. Also, in winter, the windows will be kept free from ice and snow.

529 Mark *one* answer

When may you stop on an urban clearway?

☐ **A** To set down and pick up passengers
☐ **B** To use a mobile telephone
☐ **C** To ask for directions
☐ **D** To load or unload goods

Urban clearways have their times of operation clearly signed. You may stop only for as long as is reasonable to pick up or set down passengers. You should ensure that you're not causing an obstruction for other traffic.

530 Mark *one* answer

You're looking for somewhere to park your vehicle. The area is full except for spaces marked 'disabled use'. What can you do?

- ☐ **A** You can use these spaces when elsewhere is full
- ☐ **B** You can park in one of these spaces if you stay with your vehicle
- ☐ **C** You can use one of the spaces as long as one is kept free
- ☐ **D** You can't park there, unless you're permitted to do so

It's illegal to park in a space reserved for disabled users unless you're permitted to do so. These spaces are provided for people with limited mobility, who may need extra space to get in and out of their vehicle.

531 Mark *one* answer

You're on a road that's only wide enough for one vehicle. A car is coming towards you. What should you do?

- ☐ **A** Pull into a passing place on your right
- ☐ **B** Force the other driver to reverse
- ☐ **C** Pull into a passing place if your vehicle is wider
- ☐ **D** Pull into a passing place on your left

Pull into the nearest passing place on the left if you meet another vehicle on a narrow road. If the nearest passing place is on the right, wait opposite it.

532 Mark *one* answer

You're driving at night with your headlights on full beam. A vehicle is overtaking you. When should you dip your lights?

- ☐ **A** Some time after the vehicle has passed you
- ☐ **B** Before the vehicle starts to pass you
- ☐ **C** Only if the other driver dips their headlights
- ☐ **D** As soon as the vehicle passes you

On full beam, your lights could dazzle the driver in front. Dip your lights as soon as the driver passes you and drop back so that the dipped beam falls short of the other vehicle.

533 Mark *one* answer

When may you drive a motor car in this bus lane?

- ☐ **A** Outside its hours of operation
- ☐ **B** To get to the front of a traffic queue
- ☐ **C** You may not use it at any time
- ☐ **D** To overtake slow-moving traffic

Some bus lanes operate only during peak hours and other vehicles may use them outside these hours. Make sure you check the sign for the hours of operation before driving in a bus lane.

534 Mark *one* answer
Other than direction indicators, how can you give signals to other road users?

- ☐ **A** By using brake lights
- ☐ **B** By using sidelights
- ☐ **C** By using fog lights
- ☐ **D** By using interior lights

Your brake lights will give an indication to traffic behind that you're slowing down. Good anticipation will allow you time to check your mirrors before slowing.

535 Mark *one* answer
You're parked in a busy high street. What is the safest way to turn your vehicle around so you can go the opposite way?

- ☐ **A** Find a quiet side road to turn around in
- ☐ **B** Drive into a side road and reverse into the main road
- ☐ **C** Get someone to stop the traffic
- ☐ **D** Do a U-turn

Make sure you carry out the manoeuvre without causing a hazard to other vehicles. Choose a place to turn that's safe and convenient for you and for other road users.

536 Mark *one* answer
To help keep your vehicle secure at night, where should you park?

- ☐ **A** Near a police station
- ☐ **B** In a quiet road
- ☐ **C** On a red route
- ☐ **D** In a well-lit area

Whenever possible, park in an area that will be well lit at night.

537 Mark *one* answer
You're driving in the right-hand lane of a dual carriageway. You see signs showing that the right-hand lane is closed 800 yards ahead. What should you do?

- ☐ **A** Keep in that lane until you reach the queue
- ☐ **B** Move to the left immediately
- ☐ **C** Wait and see which lane is moving faster
- ☐ **D** Move to the left in good time

Keep a lookout for traffic signs. If you're directed to change lanes, do so in good time. Don't:
- push your way into traffic in another lane
- try to gain advantage by delaying changing lanes

538 Mark *one* answer
You're driving on a road that has a cycle lane. The lane is marked by a broken white line. What does this mean?

- ☐ **A** You shouldn't drive in the lane unless it's unavoidable
- ☐ **B** There's a reduced speed limit for motor vehicles using the lane
- ☐ **C** Cyclists can travel in both directions in that lane
- ☐ **D** The lane must be used by motorcyclists in heavy traffic

Cycle lanes are marked with either a solid or a broken white line. If the line is solid, you should check the times of operation shown on the signs, and not drive or park in the lane during those times. If the line is broken, you shouldn't drive or park in the lane unless it's unavoidable.

539 Mark *one* answer
What must you have to park in a disabled space?

- ☐ **A** A Blue Badge
- ☐ **B** A wheelchair
- ☐ **C** An advanced driver certificate
- ☐ **D** An adapted vehicle

Don't park in a space reserved for disabled people unless you or your passenger are a disabled badge holder. The badge must be displayed in your vehicle, in the bottom left-hand corner of the windscreen.

540 Mark *one* answer
When must you stop your vehicle?

- ☐ **A** If you're involved in an incident that causes damage or injury
- ☐ **B** At a junction where there are 'give way' lines
- ☐ **C** At the end of a one-way street
- ☐ **D** Before merging onto a motorway

You must stop your vehicle when signalled to do so by a:
- police or traffic officer
- traffic warden
- school crossing patrol
- red traffic light

You must also stop if you're involved in an incident which causes damage or injury to any other person, vehicle, animal or property.

541 Mark *one* answer
How can you identify traffic signs that give orders?

- ☐ **A** Green rectangles
- ☐ **B** Red triangles
- ☐ **C** Blue rectangles
- ☐ **D** Red circles

There are three basic types of traffic sign: those that warn, those that inform and those that give orders. Generally, triangular signs warn, rectangular signs give information or directions, and circular signs give orders. An exception is the eight-sided 'stop' sign.

542 Mark *one* answer
Traffic signs giving orders are generally which shape?

Road signs in the shape of a circle give orders. Those with a red circle are mostly prohibitive. The 'stop' sign is octagonal to give it greater prominence. Signs giving orders must always be obeyed.

543 Mark *one* answer
Which type of sign tells you not to do something?

Signs in the shape of a circle give orders. A sign with a red circle means that you aren't allowed to do something. Study Know Your Traffic Signs to ensure that you understand what the different traffic signs mean.

544 Mark *one* answer
What does this sign mean?

- ☐ **A** Maximum speed limit with traffic calming
- ☐ **B** Minimum speed limit with traffic calming
- ☐ **C** '20 cars only' parking zone
- ☐ **D** Only 20 cars allowed at any one time

If you're in a place where there are likely to be pedestrians (for example, outside a school, near a park, in a residential area or in a shopping area), you should be cautious and keep your speed down. Many local authorities have taken steps to slow traffic down by creating traffic-calming measures such as speed humps. They're there for a reason; slow down.

545 Mark *one* answer

Which sign means no motor vehicles are allowed?

☐ **A**

☐ **B**

☐ **C**

☐ **D**

You'll generally see this sign at the approach to a pedestrian-only zone.

546 Mark *one* answer

What does this sign mean?

☐ **A** New speed limit 20 mph
☐ **B** No vehicles over 30 tonnes
☐ **C** Minimum speed limit 30 mph
☐ **D** End of 20 mph zone

Where you see this sign, the 20 mph restriction ends. Check all around for possible hazards and only increase your speed if it's safe to do so.

547 Mark *one* answer

What does this sign mean?

☐ **A** No overtaking
☐ **B** No motor vehicles
☐ **C** Clearway (no stopping)
☐ **D** Cars and motorcycles only

A sign will indicate which types of vehicles are prohibited from certain roads. Make sure that you know which signs apply to the vehicle you're using.

548 Mark *one* answer

What does this sign mean?

☐ **A** No parking
☐ **B** No road markings
☐ **C** No through road
☐ **D** No entry

'No entry' signs are used in places such as one-way streets to prevent vehicles driving against the traffic. To ignore one would be dangerous, both for yourself and for other road users, as well as being against the law.

549 Mark *one* answer
What does this sign mean?

- ☐ **A** Bend to the right
- ☐ **B** Road on the right closed
- ☐ **C** No traffic from the right
- ☐ **D** No right turn

The 'no right turn' sign may be used to warn road users that there's a 'no entry' prohibition on a road to the right ahead.

550 Mark *one* answer
Which sign means 'no entry'?

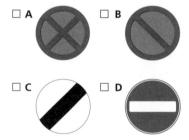

Look for and obey traffic signs. Disobeying or not seeing a sign could be dangerous. It may also be an offence for which you could be prosecuted.

551 Mark *one* answer
What does this sign mean?

- ☐ **A** Route for trams only
- ☐ **B** Route for buses only
- ☐ **C** Parking for buses only
- ☐ **D** Parking for trams only

Avoid blocking tram routes. Trams are fixed on their route and can't manoeuvre around other vehicles or pedestrians. Modern trams travel quickly and are quiet, so you might not hear them approaching.

552 Mark *one* answer
Which type of vehicle does this sign apply to?

- ☐ **A** Wide vehicles
- ☐ **B** Long vehicles
- ☐ **C** High vehicles
- ☐ **D** Heavy vehicles

The triangular shapes above and below the dimensions indicate a height restriction that applies to the road ahead.

553 Mark *one* answer
Which sign means no motor vehicles allowed?

☐ A   ☐ B

☐ C   ☐ D

This sign is used to enable pedestrians to walk free from traffic. It's often found in shopping areas.

554 Mark *one* answer
What does this sign mean?

☐ **A** You have priority
☐ **B** No motor vehicles
☐ **C** Two-way traffic
☐ **D** No overtaking

Road signs that prohibit overtaking are placed in locations where passing the vehicle in front is dangerous. If you see this sign, don't attempt to overtake. The sign is there for a reason; you must obey it.

555 Mark *one* answer
What does this sign mean?

☐ **A** Waiting restrictions apply
☐ **B** Waiting permitted
☐ **C** National speed limit applies
☐ **D** Clearway (no stopping)

There'll be a plate or additional sign to tell you when the restrictions apply.

556 Mark *one* answer
What does this sign mean?

☐ **A** End of restricted speed area
☐ **B** End of restricted parking area
☐ **C** End of clearway
☐ **D** End of cycle route

Even though you've left the restricted area, make sure that you park where you won't endanger other road users or cause an obstruction.

557 Mark *one* answer
Which sign means 'no stopping'?

☐ A   ☐ B

☐ C   ☐ D

Stopping where this clearway restriction applies is likely to cause congestion. Allow the traffic to flow by obeying the signs.

558 Mark *one* answer
You see this sign ahead. What does it mean?

☐ **A** National speed limit applies
☐ **B** Waiting restrictions apply
☐ **C** No stopping
☐ **D** No entry

Clearways are stretches of road where you aren't allowed to stop unless it's an emergency. Stopping where these restrictions apply may be dangerous and is likely to cause an obstruction. Restrictions might apply for several miles and this may be indicated on the sign.

559 Mark *one* answer
What does this sign mean?

☐ **A** Distance to parking place ahead
☐ **B** Distance to public telephone ahead
☐ **C** Distance to public house ahead
☐ **D** Distance to passing place ahead

If you intend to stop and rest, this sign allows you time to reduce speed and pull over safely.

560 Mark *one* answer
What does this sign mean?

☐ **A** Vehicles may not park on the verge or footway
☐ **B** Vehicles may park on the left-hand side of the road only
☐ **C** Vehicles may park fully on the verge or footway
☐ **D** Vehicles may park on the right-hand side of the road only

In order to keep roads free from parked cars, there are some areas where you're allowed to park on the verge. Only do this where you see the sign. Parking on verges or footways anywhere else could lead to a fine.

561 Mark *one* answer
What does this traffic sign mean?

- ☐ **A** No overtaking allowed
- ☐ **B** Give priority to oncoming traffic
- ☐ **C** Two-way traffic
- ☐ **D** One-way traffic only

Priority signs are normally shown where the road is narrow and there isn't enough room for two vehicles to pass. Examples are narrow bridges, roadworks and where there's a width restriction. Make sure you know who has priority; don't force your way through. Show courtesy and consideration to other road users.

562 Mark *one* answer
What is the meaning of this traffic sign?

- ☐ **A** End of two-way road
- ☐ **B** Give priority to vehicles coming towards you
- ☐ **C** You have priority over vehicles coming towards you
- ☐ **D** Bus lane ahead

Don't force your way through. Show courtesy and consideration to other road users. Although you have priority, make sure oncoming traffic is going to give way before you continue.

563 Mark *one* answer
What shape is a 'stop' sign at a junction?

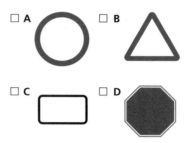

To make it easy to recognise, the 'stop' sign is the only sign of this shape. You must stop and take effective observation before proceeding.

564 Mark *one* answer
At a junction, you see this sign partly covered by snow. What does it mean?

- ☐ **A** Crossroads
- ☐ **B** Give way
- ☐ **C** Stop
- ☐ **D** Turn right

The 'stop' sign is the only road sign that's octagonal. This is so that it can be recognised and obeyed even if it's obscured (for example, by snow).

565 Mark *one* answer
What does this sign mean?

- ☐ **A** Service area 30 miles ahead
- ☐ **B** Maximum speed 30 mph
- ☐ **C** Minimum speed 30 mph
- ☐ **D** Lay-by 30 miles ahead

This sign is shown where slow-moving vehicles would impede the flow of traffic; for example, in tunnels. However, if you need to slow down or even stop to avoid an incident or potential collision, you should do so.

566 Mark *one* answer
What does this sign mean?

- ☐ **A** Give way to oncoming vehicles
- ☐ **B** Approaching traffic passes you on both sides
- ☐ **C** Turn off at the next available junction
- ☐ **D** Pass either side to get to the same destination

These signs are often seen in one-way streets that have more than one lane. When you see this sign, use the route that's the most convenient and doesn't require a late change of direction.

567 Mark *one* answer
What does this sign mean?

- ☐ **A** Route for trams
- ☐ **B** Give way to trams
- ☐ **C** Route for buses
- ☐ **D** Give way to buses

Take extra care when you encounter trams. Look out for road markings and signs that alert you to them. Modern trams are very quiet and you may not hear them approaching.

568 Mark *one* answer
What does a circular traffic sign with a blue background do?

- ☐ **A** Give warning of a motorway ahead
- ☐ **B** Give directions to a car park
- ☐ **C** Give motorway information
- ☐ **D** Give an instruction

Signs with blue circles mostly give a positive instruction. These are often found in urban areas and include signs for mini-roundabouts and directional arrows.

569 Mark *one* answer

Where would you see a contraflow bus and cycle lane?

- ☐ **A** On a dual carriageway
- ☐ **B** On a roundabout
- ☐ **C** On an urban motorway
- ☐ **D** On a one-way street

The traffic permitted to use a contraflow lane travels in the opposite direction to traffic in the other lanes on the road.

570 Mark *one* answer

What does this sign mean?

- ☐ **A** Bus station on the right
- ☐ **B** Contraflow bus lane
- ☐ **C** With-flow bus lane
- ☐ **D** Give way to buses

There will also be markings on the road surface to indicate the bus lane. You mustn't use this lane for parking or overtaking.

571 Mark *one* answer

What does a sign with a brown background show?

- ☐ **A** Tourist directions
- ☐ **B** Primary roads
- ☐ **C** Motorway routes
- ☐ **D** Minor roads

Signs with a brown background give directions to places of interest. They're often seen on a motorway, directing you along the easiest route to the attraction.

572 Mark *one* answer

What does this sign mean?

- ☐ **A** Tourist attraction
- ☐ **B** Beware of trains
- ☐ **C** Level crossing
- ☐ **D** Beware of trams

These signs indicate places of interest and are designed to guide you by the easiest route. They're particularly useful when you're unfamiliar with the area.

573 Mark *one* answer
What are triangular signs for?

- ☐ **A** To give warnings
- ☐ **B** To give information
- ☐ **C** To give orders
- ☐ **D** To give directions

This type of sign warns you of hazards ahead. Make sure you look at each sign that you pass on the road, so that you don't miss any vital instructions or information.

574 Mark *one* answer
What does this sign mean?

- ☐ **A** Turn left ahead
- ☐ **B** T-junction
- ☐ **C** No through road
- ☐ **D** Give way

This type of sign warns you of hazards ahead. Make sure you look at each sign and road marking that you pass, so that you don't miss any vital instructions or information. This particular sign shows there's a T-junction with priority over vehicles from the right.

575 Mark *one* answer
What does this sign mean?

- ☐ **A** Multi-exit roundabout
- ☐ **B** Risk of ice
- ☐ **C** Six roads converge
- ☐ **D** Place of historical interest

It will take up to ten times longer to stop when it's icy. Where there's a risk of icy conditions, you need to be aware of this and take extra care. If you think the road may be icy, don't brake or steer harshly, as your tyres could lose their grip on the road.

576 Mark *one* answer
What does this sign mean?

- ☐ **A** Crossroads
- ☐ **B** Level crossing with gate
- ☐ **C** Level crossing without gate
- ☐ **D** Ahead only

The priority through the junction is shown by the broader line. You need to be aware of the hazard posed by traffic crossing or pulling out onto a major road.

577 Mark *one* answer
What does this sign mean?

- ☐ **A** Ring road
- ☐ **B** Mini-roundabout
- ☐ **C** No vehicles
- ☐ **D** Roundabout

As you approach a roundabout, look well ahead and check all signs. Decide which exit you wish to take and move into the correct position as you approach the roundabout, signalling as required.

578 Mark *one* answer
What information would be shown in a triangular road sign?

- ☐ **A** Road narrows
- ☐ **B** Ahead only
- ☐ **C** Keep left
- ☐ **D** Minimum speed

Warning signs are there to make you aware of potential hazards on the road ahead. Take note of the signs so you're prepared and can take whatever action is necessary.

579 Mark *one* answer
What does this sign mean?

- ☐ **A** Cyclists must dismount
- ☐ **B** Cycles aren't allowed
- ☐ **C** Cycle route ahead
- ☐ **D** Cycle in single file

Where there's a cycle route ahead, a sign will show a bicycle in a red warning triangle. Watch out for children on bicycles and cyclists rejoining the main road.

580 Mark *one* answer
Which sign means that pedestrians may be walking along the road?

☐ A   ☐ B

☐ C   ☐ D

When you pass pedestrians in the road, leave plenty of room. You might have to use the right-hand side of the road, so look well ahead, as well as in your mirrors, before pulling out. Take great care if a bend in the road obscures your view ahead.

581 Mark *one* answer
Which of these signs means there's a double bend ahead?

☐ **A** ☐ **B**

☐ **C** ☐ **D**

Triangular signs give you a warning of hazards ahead. They're there to give you time to prepare for the hazard; for example, by adjusting your speed.

582 Mark *one* answer
What does this sign mean?

☐ **A** Wait at the barriers
☐ **B** Wait at the crossroads
☐ **C** Give way to trams
☐ **D** Give way to farm vehicles

Obey the 'give way' signs. Trams are unable to steer around you if you misjudge when it's safe to enter the junction.

583 Mark *one* answer
What does this sign mean?

☐ **A** Hump bridge
☐ **B** Humps in the road
☐ **C** Entrance to tunnel
☐ **D** Soft verges

These humps have been put in place to slow the traffic down. They're usually found in residential areas. Slow down to an appropriate speed.

584 Mark *one* answer
Which of these signs means the end of a dual carriageway?

☐ **A** ☐ **B**

☐ **C** ☐ **D**

If you're overtaking, make sure you move back safely into the left-hand lane before you reach the end of the dual carriageway.

585 Mark *one* answer
What does this sign mean?

☐ **A** End of dual carriageway
☐ **B** Tall bridge
☐ **C** Road narrows
☐ **D** End of narrow bridge

Don't wait until the last moment before moving into the left-hand lane. Plan ahead and don't rely on other traffic letting you in.

586 Mark *one* answer
What does this sign mean?

☐ **A** Side winds
☐ **B** Road noise
☐ **C** Airport
☐ **D** Adverse camber

A warning sign with a picture of a windsock indicates that there may be strong side winds. This sign is often found on exposed roads.

587 Mark *one* answer
What does this traffic sign mean?

☐ **A** Slippery road ahead
☐ **B** Tyres liable to punctures ahead
☐ **C** Danger ahead
☐ **D** Service area ahead

This sign is there to alert you to the likelihood of danger ahead. It may be accompanied by a plate indicating the type of hazard. Be ready to reduce your speed and take avoiding action.

588 Mark *one* answer
You're about to overtake. What should you do when you see this sign?

- ☐ **A** Overtake the other driver as quickly as possible
- ☐ **B** Move to the right to get a better view
- ☐ **C** Switch your headlights on before overtaking
- ☐ **D** Hold back until you can see clearly ahead

You won't be able to see any hazards that might be hidden in the dip. As well as oncoming traffic, the dip may conceal:
- cyclists
- horse riders
- parked vehicles
- pedestrians in the road

589 Mark *one* answer
What does this sign mean?

- ☐ **A** Level crossing with gate or barrier
- ☐ **B** Gated road ahead
- ☐ **C** Level crossing without gate or barrier
- ☐ **D** Cattle grid ahead

Some crossings have gates but no attendant or signals. You should stop, look both ways, listen and make sure that no train is approaching. If there's a telephone, contact the signal operator to make sure it's safe to cross.

590 Mark *one* answer
What does this sign mean?

- ☐ **A** No trams ahead
- ☐ **B** Oncoming trams
- ☐ **C** Trams crossing ahead
- ☐ **D** Trams only

This sign tells you to beware of trams. If you don't usually drive in a town where there are trams, remember to look out for them at junctions and look for tram rails, signs and signals.

591 Mark *one* answer
What does this sign mean?

- ☐ **A** Adverse camber
- ☐ **B** Steep hill downwards
- ☐ **C** Uneven road
- ☐ **D** Steep hill upwards

This sign gives you an early warning that the road ahead will slope downhill. Prepare to alter your speed and gear. Looking at the sign from left to right will show you whether the road slopes uphill or downhill.

592 Mark *one* answer
What does this sign mean?

- ☐ **A** Uneven road surface
- ☐ **B** Bridge over the road
- ☐ **C** Road ahead ends
- ☐ **D** Water across the road

This sign is found where a shallow stream crosses the road. Heavy rainfall could increase the flow of water. If the water looks too deep or the stream has spread over a large distance, stop and find another route.

593 Mark *one* answer
What does this sign mean?

- ☐ **A** Turn left for parking area
- ☐ **B** No through road on the left
- ☐ **C** No entry for traffic turning left
- ☐ **D** Turn left for ferry terminal

This sign shows you that you can't get through to another route by turning left at the junction ahead.

594 Mark *one* answer
What does this sign mean?

- ☐ **A** T-junction
- ☐ **B** No through road
- ☐ **C** Telephone box ahead
- ☐ **D** Toilet ahead

You won't be able to find a through route to another road. Use this road only for access.

595 Mark *one* answer
Which is the sign for a ring road?

☐ A ☐ B

☐ C ☐ D

Ring roads are designed to relieve congestion in towns and city centres.

596 Mark *one* answer
What does this sign mean?

☐ A The right-hand lane ahead is narrow
☐ B Right-hand lane for buses only
☐ C Right-hand lane for turning right
☐ D The right-hand lane is closed

Yellow-and-black temporary signs may be used to inform you about roadworks or lane restrictions. Look well ahead. If you have to change lanes, do so in good time.

597 Mark *one* answer
What does this sign mean?

☐ A Change to the left lane
☐ B Leave at the next exit
☐ C Contraflow system
☐ D One-way street

If you use the right-hand lane in a contraflow system, you'll be travelling with no permanent barrier between you and the oncoming traffic. Observe speed limits and keep a good distance from the vehicle ahead.

598 Mark *one* answer
What does this sign mean?

☐ A Leave motorway at next exit
☐ B Lane for heavy and slow vehicles
☐ C All lorries use the hard shoulder
☐ D Rest area for lorries

Where there's a long, steep, uphill gradient on a motorway, a crawler lane may be provided. This helps the traffic to flow by diverting the slower heavy vehicles into a dedicated lane on the left.

599 Mark *one* answer
What does a red traffic light mean?

- ☐ **A** You should stop unless turning left
- ☐ **B** Stop, if you're able to brake safely
- ☐ **C** You must stop and wait behind the stop line
- ☐ **D** Proceed with care

Whatever light is showing, you should know which light is going to appear next and be able to take appropriate action. For example, when amber is showing on its own, you'll know that red will appear next. This should give you ample time to anticipate and respond safely.

600 Mark *one* answer
At traffic lights, what does it mean when the amber light shows on its own?

- ☐ **A** Prepare to go
- ☐ **B** Go if the way is clear
- ☐ **C** Go if no pedestrians are crossing
- ☐ **D** Stop at the stop line

When the amber light is showing on its own, the red light will follow next. The amber light means stop, unless you've already crossed the stop line or you're so close to it that stopping may cause a collision.

601 Mark *one* answer
You're at a junction controlled by traffic lights. When shouldn't you proceed at green?

- ☐ **A** When pedestrians are waiting to cross
- ☐ **B** When your exit from the junction is blocked
- ☐ **C** When you think the lights may be about to change
- ☐ **D** When you intend to turn right

As you approach the lights, look into the road you wish to take. Only proceed if your exit road is clear. If the road is blocked, hold back, even if you have to wait for the next green signal.

602 Mark *one* answer

You're in the left-hand lane at traffic lights, waiting to turn left. At which of these traffic lights mustn't you move on?

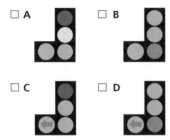

☐ **A** ☐ **B**

☐ **C** ☐ **D**

At some junctions, there may be separate signals for different lanes. These are called 'filter' lights. They're designed to help traffic flow at major junctions. Make sure that you're in the correct lane and proceed if the way is clear and the green light shows for your lane.

603 Mark *one* answer

What does this sign mean?

☐ **A** Traffic lights out of order
☐ **B** Amber signal out of order
☐ **C** Temporary traffic lights ahead
☐ **D** New traffic lights ahead

You might see this sign where traffic lights are out of order. Proceed with caution, as nobody has priority at the junction.

604 Mark *one* answer

When traffic lights are out of order, who has priority?

☐ **A** Traffic going straight on
☐ **B** Traffic turning right
☐ **C** Nobody
☐ **D** Traffic turning left

When traffic lights are out of order, you should treat the junction as an unmarked crossroads. Be cautious, as you may need to give way or stop. Look for traffic attempting to cross the junction, unaware that it doesn't have priority.

605 Mark *one* answer

These flashing red lights mean that you must stop. Where would you find them?

☐ **A** Pelican crossings
☐ **B** Motorway exits
☐ **C** Zebra crossings
☐ **D** Level crossings

These signals are found at level crossings, swing or lifting bridges, some airfields and emergency access sites. The flashing red lights mean stop whether or not the way seems to be clear.

606 Mark *one* answer

What do these zigzag lines at pedestrian crossings mean?

- ☐ **A** No parking at any time
- ☐ **B** Parking allowed only for a short time
- ☐ **C** Slow down to 20 mph
- ☐ **D** Sounding horns isn't allowed

The approach to, and exit from, a pedestrian crossing is marked with zigzag lines. You mustn't park on them or overtake the leading vehicle when approaching the crossing. Parking here would block the view for pedestrians and approaching traffic.

607 Mark *one* answer

When may you cross a double solid white line in the middle of the road?

- ☐ **A** To pass traffic that's queuing back at a junction
- ☐ **B** To pass a car signalling to turn left ahead
- ☐ **C** To pass a road maintenance vehicle travelling at 10 mph or less
- ☐ **D** To pass a vehicle that's towing a trailer

You may cross the solid white line to pass a stationary vehicle or to pass a pedal cycle, horse or road maintenance vehicle if it's travelling at 10 mph or less. You may also cross the solid white line to enter a side road or access a property.

608 Mark *one* answer

What does this road marking mean?

- ☐ **A** Don't cross the line
- ☐ **B** No stopping allowed
- ☐ **C** You're approaching a hazard
- ☐ **D** No overtaking allowed

Road markings will warn you of a hazard ahead. A single broken line along the centre of the road, with long markings and short gaps, is a hazard warning line. Don't cross it unless you can see that the road is clear well ahead.

609 Mark *one* answer
Where would you see this road marking?

- ☐ **A** At traffic lights
- ☐ **B** On road humps
- ☐ **C** Near a level crossing
- ☐ **D** At a box junction

Because the road has a dark colour, changes in level aren't easily seen. White triangles painted on the road surface give you an indication of where there are road humps.

---

610 Mark *one* answer
Which of these is a hazard warning line?

You need to know the difference between the normal centre line and a hazard warning line. If there's a hazard ahead, the markings are longer and the gaps shorter. This gives you advance warning of an unspecified hazard.

611 Mark *one* answer
At this junction, there's a 'stop' sign and a solid white line on the road surface. Why is there a 'stop' sign here?

- ☐ **A** Speed on the major road is derestricted
- ☐ **B** It's a busy junction
- ☐ **C** Visibility along the major road is restricted
- ☐ **D** There are hazard warning lines in the centre of the road

If your view at a road junction is restricted, you must stop. There may also be a 'stop' sign. Don't emerge until you're sure no traffic is approaching. If you don't know, don't go.

---

612 Mark *one* answer
You see this line across the road at the entrance to a roundabout. What does it mean?

- ☐ **A** Give way to traffic from the right
- ☐ **B** Traffic from the left has right of way
- ☐ **C** You have right of way
- ☐ **D** Stop at the line

Slow down as you approach the roundabout and check for traffic from the right. If you need to stop and give way, stay behind the broken line until it's safe to emerge onto the roundabout.

613 Mark *one* answer
How will a police officer in a patrol vehicle normally get you to stop?

☐ **A** Flash the headlights, indicate left and point to the left
☐ **B** Wait until you stop, then approach you
☐ **C** Use the siren, overtake, cut in front and stop
☐ **D** Pull alongside you, use the siren and wave you to stop

You must obey signals given by the police. If a police officer in a patrol vehicle wants you to pull over, they'll indicate this without causing danger to you or other traffic.

614 Mark *one* answer
You're approaching a junction where the traffic lights aren't working. What should you do when a police officer gives this signal?

☐ **A** Turn left only
☐ **B** Turn right only
☐ **C** Continue ahead only
☐ **D** Stop at the stop line

When a police officer or traffic warden is directing traffic, you must obey them. They'll use the arm signals shown in *The Highway Code*. Learn what these signals mean and obey them.

615 Mark *one* answer
The driver of the car in front is giving this arm signal. What does it mean?

☐ **A** The driver is slowing down
☐ **B** The driver intends to turn right
☐ **C** The driver wishes to overtake
☐ **D** The driver intends to turn left

There might be an occasion where another driver uses an arm signal. This may be because the vehicle's indicators are obscured by other traffic. In order for such signals to be effective, all drivers should know their meaning. Be aware that the 'left turn' signal might look similar to the 'slowing down' signal.

616 Mark *one* answer
Where would you see these road markings?

☐ **A** At a level crossing
☐ **B** On a motorway slip road
☐ **C** At a pedestrian crossing
☐ **D** On a single-track road

When driving on a motorway or slip road, you mustn't enter an area marked with chevrons and bordered by a solid white line for any reason, except in an emergency.

617 Mark *one* answer

What does this motorway sign mean?

☐ **A** Change to the lane on your left
☐ **B** Leave the motorway at the next exit
☐ **C** Change to the opposite carriageway
☐ **D** Pull up on the hard shoulder

On the motorway, signs sometimes show temporary warnings due to traffic or weather conditions. They may be used to indicate:
- lane closures
- temporary speed limits
- weather warnings

---

618 Mark *one* answer

What does this motorway sign mean?

☐ **A** Temporary minimum speed 50 mph
☐ **B** No services for 50 miles
☐ **C** Obstruction 50 metres (164 feet) ahead
☐ **D** Temporary maximum speed 50 mph

Look out for signs above your lane or on the central reservation. These will give you important information or warnings about the road ahead. To allow for the high speed of motorway traffic, these signs may light up some distance from any hazard. Don't ignore the signs just because the road looks clear to you.

619 Mark *one* answer

What does this sign mean?

☐ **A** Through traffic to use left lane
☐ **B** Right-hand lane T-junction only
☐ **C** Right-hand lane closed ahead
☐ **D** 11 tonne weight limit

You should change lanes as directed by the sign. Here, the right-hand lane is closed but the left-hand and centre lanes are available. Merging in turn is recommended when it's safe and traffic is going slowly; for example, at roadworks or a road traffic incident. When vehicles are travelling at speed, this isn't advisable and you should move into the appropriate lane in good time.

620 Mark *one* answer
What does '25' mean on this motorway sign?

- ☐ **A** The distance to the nearest town
- ☐ **B** The route number of the road
- ☐ **C** The number of the next junction
- ☐ **D** The speed limit on the slip road

Before you set out on your journey, use a road map to plan your route. When you see an advance warning of your junction, make sure you get into the correct lane in plenty of time. Last-minute harsh braking and cutting across lanes at speed is extremely hazardous.

621 Mark *one* answer
How should the right-hand lane of a three-lane motorway be used?

- ☐ **A** As a high-speed lane
- ☐ **B** As an overtaking lane
- ☐ **C** As a right-turn lane
- ☐ **D** As an acceleration lane

You should stay in the left-hand lane of a motorway unless you're overtaking another vehicle. The right-hand lane of a motorway is an overtaking lane; it isn't the 'fast lane'. After overtaking, move back to the left when it's safe to do so.

622 Mark *one* answer
Where can you find reflective amber studs on a motorway?

- ☐ **A** Separating the slip road from the motorway
- ☐ **B** On the left-hand edge of the road
- ☐ **C** On the right-hand edge of the road
- ☐ **D** Separating the lanes

At night or in poor visibility, reflective studs on the road help you to judge your position on the carriageway.

623 Mark *one* answer
Where on a motorway would you find green reflective studs?

- ☐ **A** Separating driving lanes
- ☐ **B** Between the hard shoulder and the carriageway
- ☐ **C** At slip-road entrances and exits
- ☐ **D** Between the carriageway and the central reservation

Knowing the colours of the reflective studs on the road will help you judge your position, especially at night, in foggy conditions or when visibility is poor.

624 Mark *one* answer

What should you do when you see this sign as you travel along a motorway?

- ☐ **A** Leave the motorway at the next exit
- ☐ **B** Turn left immediately
- ☐ **C** Change lane
- ☐ **D** Move onto the hard shoulder

You'll see this sign if the motorway is closed ahead. Pull into the left-hand lane as soon as it's safe to do so. Don't wait until the last moment before you move across, because the lane may be busy and you'll have to rely on another driver making room for you.

---

625 Mark *one* answer

What does this sign mean?

- ☐ **A** No motor vehicles
- ☐ **B** End of motorway
- ☐ **C** No through road
- ☐ **D** End of bus lane

When you leave the motorway, make sure that you check your speedometer. You may be going faster than you realise. Slow down and look for speed-limit signs.

626 Mark *one* answer

Which of these signs means that the national speed limit applies?

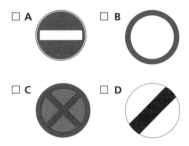

- ☐ **A**
- ☐ **B**
- ☐ **C**
- ☐ **D**

You should know the speed limit for the road on which you're travelling and the vehicle that you're driving. The different speed limits are shown in *The Highway Code*.

---

627 Mark *one* answer

What is the maximum speed on a single carriageway road?

- ☐ **A** 50 mph
- ☐ **B** 60 mph
- ☐ **C** 40 mph
- ☐ **D** 70 mph

If you're travelling on a dual carriageway that becomes a single carriageway road, reduce your speed gradually so that you aren't exceeding the limit as you enter. There might not be a sign to remind you of the limit, so make sure you know the speed limits for different types of road and vehicle.

628 Mark *one* answer
What does this sign mean?

- ☐ **A** End of motorway
- ☐ **B** End of restriction
- ☐ **C** Lane ends ahead
- ☐ **D** Free recovery ends

Temporary restrictions on motorways are shown on signs that have flashing amber lights. At the end of the restriction, you'll see this sign without any flashing lights.

629 Mark *one* answer
What does this sign indicate?

- ☐ **A** A diversion route
- ☐ **B** A picnic area
- ☐ **C** A pedestrian zone
- ☐ **D** A cycle route

When a diversion route has been put in place, drivers are advised to follow a symbol, which may be a black triangle, square, circle or diamond shape on a yellow background.

630 Mark *one* answer
What does this temporary sign indicate?

- ☐ **A** The speed-limit change at the end of the motorway
- ☐ **B** An advisory change of speed limit ahead
- ☐ **C** A variable speed limit ahead
- ☐ **D** A mandatory speed-limit change ahead

In the interests of road safety, temporary mandatory speed limits are imposed at all major roadworks. Signs like this, giving advance warning of the speed limit, are normally placed about three-quarters of a mile ahead of where the speed limit comes into force.

631 Mark *one* answer
What does this traffic sign mean?

- ☐ **A** Compulsory maximum speed limit
- ☐ **B** Advisory maximum speed limit
- ☐ **C** Compulsory minimum speed limit
- ☐ **D** Advised separation distance

The sign gives you an early warning of a speed restriction. If you're travelling at a higher speed, slow down in good time. You could come across queuing traffic due to roadworks or a temporary obstruction.

632 Mark *one* answer
What should you do when you see this sign at a crossroads?

- ☐ **A** Maintain the same speed
- ☐ **B** Carry on with great care
- ☐ **C** Find another route
- ☐ **D** Telephone the police

When traffic lights are out of order, treat the junction as an unmarked crossroads. Be very careful and be prepared to stop; no-one has priority.

633 Mark *one* answer
You're signalling to turn right in busy traffic. How would you confirm your intention safely?

- ☐ **A** Sound the horn
- ☐ **B** Give an arm signal
- ☐ **C** Flash your headlights
- ☐ **D** Position over the centre line

In some situations, you may feel your indicators can't be seen by other road users. If you think you need to make your intention more obvious, give the arm signal shown in *The Highway Code*.

634 Mark *one* answer
What does this sign mean?

- ☐ **A** Motorcycles only
- ☐ **B** No cars
- ☐ **C** Cars only
- ☐ **D** No motorcycles

You must comply with all traffic signs and be especially aware of those signs that apply specifically to the type of vehicle you're using.

635 Mark *one* answer
You're on a motorway. A lorry has stopped in the right-hand lane. What should you do when you see this sign on the lorry?

- ☐ **A** Move into the right-hand lane
- ☐ **B** Stop behind the flashing lights
- ☐ **C** Pass the lorry on the left
- ☐ **D** Leave the motorway at the next exit

Sometimes work is carried out on the motorway without closing the lanes. When this happens, signs are mounted on the back of lorries to warn other road users of the roadworks ahead.

636 Mark *one* answer

You're on a motorway. Red flashing lights appear above your lane only. What should you do?

- ☐ **A** Continue in that lane and look for further information
- ☐ **B** Move into another lane in good time
- ☐ **C** Pull onto the hard shoulder
- ☐ **D** Stop and wait for an instruction to proceed

Flashing red lights above your lane show that your lane is closed. You should move into another lane as soon as you can do so safely.

637 Mark *one* answer

When may you sound the horn?

- ☐ **A** To give you right of way
- ☐ **B** To attract a friend's attention
- ☐ **C** To warn others of your presence
- ☐ **D** To make slower drivers move over

Never sound the horn aggressively. You mustn't sound it when driving in a built-up area between 11.30 pm and 7.00 am, or when you're stationary, unless another road user poses a danger. Don't scare animals by sounding your horn.

638 Mark *one* answer

Your vehicle is stationary. When may you use its horn?

- ☐ **A** When another road user poses a danger
- ☐ **B** When the road is blocked by queuing traffic
- ☐ **C** When it's used only briefly
- ☐ **D** When signalling that you've just arrived

When your vehicle is stationary, only sound the horn if you think there's a risk of danger from another road user. Don't use it just to attract someone's attention. This causes unnecessary noise and could be misleading.

639 Mark *one* answer

What does this sign mean?

- ☐ **A** You can park on the days and times shown
- ☐ **B** No parking on the days and times shown
- ☐ **C** No parking at all from Monday to Friday
- ☐ **D** End of the urban clearway restrictions

Urban clearways are provided to keep traffic flowing at busy times. You may stop only briefly to set down or pick up passengers. Times of operation will vary from place to place, so always check the signs.

640 Mark *one* answer
What does this sign mean?

- ☐ **A** Quayside or river bank
- ☐ **B** Steep hill downwards
- ☐ **C** Uneven road surface
- ☐ **D** Road liable to flooding

You should be careful in these locations, as the road surface is likely to be wet and slippery. There may be a steep drop to the water, and there may not be a barrier along the edge of the road.

641 Mark *one* answer
What does this white line along the centre of the road mean?

- ☐ **A** Bus lane marking
- ☐ **B** Hazard warning
- ☐ **C** Give way warning
- ☐ **D** Lane marking

The centre of the road is usually marked by a broken white line, with lines that are shorter than the gaps. When the lines become longer than the gaps, this is a hazard warning line. Look well ahead for these, especially when you're planning to overtake or turn off.

642 Mark *one* answer
What is the reason for the yellow crisscross lines painted on the road here?

- ☐ **A** To mark out an area for trams only
- ☐ **B** To prevent queuing traffic from blocking the junction on the left
- ☐ **C** To mark the entrance lane to a car park
- ☐ **D** To warn you of the tram lines crossing the road

Yellow 'box junctions' like this are often used where it's busy. Their purpose is to keep the junction clear for crossing traffic. Don't enter the painted area unless your exit is clear. The one exception is when you're turning right and are only prevented from doing so by oncoming traffic or by other vehicles waiting to turn right.

643 Mark *one* answer

What is the reason for the area marked in red and white along the centre of this road?

- ☐ **A** It separates traffic flowing in opposite directions
- ☐ **B** It marks an area to be used by overtaking motorcyclists
- ☐ **C** It's a temporary marking to warn of the roadworks
- ☐ **D** It separates the two sides of the dual carriageway

Areas of 'hatched markings' such as these separate traffic streams that could be a danger to each other. They're often seen on bends or where the road becomes narrow. If the area is bordered by a solid white line, you mustn't enter it except in an emergency.

644 Mark *one* answer

Other drivers may sometimes flash their headlights at you. In which situation are they allowed to do this?

- ☐ **A** To warn of a radar speed trap ahead
- ☐ **B** To show that they're giving way to you
- ☐ **C** To warn you of their presence
- ☐ **D** To let you know there's a fault with your vehicle

If other drivers flash their headlights, this isn't a signal to show priority. The flashing of headlights has the same meaning as sounding the horn: it's a warning of their presence.

645 Mark *one* answer

What speed limit is often found in narrow residential streets?

- ☐ **A** 20 mph
- ☐ **B** 25 mph
- ☐ **C** 35 mph
- ☐ **D** 40 mph

In some built-up areas, you may find the speed limit reduced to 20 mph. Driving at a slower speed will help give you the time and space to see and deal safely with hazards such as pedestrians and other vulnerable road users.

646 Mark *one* answer

What does this signal mean?

- ☐ **A** Cars must stop
- ☐ **B** Trams must stop
- ☐ **C** Both trams and cars must stop
- ☐ **D** Both trams and cars can continue

The white light shows that trams must stop. The green light shows that other vehicles can go if the way is clear. Trams are being introduced into more cities, so you're likely to come across them and you should learn which signs apply to them.

647 Mark *one* answer
Where would you find these road markings?

- ☐ **A** At a railway crossing
- ☐ **B** At a mini-roundabout
- ☐ **C** On a motorway
- ☐ **D** On a pedestrian crossing

These markings show the direction in which the traffic should go at a mini-roundabout.

648 Mark *one* answer
A police car is following you. The police officer flashes the headlights and points to the left. What should you do?

- ☐ **A** Turn left at the next junction
- ☐ **B** Pull up on the left
- ☐ **C** Stop immediately
- ☐ **D** Move over to the left

You must pull up on the left as soon as it's safe to do so and switch off your engine.

649 Mark *one* answer
You see this amber traffic light ahead. Which light, or lights, will come on next?

- ☐ **A** Red alone
- ☐ **B** Red and amber together
- ☐ **C** Green and amber together
- ☐ **D** Green alone

At junctions controlled by traffic lights, you must stop behind the white line until the lights change to green. A red light, an amber light, and red and amber lights showing together all mean stop.

You may proceed when the light is green unless your exit road is blocked or pedestrians are crossing in front of you.

If you're approaching traffic lights that are visible from a distance and the light has been green for some time, be ready to slow down and stop, because the lights are likely to change.

650 Mark *one* answer

You see this signal overhead on the motorway. What does it mean?

- ☐ **A** Leave the motorway at the next exit
- ☐ **B** All vehicles use the hard shoulder
- ☐ **C** Sharp bend to the left ahead
- ☐ **D** Stop: all lanes ahead closed

You'll see this sign if there has been an incident ahead and the motorway is closed. You must obey the sign. Make sure that you prepare to leave in good time. Don't cause drivers to take avoiding action by cutting in at the last moment.

651 Mark *one* answer

What must you do when you see this sign?

- ☐ **A** Stop only if traffic is approaching
- ☐ **B** Stop even if the road is clear
- ☐ **C** Stop only if children are waiting to cross
- ☐ **D** Stop only if a red light is showing

Stop' signs are situated at junctions where visibility is restricted or where there's heavy traffic. They must be obeyed: you must stop. Take good all-round observation before moving off.

652 Mark *one* answer

Which shape is used for a 'give way' sign?

- ☐ **A**
- ☐ **B**
- ☐ **C**
- ☐ **D**

Other warning signs are the same shape and colour, but the 'give way' triangle points downwards. When you see this sign, you must give way to traffic on the road that you're about to enter.

653 Mark *one* answer

What does this sign mean?

- ☐ **A** Buses turning
- ☐ **B** Ring road
- ☐ **C** Mini-roundabout
- ☐ **D** Keep right

When you see this sign, look out for any direction signs and judge whether you need to signal your intentions. Do this in good time so that other road users approaching the roundabout know what you're planning to do.

654 Mark *one* answer
What does this sign mean?

- ☐ **A** Two-way traffic straight ahead
- ☐ **B** Two-way traffic crosses a one-way road
- ☐ **C** Two-way traffic over a bridge
- ☐ **D** Two-way traffic crosses a two-way road

Be prepared for traffic approaching from junctions on either side of you. Try to avoid unnecessary changing of lanes just before the junction.

655 Mark *one* answer
What does this sign mean?

- ☐ **A** Two-way traffic crosses a one-way road
- ☐ **B** Traffic approaching you has priority
- ☐ **C** Two-way traffic straight ahead
- ☐ **D** Motorway contraflow system ahead

This sign may be at the end of a dual carriageway or a one-way street. It's there to warn you of oncoming traffic.

656 Mark *one* answer
What does this sign mean?

- ☐ **A** Hump bridge
- ☐ **B** Traffic-calming hump
- ☐ **C** Low bridge
- ☐ **D** Uneven road

You'll need to slow down. At hump bridges, your view ahead will be restricted and the road will often be narrow. If the bridge is very steep, sound your horn to warn others of your approach. Going over the bridge too fast is highly dangerous to other road users and could even cause your wheels to leave the road, with a resulting loss of control.

657 Mark *one* answer
What does this sign mean?

- ☐ **A** Direction to park-and-ride car park
- ☐ **B** No parking for buses or coaches
- ☐ **C** Direction to bus and coach park
- ☐ **D** Parking area for cars and coaches

To ease the congestion in town centres, some cities and towns provide park-and-ride schemes. These allow you to park in a designated area and ride by bus into the centre. Park-and-ride schemes are usually cheaper and easier than car parking in the town centre.

658 Mark *one* answer

What should you do when approaching traffic lights where red and amber are showing together?

- ☐ **A** Pass the lights if the road is clear
- ☐ **B** Take care because there's a fault with the lights
- ☐ **C** Wait for the green light
- ☐ **D** Stop because the lights are changing to red

Be aware that other traffic might still be clearing the junction as you approach. A green light means you may go on, but only if the way is clear.

659 Mark *one* answer

Where does this marking normally appear on a road?

- ☐ **A** Just before a 'no entry' sign
- ☐ **B** Just before a 'give way' sign
- ☐ **C** Just before a 'stop' sign
- ☐ **D** Just before a 'no through road' sign

This road marking means you should give way to traffic on the main road. It might not be used at junctions where there isn't much traffic. However, if there's a double broken line across the junction, the 'give way' rules still apply.

660 Mark *one* answer

At a railway level crossing, the red lights continue to flash after a train has gone by. What should you do?

- ☐ **A** Phone the signal operator
- ☐ **B** Alert drivers behind you
- ☐ **C** Wait
- ☐ **D** Proceed with caution

You must always obey red flashing stop lights. If a train passes but the lights continue to flash, another train will be passing soon. Cross only when the lights go off and the barriers open.

661 Mark *one* answer

You're in a tunnel and you see this sign. What does it mean?

- ☐ **A** Direction to emergency pedestrian exit
- ☐ **B** Beware of pedestrians: no footpath ahead
- ☐ **C** No access for pedestrians
- ☐ **D** Beware of pedestrians crossing ahead

If you have to leave your vehicle and get out of a tunnel by an emergency exit, do so as quickly as you can. Follow the signs directing you to the nearest exit point. If there are several people using the exit, don't panic but try to leave in a calm and orderly manner.

662 Mark *one* answer

Which of these signs shows that you're entering a one-way system?

☐ A   ☐ B

☐ C   ☐ D

If the road has two lanes, you can use either lane and overtake on either side. Use the lane that's more convenient for your destination unless signs or road markings indicate otherwise.

663 Mark *one* answer

What does this sign mean?

☐ **A** With-flow bus and cycle lane
☐ **B** Contraflow bus and cycle lane
☐ **C** No buses and cycles allowed
☐ **D** No waiting for buses and cycles

Buses and cycles can travel in this lane. In this example, they'll flow in the same direction as other traffic. If it's busy, they may be passing you on the left, so watch out for them. Times on the sign will show the lane's hours of operation; if no times are shown, or there's no sign at all, this means the lane is in operation 24 hours a day. In some areas, other vehicles, such as taxis and motorcycles, are allowed to use bus lanes. The sign will show if this is the case.

664 Mark *one* answer
What does this sign mean?

- ☐ **A** School crossing patrol
- ☐ **B** No pedestrians allowed
- ☐ **C** Pedestrian zone – no vehicles
- ☐ **D** Zebra crossing ahead

Look well ahead and be ready to stop for any pedestrians crossing, or about to cross, the road. Also check the pavements for anyone who looks like they might step or run into the road.

665 Mark *one* answer
Which arm signal tells you that the car you're following is going to pull up?

☐ **A** ☐ **B**

☐ **C** ☐ **D**

There may be occasions when drivers need to give an arm signal to confirm their intentions. This could include in bright sunshine, at a complex road layout, when stopping at a pedestrian crossing or when turning right just after passing a parked vehicle. You should understand what each arm signal means. If you give arm signals, make them clear, correct and decisive.

666 Mark *one* answer
Which of these signs means turn left ahead?

☐ **A** ☐ **B**

☐ **C** ☐ **D**

Blue circles tell you what you must do and this sign gives a clear instruction to turn left ahead. You should be looking out for signs at all times and know what they mean.

667 Mark *one* answer

You're approaching a red traffic light. What will the signal show next?

- ☐ **A** Red and amber
- ☐ **B** Green alone
- ☐ **C** Amber alone
- ☐ **D** Green and amber

If you know which light is going to show next, you can plan your approach accordingly. This can help prevent excessive braking or hesitation at the junction.

668 Mark *one* answer

What does this sign mean?

- ☐ **A** Low bridge ahead
- ☐ **B** Tunnel ahead
- ☐ **C** Ancient monument ahead
- ☐ **D** Traffic danger spot ahead

When approaching a tunnel, switch on your dipped headlights. Be aware that your eyes might need to adjust to the sudden darkness. You may need to reduce your speed.

669 Mark *one* answer

You're approaching a zebra crossing where pedestrians are waiting. Which arm signal might you give?

☐ **A**   ☐ **B**

☐ **C**   ☐ **D**

A 'slowing down' signal will indicate your intentions to oncoming and following vehicles. Be aware that pedestrians might start to cross as soon as they see this signal.

670 Mark *one* answer

What does the white line along the side of the road indicate?

- ☐ **A** The edge of the carriageway
- ☐ **B** The approach to a hazard
- ☐ **C** No parking
- ☐ **D** No overtaking

A continuous white line is used on many roads to indicate the edge of the carriageway. This can be useful when visibility is restricted. The line is discontinued at junctions, lay-bys, and entrances to or exits from private drives.

671 Mark *one* answer

What does this white arrow on the road ahead mean?

- ☐ **A** Entrance on the left
- ☐ **B** All vehicles turn left
- ☐ **C** Keep left of the hatched markings
- ☐ **D** Road bends to the left

Don't attempt to overtake here, as there might be unseen hazards over the brow of the hill. Keep to the left.

---

672 Mark *one* answer

How should you give an arm signal to turn left?

☐ **A**   ☐ **B**

☐ **C**   ☐ **D**

There may be occasions when other road users are unable to see your indicator, such as in bright sunlight or at a busy, complicated junction. In these cases, an arm signal will help others to understand your intentions.

673 Mark *one* answer

You're waiting at a T-junction. A vehicle is coming from the right, with its left indicator flashing. What should you do?

- ☐ **A** Move out and accelerate hard
- ☐ **B** Wait until the vehicle starts to turn in
- ☐ **C** Pull out before the vehicle reaches the junction
- ☐ **D** Move out slowly

Other road users may give misleading signals. When you're waiting at a junction, don't emerge until you're sure of their intentions.

---

674 Mark *one* answer

When may you use hazard warning lights while you're driving?

- ☐ **A** Instead of sounding the horn in a built-up area between 11.30 pm and 7.00 am
- ☐ **B** On a motorway or unrestricted dual carriageway, to warn of a hazard ahead
- ☐ **C** On rural routes, after a sign warning of animals
- ☐ **D** On the approach to toucan crossings where cyclists are waiting to cross

When there's queuing traffic ahead and you have to slow down or even stop, briefly showing your hazard warning lights will help alert following traffic to the hazard.

675 Mark *one* answer

When can you park on these markings outside a school?

- ☐ **A** When you're picking up children
- ☐ **B** Not under any circumstances
- ☐ **C** When there's nowhere else available
- ☐ **D** When you're dropping off children

You shouldn't stop on yellow zigzag lines outside schools, not even to set down or pick up children or other passengers. This is to make sure passing drivers and pedestrians have an unobstructed view.

676 Mark *one* answer

Why should you make sure that your indicators are cancelled after turning?

- ☐ **A** To avoid flattening the battery
- ☐ **B** To avoid misleading other road users
- ☐ **C** To avoid dazzling other road users
- ☐ **D** To avoid damage to the indicator relay

Leaving your indicators on could confuse other road users and may even lead to a crash. Be aware that if you haven't taken a sharp turn, your indicators may not self-cancel and you'll need to turn them off manually.

677 Mark *one* answer

You're driving in busy traffic. You want to pull up on the left just after a junction on the left. When should you signal?

- ☐ **A** As you're passing or just after the junction
- ☐ **B** Just before you reach the junction
- ☐ **C** Well before you reach the junction
- ☐ **D** It would be better not to signal at all

You need to signal to let other drivers know your intentions. However, if you indicate too early, they may think you're turning left into the junction. Correct timing of the signal is very important to avoid misleading others.

678 Mark *one* answer
For how long is an MOT certificate normally valid?

- ☐ **A** Three years after the date it was issued
- ☐ **B** 10,000 miles
- ☐ **C** One year after the date it was issued
- ☐ **D** 30,000 miles

Some garages will remind you that your vehicle is due for its annual MOT test, but not all do. To ensure continuous cover, you may take your vehicle for its MOT up to one month before its existing MOT certificate runs out. The expiry date on the new certificate will be 12 months after the expiry date on the old certificate.

679 Mark *one* answer
What is a cover note?

- ☐ **A** A document issued before you receive your driving licence
- ☐ **B** A document issued before you receive your insurance certificate
- ☐ **C** A document issued before you receive your registration document
- ☐ **D** A document issued before you receive your MOT certificate

Sometimes an insurance company will issue a temporary insurance certificate called a cover note. It gives you the same insurance cover as your certificate but lasts for a limited period, usually one month.

680 Mark *one* answer
You've just passed your practical test. You don't hold a full licence in another category. Within two years you get six penalty points on your licence. What will you have to do?

- ☐ **A** Retake only your theory test
- ☐ **B** Retake your theory and practical tests
- ☐ **C** Retake only your practical test
- ☐ **D** Reapply for your full licence immediately

If you accumulate six or more penalty points within two years of gaining your first full licence, it will be revoked. The six or more points include any gained due to offences you committed before passing your test. If this happens, you may only drive as a learner until you pass both the theory and practical tests again.

681 Mark *one* answer
For how long is a Statutory Off-Road Notification (SORN) valid?

- ☐ **A** Until the vehicle is taxed, sold or scrapped
- ☐ **B** Until the vehicle is insured and MOT'd
- ☐ **C** Until the vehicle is repaired or modified
- ☐ **D** Until the vehicle is used on the road

A SORN allows you to keep a vehicle off-road and untaxed. SORN will end when the vehicle is taxed, sold or scrapped.

682 Mark *one* answer   NI
What is a Statutory Off-Road Notification (SORN)?

☐ **A** A notification to tell DVSA that a vehicle doesn't have a current MOT
☐ **B** Information kept by the police about the owner of a vehicle
☐ **C** A notification to tell DVLA that a vehicle isn't being used on the road
☐ **D** Information held by insurance companies to check a vehicle is insured

If you want to keep a vehicle untaxed and off the public road, you must make a SORN. It's an offence not to do so. Your SORN is valid until your vehicle is taxed, sold or scrapped.

683 Mark *one* answer
What is the maximum fine for driving without insurance?

☐ **A** Unlimited
☐ **B** £500
☐ **C** £1000
☐ **D** £5000

Driving without insurance is a serious offence. As well as an unlimited fine, you may be disqualified or incur penalty points.

684 Mark *one* answer
Who's legally responsible for ensuring that a vehicle registration certificate (V5C) is updated?

☐ **A** The registered vehicle keeper
☐ **B** The vehicle manufacturer
☐ **C** Your insurance company
☐ **D** The licensing authority

It's your legal responsibility to keep the details on your vehicle registration certificate (V5C) up to date. You should tell the licensing authority about any changes. These include your name, address or vehicle details. If you don't do this, you may have problems when you try to sell your vehicle.

685 Mark *one* answer
In which of these circumstances must you show your insurance certificate?

☐ **A** When making a SORN
☐ **B** When buying or selling a vehicle
☐ **C** When a police officer asks you for it
☐ **D** When having an MOT inspection

You must produce a valid insurance certificate when requested by a police officer. If you can't do this immediately, you may be asked to take it to a police station. Other documents you may be asked to produce are your driving licence and the vehicle's MOT certificate.

686 Mark *one* answer

Which of these is needed before you can legally use a vehicle on the road?

- ☐ **A** A valid driving licence
- ☐ **B** Breakdown cover
- ☐ **C** Proof of your identity
- ☐ **D** A vehicle handbook

Using a vehicle on the road illegally carries a heavy fine and can lead to penalty points on your driving licence. You must have:
- a valid driving licence
- paid the appropriate vehicle excise duty (road tax)
- proper insurance cover

687 Mark *one* answer

What must you have when you apply to renew your vehicle excise licence?

- ☐ **A** Valid insurance
- ☐ **B** The vehicle's chassis number
- ☐ **C** The handbook
- ☐ **D** A valid driving licence

The vehicle excise licence (road tax) can be renewed at post offices, vehicle registration offices, online or by phone. When applying, make sure you have all the relevant valid documents, including a valid MOT test certificate where applicable.

688 Mark *one* answer

A police officer asks to see your documents. You don't have them with you. Within what time must you produce them at a police station?

- ☐ **A** 5 days
- ☐ **B** 7 days
- ☐ **C** 14 days
- ☐ **D** 21 days

You don't have to carry around your vehicle's documents wherever you go. If a police officer asks to see them and you don't have them with you, you may be asked to produce them at a police station within 7 days.

689 Mark *one* answer

What must learner drivers do before they start driving on the road?

- ☐ **A** Pass their theory test
- ☐ **B** Take professional instruction
- ☐ **C** Sign their provisional licence
- ☐ **D** Apply for a driving test

Before a learner starts to drive on the road, they must have a valid provisional licence for the category of vehicle that they're driving. They must sign the licence because, without a signature, the licence isn't valid.

690 Mark *one* answer
What must you make sure of before you drive someone else's vehicle?

☐ **A** That the vehicle owner has third-party insurance cover
☐ **B** That your own vehicle has insurance cover
☐ **C** That the vehicle is insured for your use
☐ **D** That the insurance documents are in the vehicle

Driving a vehicle without insurance cover is illegal, so be sure that, whoever's car you drive, you're insured – whether on their policy or on your own. If you need to take out insurance, it's worth comparing several quotes before you decide which insurance provider best meets your needs.

691 Mark *one* answer
Your car needs to pass an MOT test. What may be invalidated if you drive the car without a current MOT certificate?

☐ **A** The vehicle service record
☐ **B** Your insurance
☐ **C** The vehicle excise licence (road tax)
☐ **D** Your vehicle registration document

If your vehicle requires an MOT certificate, it's illegal to drive it without one and your insurance may be invalid if you do so. The only exceptions are that you may drive to a pre-arranged MOT test appointment, or to a garage for repairs required for the test.

692 Mark *one* answer
What must a newly qualified driver do?

☐ **A** Display green L plates
☐ **B** Keep under 40 mph for 12 months
☐ **C** Be accompanied on a motorway
☐ **D** Have valid motor insurance

It's your responsibility to make sure you're properly insured for the vehicle you're driving. This is the case regardless of whether you're a newly qualified driver or one with more experience.

693 Mark *one* answer
You have third-party insurance. What does this cover?

☐ **A** Damage to your vehicle
☐ **B** Fire damage to your vehicle
☐ **C** Flood damage to your vehicle
☐ **D** Damage to other vehicles

Third-party insurance doesn't cover damage to your own vehicle or injury to yourself. If you have a crash and your vehicle is damaged, you might have to carry out the repairs at your own expense.

694 Mark *one* answer
Who's responsible for paying the vehicle excise duty (road tax)?

☐ **A** The driver of the vehicle
☐ **B** The registered keeper of the vehicle
☐ **C** The car dealer
☐ **D** The Driver and Vehicle Licensing Agency (DVLA)

The registered keeper of the vehicle is responsible for paying the vehicle excise duty or making a Statutory Off-Road Notification (SORN) if the vehicle is to be kept untaxed and off the road.

695 Mark *one* answer
What information is found on a vehicle registration document?

☐ **A** The registered keeper
☐ **B** The type of insurance cover
☐ **C** The service history details
☐ **D** The date of the MOT

Every vehicle used on the road has a registration document. This shows the vehicle's details, including date of first registration, registration number, registered keeper, previous keeper, make of vehicle, engine size, chassis number, year of manufacture and colour.

696 Mark *one* answer
When must you contact the vehicle licensing authority?

☐ **A** When you take your vehicle abroad on holiday
☐ **B** When you change your vehicle
☐ **C** When you use your vehicle for work
☐ **D** When your vehicle's insurance is due

The licensing authority needs to keep its records up to date. It sends out a reminder when a vehicle's excise licence (road tax) is due for renewal. To do this, it needs to know the name and address of the registered keeper. Every vehicle in the country is registered, so it's possible to trace its history.

697 Mark *one* answer
When must you notify the licensing authority?

☐ **A** When your health affects your driving
☐ **B** When you have to work abroad
☐ **C** When you lend your vehicle to someone
☐ **D** When your vehicle needs an MOT certificate

The licensing authorities hold the records of all vehicles, drivers and riders in Great Britain and Northern Ireland. They need to know if you have a medical condition that might affect your ability to drive safely. You must tell them if your health deteriorates and you become unfit to drive.

698 Mark *one* answer　　NI

When may the cost of your insurance come down?

☐ **A** When you're under 25 years old
☐ **B** When you don't wear glasses
☐ **C** When you pass the driving test first time
☐ **D** When you complete the Pass Plus scheme

The cost of insurance varies with your age and how long you've been driving. Usually, the younger you are, the more expensive it is, especially if you're under 25. Pass Plus provides additional training to newly qualified drivers. The scheme is recognised by many insurance companies, and taking this extra training could give you reduced insurance premiums, as well as improving your skills and experience.

699 Mark *one* answer

What qualifies you to supervise a learner driver?

☐ **A** You must have held a licence for at least a year
☐ **B** You must be at least 21 years old
☐ **C** You must be an approved driving instructor
☐ **D** You must hold an advanced driving certificate

Learner drivers benefit by combining professional driving lessons with private practice. However, you need to be at least 21 years old and have held your driving licence for at least 3 years before you can supervise a learner driver.

700 Mark *one* answer

Your car requires an MOT certificate. When is it legal to drive it without an MOT certificate?

☐ **A** Up to seven days after the old certificate has run out
☐ **B** When driving to an MOT centre to arrange an appointment
☐ **C** When driving the car with the owner's permission
☐ **D** When driving to an appointment at an MOT centre

When a car is three years old (four years old in Northern Ireland), it must pass an MOT test and have a valid MOT certificate before it can be used on the road. Exceptionally, you may:
- drive to a pre-arranged test appointment or to a garage for repairs required for the test
- drive vehicles made before 1960 without an MOT test, but they must be in a roadworthy condition before being used on the road

701 Mark *one* answer `NI`

A new car will need its first MOT test when it's how old?

☐ **A** One year
☐ **B** Three years
☐ **C** Five years
☐ **D** Seven years

The vehicle you drive must be roadworthy and in good condition. If it's over three years old, it must pass an MOT test to remain in use on the road. Vehicles made before 1960 are exempt from the MOT test, but they must be in a roadworthy condition before being driven on the road.

702 Mark *one* answer `NI`

The Pass Plus scheme has been created for new drivers. What is its main purpose?

☐ **A** To allow you to drive faster
☐ **B** To allow you to carry passengers
☐ **C** To improve your basic skills
☐ **D** To let you drive on motorways

New drivers are far more vulnerable on the road and more likely to be involved in incidents. The Pass Plus scheme has been designed to improve new drivers' basic skills and help widen their driving experience.

703 Mark *one* answer

Your vehicle is insured third-party only. What does this cover?

☐ **A** Damage to your vehicle
☐ **B** Damage to other vehicles
☐ **C** Injury to yourself
☐ **D** All damage and injury

Third-party insurance cover is usually cheaper than comprehensive cover. However, it doesn't cover any damage caused to your own vehicle or property. It only covers damage and injury you cause to others.

704 Mark *one* answer

What is the legal minimum insurance cover you must have to drive on public roads?

☐ **A** Third party, fire and theft
☐ **B** Comprehensive
☐ **C** Third party only
☐ **D** Personal injury cover

The minimum insurance required by law is third-party cover. This covers your liability to others involved in a collision but not damage to your vehicle. Basic third-party insurance also won't cover theft or fire damage. Ask your insurance company for advice on the best cover for you and make sure that you read the policy carefully.

705 Mark *one* answer

You claim on your insurance to have your car repaired. Your policy has an excess of £100. What does this mean?

- ☐ **A** The insurance company will pay the first £100 of any claim
- ☐ **B** You'll be paid £100 if you don't claim within one year
- ☐ **C** Your vehicle is insured for a value of £100 if it's stolen
- ☐ **D** You'll have to pay the first £100 of the cost of repairs to your car

Having an excess on your policy will help to keep the premium down. However, if you make a claim, you'll have to pay the excess yourself – in this case, £100.

706 Mark *one* answer NI

What is the purpose of the Pass Plus scheme?

- ☐ **A** To give you a discount on your MOT
- ☐ **B** To improve your basic driving skills
- ☐ **C** To increase your mechanical knowledge
- ☐ **D** To allow you to drive anyone else's vehicle

After passing your practical driving test, you can take further training. One option is known as the Pass Plus scheme. It's designed to improve your basic driving skills and involves a series of modules, including night-time and motorway driving.

707 Mark *one* answer NI

What does the Pass Plus scheme enable newly qualified drivers to do?

- ☐ **A** Widen their driving experience
- ☐ **B** Supervise a learner driver
- ☐ **C** Increase their insurance premiums
- ☐ **D** Avoid mechanical breakdowns

The Pass Plus scheme was created for newly qualified drivers. It aims to widen their driving experience and improve basic skills. After passing the practical driving test, additional professional training can be taken with an approved driving instructor (ADI). Some insurance companies also offer discounts to holders of a Pass Plus certificate.

708 Mark *one* answer

You see a car on the hard shoulder of a motorway with a 'help' pennant displayed. What does this mean?

- ☐ **A** The driver is likely to be a disabled person
- ☐ **B** The driver is first-aid trained
- ☐ **C** The driver is a foreign visitor
- ☐ **D** The driver is a rescue patrol officer

If a disabled driver's vehicle breaks down and they're unable to walk to an emergency phone, they're advised to stay in their car and switch on the hazard warning lights. They may also display a 'help' pennant in their vehicle.

709 Mark *one* answer

When should you use hazard warning lights?

- ☐ **A** When you slow down quickly on a motorway because of a hazard ahead
- ☐ **B** When you leave your car at the roadside to visit a shop
- ☐ **C** When you wish to stop on double yellow lines
- ☐ **D** When you need to park on the pavement

Hazard warning lights are fitted to all modern cars and some motorcycles. They should be used to warn:

- other road users when your vehicle is causing a temporary obstruction; for example, after a collision or when it's broken down
- following drivers on a motorway of a hazard or obstruction ahead

They shouldn't be used as an excuse for dangerous or illegal parking.

710 Mark *one* answer

When are you allowed to use hazard warning lights?

- ☐ **A** When stopped and temporarily obstructing traffic
- ☐ **B** When travelling during darkness without headlights
- ☐ **C** When parked on double yellow lines to visit a shop
- ☐ **D** When travelling slowly because you're lost

You mustn't use hazard warning lights while moving, except to warn traffic behind when you slow suddenly on a motorway or unrestricted dual carriageway. Never use hazard warning lights to excuse dangerous or illegal parking.

711 Mark *one* answer

You're going through a congested tunnel and have to stop. What should you do?

- ☐ **A** Pull up very close to the vehicle in front to save space
- ☐ **B** Ignore any message signs, as they're never up to date
- ☐ **C** Keep a safe distance from the vehicle in front
- ☐ **D** Make a U-turn and find another route

It's important to keep a safe distance from the vehicle in front at all times. This still applies in congested tunnels, even if you're moving very slowly or have stopped. If the vehicle in front breaks down, you may need room to manoeuvre past it.

712 Mark *one* answer
On a motorway, when should the hard shoulder be used?

☐ **A** When answering a mobile phone
☐ **B** When an emergency arises
☐ **C** When taking a short rest
☐ **D** When checking a road map

The hard shoulder should only be used in a genuine emergency. If possible, and if it's safe, use a roadside telephone to call for help. This will give your exact location to the operator. Never cross the carriageway or a slip road to use a telephone on the other side of the road.

713 Mark *one* answer
You arrive at the scene of a crash. Someone is bleeding badly from an arm wound. Nothing is embedded in it. What should you do?

☐ **A** Apply pressure over the wound and keep the arm down
☐ **B** Dab the wound
☐ **C** Get them a drink
☐ **D** Apply pressure over the wound and raise the arm

If possible, lay the casualty down. Check for anything that may be in the wound. Apply firm pressure to the wound using clean material, without pressing on anything that might be in it. Raising the arm above the level of the heart will also help to stem the flow of blood.

714 Mark *one* answer
At an incident, a casualty is unconscious. You need to check whether they're breathing. How long should you allow for this check?

☐ **A** At least 2 seconds
☐ **B** At least 10 seconds
☐ **C** At least 1 minute
☐ **D** At least 2 minutes

Once the casualty's airway is open, listen and feel for breath. Do this by placing your cheek over their mouth and nose, and look to see if their chest rises. This should be done for up to 10 seconds. If you cannot detect any breathing, you should begin compressions.

715 Mark *one* answer
Following a collision, someone has suffered a burn. The burn needs to be cooled. What is the shortest time that it should be cooled for?

☐ **A** 5 minutes
☐ **B** 10 minutes
☐ **C** 15 minutes
☐ **D** 20 minutes

Check the casualty for shock and, if possible, try to cool the burn for at least 10 minutes. Use a clean, cool, non-toxic liquid, preferably water.

716 Mark *one* answer
A casualty isn't breathing normally. Chest compressions should be given. At what rate?

- ☐ **A** 10 per minute
- ☐ **B** 120 per minute
- ☐ **C** 60 per minute
- ☐ **D** 240 per minute

If a casualty isn't breathing normally, chest compressions may be needed to maintain circulation. Place two hands on the centre of the chest and press down hard and fast – around 5–6 centimetres and about twice a second.

717 Mark *one* answer
A person has been injured. They may be suffering from shock. What are the warning signs to look for?

- ☐ **A** Flushed complexion
- ☐ **B** Warm dry skin
- ☐ **C** Slow pulse
- ☐ **D** Pale grey skin

The effects of shock may not be immediately obvious. Warning signs are rapid pulse, sweating, pale grey skin and rapid shallow breathing.

718 Mark *one* answer
An injured person has been placed in the recovery position. They're unconscious but breathing normally. What else should be done?

- ☐ **A** Press firmly between their shoulders
- ☐ **B** Place their arms by their side
- ☐ **C** Give them a hot sweet drink
- ☐ **D** Check their airway remains clear

After a casualty has been placed in the recovery position, make sure their airway remains open and monitor their condition until medical help arrives. Where possible, don't move a casualty unless there's further danger.

719 Mark *one* answer
An injured motorcyclist is lying unconscious in the road. The traffic has stopped and there's no further danger. What should you do to help?

- ☐ **A** Remove their safety helmet
- ☐ **B** Seek medical assistance
- ☐ **C** Move the person off the road
- ☐ **D** Remove their leather jacket

If someone has been injured, the sooner proper medical attention is given the better. Ask someone to phone for help or do it yourself. An injured person should only be moved if they're in further danger. An injured motorcyclist's helmet shouldn't be removed unless it's essential.

720 Mark *one* answer

What should you do if you see a large box fall from a lorry onto the motorway?

- ☐ **A** Go to the next emergency telephone and report the hazard
- ☐ **B** Catch up with the lorry and try to get the driver's attention
- ☐ **C** Stop close to the box until the police arrive
- ☐ **D** Pull over to the hard shoulder, then remove the box

Lorry drivers can be unaware of objects falling from their vehicles. If you see something fall onto a motorway, look to see if the driver pulls over. If they don't stop, don't attempt to retrieve the object yourself. Pull onto the hard shoulder near an emergency telephone and report the hazard.

721 Mark *one* answer

You're going through a long tunnel. What will warn you of congestion or an incident ahead?

- ☐ **A** Hazard warning lines
- ☐ **B** Other drivers flashing their lights
- ☐ **C** Variable message signs
- ☐ **D** Areas with hatch markings

Follow the instructions given by the signs or by tunnel officials. In congested tunnels, a minor incident can soon turn into a major one, with serious or even fatal results.

722 Mark *one* answer

An adult casualty isn't breathing. To maintain circulation, compressions should be given. What is the correct depth to press for each compression?

- ☐ **A** 1 to 2 centimetres
- ☐ **B** 5 to 6 centimetres
- ☐ **C** 10 to 15 centimetres
- ☐ **D** 15 to 20 centimetres

An adult casualty isn't breathing normally. To maintain circulation, place two hands on the centre of the chest. Then press down hard and fast – around 5–6 centimetres and about twice a second.

723 Mark *one* answer

You're the first to arrive at the scene of a crash. What should you do?

- ☐ **A** Leave as soon as another motorist arrives
- ☐ **B** Flag down other motorists to help you
- ☐ **C** Drag all casualties away from the vehicles
- ☐ **D** Call the emergency services promptly

At a crash scene you can help in practical ways, even if you aren't trained in first aid. Call the emergency services and make sure you don't put yourself or anyone else in danger. The safest way to warn other traffic is by switching on your hazard warning lights.

724 Mark *one* answer

You're the first person to arrive at an incident where people are badly injured. You've switched on your hazard warning lights and checked all engines are stopped. What else should you do?

☐ **A** Make sure that an ambulance is called for
☐ **B** Stop other cars and ask the drivers for help
☐ **C** Try and get people who are injured to drink something
☐ **D** Move the people who are injured clear of their vehicles

If you're the first to arrive at a crash scene, the first concerns are the risk of further collision and fire. Ensuring that vehicle engines are switched off will reduce the risk of fire. Use hazard warning lights so that other traffic knows there's a need for caution. Make sure the emergency services are contacted; don't assume this has already been done.

725 Mark *one* answer

You arrive at the scene of a motorcycle crash. The rider is injured. When should their helmet be removed?

☐ **A** Only when it's essential
☐ **B** Always straight away
☐ **C** Only when the motorcyclist asks
☐ **D** Always, unless they're in shock

Don't remove a motorcyclist's helmet unless it's essential. Remember they may be suffering from shock. Don't give them anything to eat or drink, but do reassure them confidently.

726 Mark *one* answer

You arrive at an incident. There's no danger from fire or further collisions. What is your first priority when attending to an unconscious motorcyclist?

☐ **A** Check whether they're breathing
☐ **B** Check whether they're bleeding
☐ **C** Check whether they have any broken bones
☐ **D** Check whether they have any bruising

At the scene of an incident, always be aware of danger from further collisions or fire. The first priority when dealing with an unconscious person is to ensure they can breathe. This may involve clearing their airway if you can see an obstruction or if they're having difficulty breathing.

727 Mark *one* answer

At an incident, someone is unconscious. What would your priority be?

☐ **A** Find out their name
☐ **B** Wake them up
☐ **C** Make them comfortable
☐ **D** Check their airway is clear

Remember this procedure by saying DR ABC. This stands for Danger, Response, Airway, Breathing, Compressions. Give whatever first aid you can and stay with the injured person until the emergency services arrive.

728 Mark *one* answer
You've stopped at an incident to give help. What should you do?

☐ **A** Keep injured people warm and comfortable
☐ **B** Give injured people something to eat
☐ **C** Keep injured people on the move by walking them around
☐ **D** Give injured people a warm drink

There are a number of things you can do to help, even without expert training. Be aware of further danger from other traffic and fire; make sure the area is safe. People may be in shock. Don't give them anything to eat or drink. Keep them warm and comfortable and reassure them. Don't move injured people unless there's a risk of further danger.

729 Mark *one* answer
There's been a collision. A driver is suffering from shock. What should you do?

☐ **A** Give them a drink
☐ **B** Reassure them
☐ **C** Ask who caused the incident
☐ **D** Offer them a cigarette

A casualty suffering from shock may have injuries that aren't immediately obvious. Call the emergency services, then stay with the person in shock, offering reassurance until the experts arrive.

730 Mark *one* answer
You arrive at the scene of a motorcycle crash. No other vehicle is involved. The rider is unconscious and lying in the middle of the road. What is the first thing you should do at the scene?

☐ **A** Move the rider out of the road
☐ **B** Warn other traffic
☐ **C** Clear the road of debris
☐ **D** Give the rider reassurance

The motorcyclist is in an extremely vulnerable position, exposed to further danger from traffic. Approaching vehicles need advance warning in order to slow down and safely take avoiding action or stop. Don't put yourself or anyone else at risk. Use the hazard warning lights on our vehicle to alert other road users to the danger.

731 Mark *one* answer
At an incident, a small child isn't breathing. To restore normal breathing, how should you breathe into their mouth?

☐ **A** Sharply
☐ **B** Gently
☐ **C** Heavily
☐ **D** Rapidly

If a young child has stopped breathing, first check that their airway is clear. Then give compressions to the chest using one hand (two fingers for an infant) and begin mouth-to-mouth resuscitation. Breathe very gently and continue the procedure until they can breathe without help.

732 Mark *one* answer
At an incident, a casualty isn't breathing. What should you do while helping them to start breathing again?

☐ **A** Put their arms across their chest
☐ **B** Shake them firmly
☐ **C** Roll them onto their side
☐ **D** Tilt their head back gently

It's important to ensure that the airways are clear before you start mouth-to-mouth resuscitation. Gently tilt their head back and use your finger to check for and remove any obvious obstruction in the mouth.

733 Mark *one* answer
At an incident, someone is suffering from severe burns. What should you do to help them?

☐ **A** Apply lotions to the injury
☐ **B** Burst any blisters
☐ **C** Remove anything sticking to the burns
☐ **D** Douse the burns with clean, cool, non-toxic liquid

Your priority is to cool the burns with a clean, cool, non-toxic liquid, preferably water. Its coolness will help take the heat out of the burns and relieve the pain. Keep the wound doused for at least 10 minutes. If blisters appear, don't attempt to burst them, as this could lead to infection.

734 Mark *one* answer
You arrive at an incident. A pedestrian is bleeding heavily from a leg wound. The leg isn't broken and there's nothing in the wound. What should you do?

☐ **A** Dab the wound to stop bleeding
☐ **B** Keep both legs flat on the ground
☐ **C** Fetch them a warm drink
☐ **D** Raise the leg to lessen bleeding

If there's nothing in the wound, applying a pad of clean cloth or bandage will help stem the bleeding. Raising the leg will also lessen the flow of blood. Don't tie anything tightly round the leg, as this will restrict circulation and could result in long-term injury.

735 Mark *one* answer
At an incident, a casualty is unconscious but breathing. When should you move them?

☐ **A** When an ambulance is on its way
☐ **B** When bystanders advise you to
☐ **C** When there's further danger
☐ **D** When bystanders will help you

Don't move a casualty unless there's further danger; for example, from other traffic or fire. They may have unseen or internal injuries. Moving them unnecessarily could cause further injury. Don't remove a motorcyclist's helmet unless it's essential.

736 Mark *one* answer

At an incident, it's important to look after any casualties. What should you do with them when the area is safe?

☐ **A** Move them away from the vehicles
☐ **B** Ask them how it happened
☐ **C** Give them something to eat
☐ **D** Keep them where they are

When the area is safe and there's no danger from other traffic or fire, it's better not to move casualties. Moving them may cause further injury.

737 Mark *one* answer

A tanker is involved in a collision. Which sign shows that it's carrying dangerous goods?

☐ **A**   ☐ **B**

☐ **C**   ☐ **D**

There will be an orange label on the side and rear of the tanker. Look at this carefully and report what it says when you phone the emergency services. Details of hazard warning plates are given in *The Highway Code*.

738 Mark *one* answer

You're involved in a collision. Afterwards, which document may the police ask you to produce?

☐ **A** Vehicle registration document
☐ **B** Driving licence
☐ **C** Theory test certificate
☐ **D** Vehicle service record

You must stop if you've been involved in a collision which results in injury or damage. The police may ask to see your driving licence and insurance details at the time or later at a police station.

739 Mark *one* answer

After a collision, someone is unconscious in their vehicle. When should you call the emergency services?

☐ **A** Only as a last resort
☐ **B** As soon as possible
☐ **C** After you've woken them up
☐ **D** After checking for broken bones

It's important to make sure that the emergency services arrive as soon as possible. When a person is unconscious, they could have serious injuries that aren't immediately obvious.

740 Mark *one* answer

A casualty has an injured arm. They can move it freely but it's bleeding. Why should you get them to keep it in a raised position?

☐ **A** It will ease the pain
☐ **B** It will help them to be seen more easily
☐ **C** To stop them touching other people
☐ **D** It will help to reduce the blood flow

If a casualty is bleeding heavily, raise the limb to a higher position. This will help to reduce the blood flow. Before raising the limb, you should make sure that it isn't broken.

741 Mark *one* answer

A collision has just happened. An injured person is lying in a busy road. What is the first thing you should do to help?

☐ **A** Treat the person for shock
☐ **B** Warn other traffic
☐ **C** Place them in the recovery position
☐ **D** Make sure the injured person is kept warm

The most immediate danger is further collisions and fire. You could warn other traffic by switching on hazard warning lights, displaying an advance warning triangle or sign (but not on a motorway), or by any other means that doesn't put you or others at risk.

742 Mark *one* answer

At an incident, what should you do with a casualty who has stopped breathing?

☐ **A** Keep their head tilted forwards as far as possible
☐ **B** Remove anything that's blocking their airway
☐ **C** Raise their legs to help with circulation
☐ **D** Try to give them something to drink

Unblocking the casualty's airway and gently tilting their head back will help them to breathe. They'll then be in the correct position if mouth-to-mouth resuscitation is required. Don't move a casualty unless there's further danger.

743 Mark *one* answer

You're at the scene of an incident. Someone is suffering from shock. How should you treat them?

☐ **A** Reassure them confidently
☐ **B** Offer them a cigarette
☐ **C** Give them a warm drink
☐ **D** Offer them some food

If someone is suffering from shock, try to keep them warm and as comfortable as you can. Don't give them anything to eat or drink but reassure them confidently and try not to leave them alone.

744 Mark *one* answer

There's been a collision. A motorcyclist is lying injured and unconscious. Unless it's essential, why should you not usually attempt to remove their helmet?

- ☐ **A** They might not want you to
- ☐ **B** This could result in more serious injury
- ☐ **C** They'll get too cold if you do this
- ☐ **D** You could scratch the helmet

When someone is injured, any movement that isn't absolutely necessary should be avoided, since it could make the injuries worse. Unless it's essential to remove a motorcyclist's helmet, it's generally safer to leave it in place.

745 Mark *one* answer

You've broken down on a two-way road. You have a warning triangle. At least how far from your vehicle should you place the warning triangle?

- ☐ **A** 5 metres (16 feet)
- ☐ **B** 25 metres (82 feet)
- ☐ **C** 45 metres (147 feet)
- ☐ **D** 100 metres (328 feet)

Advance warning triangles fold flat and don't take up much room. Use one to warn other road users if your vehicle has broken down or if there has been an incident. Place it at least 45 metres (147 feet) behind your vehicle (or the incident), on the same side of the road or verge. Place it further back if the scene is hidden by, for example, a bend, hill or dip in the road. Don't use warning triangles on motorways.

746 Mark *one* answer

You break down on a level crossing. The lights haven't yet begun to flash. What is the first thing you should do?

- ☐ **A** Tell drivers behind what has happened
- ☐ **B** Leave your vehicle and get everyone clear
- ☐ **C** Walk down the track and signal the next train
- ☐ **D** Stay in your car until you're told to move

If your vehicle breaks down on a level crossing, your first priority is to get everyone out of the vehicle and clear of the crossing. Then use the railway telephone, if there is one, to tell the signal operator. If you have time before the train arrives, move the vehicle clear of the crossing, but only do this if alarm signals are not on.

747 Mark *one* answer

Your tyre bursts while you're driving. What should you do?

- ☐ **A** Pull on the handbrake
- ☐ **B** Brake as quickly as possible
- ☐ **C** Pull up slowly at the side of the road
- ☐ **D** Continue on at a normal speed

A tyre bursting can lead to a loss of control, especially if you're travelling at high speed. Using the correct procedure should help you to stop the vehicle safely.

748 Mark *one* answer

Your vehicle has a puncture on a motorway. What should you do?

- ☐ **A** Drive slowly to the next service area to get assistance
- ☐ **B** Pull up on the hard shoulder. Change the wheel as quickly as possible
- ☐ **C** Pull up on the hard shoulder. Use the emergency phone to get assistance
- ☐ **D** Switch on your hazard warning lights. Stop in your lane

Pull up on the hard shoulder and make your way to the nearest emergency telephone to call for assistance. Don't attempt to repair your vehicle while it's on the hard shoulder, because of the risk posed by traffic passing at high speeds.

749 Mark *one* answer

You've stalled in the middle of a level crossing and can't restart the engine. The warning bells start to ring. What should you do?

- ☐ **A** Get out of the car and clear of the crossing
- ☐ **B** Run down the track to warn the signal operator
- ☐ **C** Carry on trying to restart the engine
- ☐ **D** Push the vehicle clear of the crossing

Try to stay calm, especially if you have passengers with you. If you can't restart your engine before the warning bells ring, leave the vehicle and get yourself and any passengers well clear of the crossing.

750 Mark *one* answer
You're driving on a motorway. When can you use hazard warning lights?

☐ **A** When a vehicle is following too closely
☐ **B** When you slow down quickly because of danger ahead
☐ **C** When you're towing another vehicle
☐ **D** When you're driving on the hard shoulder

Briefly using your hazard warning lights will warn the traffic travelling behind you that there's a hazard ahead. This can reduce the chance of vehicles crashing into the back of each other.

751 Mark *one* answer
You've broken down on a motorway. When you use the emergency telephone, what will you be asked for?

☐ **A** Details about your vehicle
☐ **B** Your driving licence details
☐ **C** The name of your vehicle's insurance company
☐ **D** Your employer's details

Have the correct details ready before you use the emergency telephone. The operator will need to know the details of your vehicle and its fault. For your own safety, always face the traffic when you speak on a roadside telephone.

752 Mark *one* answer
Before driving through a tunnel, what should you do?

☐ **A** Switch off your radio
☐ **B** Remove any sunglasses
☐ **C** Close your sunroof
☐ **D** Switch on your windscreen wipers

If you're wearing sunglasses, you should remove them before driving into a tunnel. If you don't, your vision will be restricted, even in tunnels that appear to be well lit.

753 Mark *one* answer
You're driving through a tunnel and the traffic is flowing normally. What should you do?

☐ **A** Use parking lights
☐ **B** Use front spotlights
☐ **C** Use dipped headlights
☐ **D** Use rear fog lights

Before entering a tunnel, you should switch on your dipped headlights, as this will allow you to see and be seen. In many tunnels, it's a legal requirement. Don't wear sunglasses while driving in a tunnel. You may wish to tune your radio to a local channel for traffic information.

754 Mark *one* answer
What safeguard could you take against fire risk to your vehicle?

☐ **A** Keep water levels above maximum
☐ **B** Check out any strong smell of fuel
☐ **C** Avoid driving with a full tank of fuel
☐ **D** Use fuel additives

The fuel in your vehicle can be a dangerous fire hazard. If you smell fuel, check out where it's coming from. Never:
• use a naked flame near the vehicle if you can smell fuel
• smoke when refuelling your vehicle

755 Mark *one* answer
You're on the motorway. Luggage falls from your vehicle. What should you do?

☐ **A** Stop at the next emergency telephone and contact the police
☐ **B** Stop on the motorway and switch on hazard warning lights while you pick it up
☐ **C** Walk back up the motorway to pick it up
☐ **D** Pull up on the hard shoulder and wave traffic down

If any object falls onto the motorway carriageway from your vehicle, pull onto the hard shoulder near an emergency telephone and call for assistance. Don't stop on the carriageway or attempt to retrieve anything.

756 Mark *one* answer
While you're driving, a warning light on your vehicle's instrument panel comes on. What should you do?

☐ **A** Continue if the engine sounds all right
☐ **B** Hope that it's just a temporary electrical fault
☐ **C** Deal with the problem when there's more time
☐ **D** Check out the problem quickly and safely

Make sure you know what the different warning lights mean. An illuminated warning light could mean that your car is unsafe to drive. If you aren't sure about the problem, get a qualified mechanic to check it.

757 Mark *one* answer
Your vehicle breaks down in a tunnel. What should you do?

☐ **A** Stay in your vehicle and wait for the police
☐ **B** Stand in the lane behind your vehicle to warn others
☐ **C** Stand in front of your vehicle to warn oncoming drivers
☐ **D** Switch on hazard warning lights, then go and call for help

A broken-down vehicle in a tunnel can cause serious congestion and danger to other road users. If your vehicle breaks down, get help without delay. Switch on your hazard warning lights, then go to an emergency telephone to call for help.

758 Mark *one* answer

Your vehicle catches fire while driving through a tunnel. It's still driveable. What should you do?

- ☐ **A** Leave it where it is, with the engine running
- ☐ **B** Pull up, then walk to an emergency telephone
- ☐ **C** Park it away from the carriageway
- ☐ **D** Drive it out of the tunnel if you can do so

If it's possible, and you can do so without causing further danger, it may be safer to drive a vehicle that's on fire out of a tunnel. The greatest danger in a tunnel fire is smoke and suffocation.

759 Mark *one* answer

You're in a tunnel. Your vehicle is on fire and you can't drive it. What should you do?

- ☐ **A** Stay in the vehicle and close the windows
- ☐ **B** Switch on hazard warning lights
- ☐ **C** Leave the engine running
- ☐ **D** Switch off all of your lights

It's usually better to drive a burning vehicle out of a tunnel. If you can't do this, pull over and stop at an emergency point if possible. Switch off the engine, use hazard warning lights, and leave the vehicle immediately. Call for help from the nearest emergency point. If you have an extinguisher it may help to put out a small fire, but don't try to tackle a large one.

760 Mark *one* answer

What should you do as you approach a long road tunnel?

- ☐ **A** Put on your sunglasses and use the sun visor
- ☐ **B** Turn your headlights on to main beam
- ☐ **C** Change down to a lower gear
- ☐ **D** Make sure your radio is tuned to the frequency shown

On the approach to tunnels, a sign will usually show a local radio channel. This should give a warning of any incidents or congestion in the tunnel ahead. Many radios can be set to automatically pick up traffic announcements and local frequencies. If you have to tune the radio manually, don't be distracted while doing so. Incidents in tunnels can lead to serious casualties. The greatest hazard is fire. Getting an advance warning of problems could save your life and others.

761 Mark *one* answer

Your vehicle has broken down on an automatic railway level crossing. What should you do first?

- ☐ **A** Get everyone out of the vehicle and clear of the crossing
- ☐ **B** Telephone your vehicle recovery service to move it
- ☐ **C** Walk along the track to give warning to any approaching trains
- ☐ **D** Try to push the vehicle clear of the crossing as soon as possible

First, get yourself and anyone else well away from the crossing. If there's a railway telephone, use that to get instructions from the signal operator. Then, if there's time, move the vehicle clear of the crossing.

762 Mark *one* answer

What should you carry for use in the event of a collision?

- ☐ **A** Road map
- ☐ **B** Can of petrol
- ☐ **C** Jump leads
- ☐ **D** Fire extinguisher

Various items – such as a first aid kit and a fire extinguisher – can provide invaluable help in the event of a collision or breakdown. They could even save a life.

---

763 Mark *one* answer

You have a collision while your car is moving. What is the first thing you must do?

- ☐ **A** Stop only if someone waves at you
- ☐ **B** Call the emergency services
- ☐ **C** Stop at the scene of the incident
- ☐ **D** Call your insurance company

If you're in a collision that causes damage or injury to any other person, vehicle, animal or property, by law you must stop. Give your name, the vehicle owner's name and address, and the vehicle's registration number to anyone who has reasonable grounds for requesting them.

764 Mark *one* answer

You're in collision with another moving vehicle. Someone is injured and your vehicle is damaged. What information should you find out?

- ☐ **A** Whether the other driver is licensed to drive
- ☐ **B** The other driver's name, address and telephone number
- ☐ **C** The destination of the other driver
- ☐ **D** The occupation of the other driver

Try to keep calm and don't rush. Make sure that you've shared all the relevant details with the other driver before you leave the scene. If possible, take pictures and note the positions of all the vehicles involved.

---

765 Mark *one* answer

You lose control of your car and damage a garden wall. No-one is around. What must you do?

- ☐ **A** Report the incident to the police within 24 hours
- ☐ **B** Go back to tell the house owner the next day
- ☐ **C** Report the incident to your insurance company when you get home
- ☐ **D** Find someone in the area to tell them about it immediately

If the property owner isn't available at the time, you must inform the police about the incident. This should be done as soon as possible, and in any case within 24 hours.

766 Mark *one* answer
You're towing a small trailer on a busy three-lane motorway. What must you do if all the lanes are open?

☐ **A** Not exceed 50 mph
☐ **B** Not overtake
☐ **C** Have a stabiliser fitted
☐ **D** Use only the left-hand and centre lanes

The motorway regulations for towing a trailer state that you mustn't:
- use the right-hand lane of a three-lane motorway unless directed to do so (for example, at roadworks or due to a lane closure)
- exceed 60 mph

767 Mark *one* answer
What should you do if a trailer starts to swing from side to side while you're towing it?

☐ **A** Ease off the accelerator to reduce your speed
☐ **B** Let go of the steering wheel and let it correct itself
☐ **C** Brake hard and hold the pedal down
☐ **D** Accelerate until it stabilises

Strong winds or buffeting from large vehicles can cause a trailer or caravan to swing from side to side ('snake'). If this happens, ease off the accelerator. Don't brake harshly, steer sharply or increase your speed.

768 Mark *one* answer
On which occasion should you inflate your tyres to more than their normal pressure?

☐ **A** When the roads are slippery
☐ **B** When the vehicle is fitted with anti-lock brakes
☐ **C** When the tyre tread is worn below 2 mm
☐ **D** When carrying a heavy load

Check the vehicle handbook. This should give you guidance on the correct tyre pressures for your vehicle and when you may need to adjust them. If you're carrying a heavy load, you may need to adjust the headlights as well. Most cars have a switch on the dashboard to do this.

769 Mark *one* answer

How will a heavy load on your roof rack affect your vehicle's handling?

☐ **A** It will improve the road holding
☐ **B** It will reduce the stopping distance
☐ **C** It will make the steering lighter
☐ **D** It will reduce stability

A heavy load on your roof rack will reduce the stability of the vehicle because it moves the centre of gravity away from that designed by the manufacturer. Be aware of this when you drive round bends and corners. If you change direction at speed, your vehicle and/or load could become unstable and you could lose control.

770 Mark *one* answer

What can be badly affected when you overload your vehicle?

☐ **A** The vehicle's gearbox
☐ **B** The vehicle's ventilation
☐ **C** The vehicle's handling
☐ **D** The vehicle's battery

Any load will have an effect on the handling of your vehicle, and this becomes worse as you increase the load. You need to be aware of this when carrying passengers or heavy loads, fitting a roof rack or towing a trailer.

771 Mark *one* answer

Who's responsible for making sure that a vehicle isn't overloaded?

☐ **A** The driver of the vehicle
☐ **B** The owner of the items being carried
☐ **C** The person who loaded the vehicle
☐ **D** The licensing authority

Carrying heavy loads will affect control and the vehicle's handling characteristics. If the vehicle you're driving is overloaded, you'll be held responsible.

772 Mark *one* answer

You're planning to tow a caravan. Which of these will be the biggest aid to the vehicle handling?

☐ **A** A jockey wheel fitted to the towbar
☐ **B** Power steering fitted to the towing vehicle
☐ **C** Anti-lock brakes fitted to the towing vehicle
☐ **D** A stabiliser fitted to the towbar

Towing a caravan or trailer affects the way the towing vehicle handles. A stabiliser device is not designed to overcome instability caused by incorrect loading but it can give added security in side winds and from buffeting caused by large vehicles.

773 Mark *one* answer

Are passengers allowed to ride in a caravan that's being towed?

☐ **A** Yes, if they're over 14
☐ **B** No, not at any time
☐ **C** Only if all the seats in the towing vehicle are full
☐ **D** Only if a stabiliser is fitted

Riding in a towed caravan is highly dangerous. The safety of the entire unit is dependent on the stability of the trailer. Moving passengers would make the caravan unstable and could cause loss of control.

774 Mark *one* answer

A trailer must stay securely hitched to the towing vehicle. What additional safety device must be fitted to a trailer braking system?

☐ **A** Stabiliser
☐ **B** Jockey wheel
☐ **C** Corner steadies
☐ **D** Breakaway cable

In the event that the trailer becomes detached from the towing vehicle, the breakaway cable activates the trailer brakes before snapping. This allows the towing vehicle to get free of the trailer and out of danger.

775 Mark *one* answer

You wish to tow a trailer. Where would you find the maximum noseweight allowed on your vehicle's tow hitch?

- ☐ **A** In the vehicle handbook
- ☐ **B** In *The Highway Code*
- ☐ **C** In your vehicle registration certificate
- ☐ **D** In your licence documents

You must know how to load your trailer or caravan so that the hitch exerts an appropriate downward force on the tow ball. Information about the maximum permitted noseweight can be found in your vehicle handbook or obtained from your vehicle manufacturer's agent.

776 Mark *one* answer

How should a load be carried on your roof rack?

- ☐ **A** Securely fastened with suitable restraints
- ☐ **B** Loaded towards the rear of the vehicle
- ☐ **C** Visible in your exterior mirror
- ☐ **D** Covered with plastic sheeting

Any load must be securely fastened to the vehicle. The safest way to carry items on the roof is in a specially designed roof box. This will help to keep your luggage secure and dry, and it also has less wind resistance than loads carried exposed on a roof rack.

777 Mark *one* answer

You're carrying a child in your car. They're under three years old. Which of these is a suitable restraint?

- ☐ **A** A child seat
- ☐ **B** An adult holding a child
- ☐ **C** An adult seat belt
- ☐ **D** An adult lap belt

It's your responsibility to ensure that all children in your car are secure. Suitable restraints include a child seat, baby seat, booster seat or booster cushion. It's essential that any restraint used is suitable for the child's size and weight, and fitted according to the manufacturer's instructions.

Glossary

Glossary

Accelerate

To make the vehicle move faster by pressing the right-hand pedal.

Advanced stop lines

A marked area on the road at traffic lights, which permits cyclists or buses to wait in front of other traffic.

Adverse weather

Bad weather that makes driving difficult or dangerous.

Alert

Quick to notice possible hazards.

Anticipation

Looking out for hazards and taking action before a problem starts.

Anti-lock brakes

Brakes that stop the wheels locking so that you are less likely to skid on a slippery road.

Aquaplane

To slide out of control on a wet road surface.

Articulated vehicle

A long vehicle that is divided into two or more sections joined by cables.

Attitude

The way you think or feel, which affects the way you drive. Especially, whether you are patient and polite, or impatient and aggressive.

Automatic

A vehicle with gears that change by themselves as you speed up or slow down.

Awareness

Taking notice of the road and traffic conditions around you at all times.

Black ice

An invisible film of ice that forms over the road surface, creating very dangerous driving conditions.

Blind spot

The section of road behind you which you cannot see in your mirrors. You 'cover' your blind spot by looking over your shoulder before moving off or overtaking.

Brake fade

Loss of power to the brakes when you have been using them for a long time without taking your foot off the brake pedal. For example, when driving down a steep hill. The brakes will overheat and not work properly.

Braking distance

The distance you must allow to slow the vehicle in order to come to a stop.

Brow

The highest point of a hill.

Built-up area

A town, or place with lots of buildings.

Carriageway

One side of a road or motorway. A 'dual carriageway' has a central reservation.

Catalytic converter

A piece of equipment fitted in the exhaust system that changes harmful gases into less harmful ones.

Chicane

A sharp double bend that has been put into a road to make traffic slow down.

Child restraint

A child seat or special seat belt for children. It keeps them safe and stops them moving around in the car.

Clearway

A road where no stopping is allowed at any time. The sign for a clearway is a red cross in a red circle on a blue background.

Coasting

Driving a vehicle without using any of the gears. That is, with your foot on the clutch pedal and the car in neutral.

Commentary driving

Talking to yourself about what you see on the road ahead and what action you are going to take – an aid to concentration.

Comprehensive insurance

A motor insurance policy that pays for all repairs even if you cause an accident.

Concentration

Keeping all your attention on your driving.

Conditions

How good or bad the road surface is, volume of traffic on the road, and what the weather is like.

Congestion

Heavy traffic that makes it difficult to get to where you want to go.

Consideration

Thinking about other road users and not just yourself. For example, letting another driver go first at a junction, or stopping at a zebra crossing to let pedestrians cross over.

Contraflow

When traffic on a motorway follows signs to move to the opposite carriageway for a short distance because of roadworks. (During a contraflow, there is traffic driving in both directions on the same side of the motorway.)

Coolant

Liquid in the radiator that removes heat from the engine.

Defensive driving

Driving safely without taking risks, looking out for hazards and thinking for others.

Disqualified

Stopped from doing something (eg driving) by law, because you have broken the law.

Distraction

Anything that stops you concentrating on your driving, such as chatting to passengers or on your mobile phone.

Document

An official paper or card, eg your driving licence.

Dual carriageway

A road or motorway with a central reservation.

Engine braking – *see also* gears

Using the low gears to keep your speed down. For example, when you are driving down a steep hill and you want to stop the vehicle running away. Using the gears instead of braking will help to prevent brake fade.

Environment

The world around us and the air we breathe.

Equestrian crossing

An unusual kind of crossing. It has a button high up for horse riders to push.

Exceed

Go higher than an upper limit.

Exhaust emissions

Gases that come out of the exhaust pipe to form part of the outside air.

Field of vision

How far you can see in front and around you when you are driving.

Filler cap

Provides access to the vehicle's fuel tank, for filling up with petrol or diesel.

Fog lights

Extra bright rear (and sometimes front) lights which may be switched on in conditions of very poor visibility. You must remember to switch them off when visibility improves, as they can dazzle and distract other drivers.

Ford

A place in a stream or river which is shallow enough to drive across with care.

Four-wheel drive (4WD)

On a conventional vehicle, steering and engine speed affect just two 'drive' wheels. On 4WD, they affect all four wheels, ensuring optimum grip on loose ground.

Frustration

Feeling annoyed because you cannot drive as fast as you want to because of other drivers or heavy traffic.

Fuel consumption

The amount of fuel (petrol or diesel) that your vehicle uses. Different vehicles have different rates of consumption. Increased fuel consumption means using more fuel. Decreased fuel consumption means using less fuel.

Fuel gauge

A display or dial on the instrument panel that tells you how much fuel (petrol or diesel) you have left.

Gantry

An overhead platform like a high narrow bridge that displays electric signs on a motorway.

Gears

Control the speed of the engine in relation to the vehicle's speed. May be hand operated (manual) or automatically controlled. In a low gear (such as first or second) the engine runs more slowly. In a high gear (such as fourth or fifth), it runs more quickly. Putting the car into a lower gear as you drive can create the effect of engine braking – forcing the engine to run more slowly.

Handling

How well your vehicle moves or responds when you steer or brake.

Harass

To drive in away that makes other road users afraid.

Hard shoulder

The single lane to the left of the inside lane on a motorway, which is for emergency use only. You should not drive on the hard shoulder except in an emergency, or when there are signs telling you to use the hard shoulder because of roadworks.

Harsh braking (or harsh acceleration)

Using the brake or accelerator too hard so as to cause wear on the engine.

Hazard warning lights

Flashing amber lights which you should use only when you have broken down. On a motorway you can use them to warn other drivers behind of a hazard ahead.

High-sided vehicle

A van or truck with tall sides, or a tall trailer such as a caravan or horse-box, that is at risk of being blown off-course in strong winds.

Impatient

Not wanting to wait for pedestrians and other road users.

Inflate

To blow up – to put air in your tyres until they are at the right pressures.

Instrument panel

The car's electrical controls and gauges, set behind the steering wheel. Also called the dashboard.

Intimidate

To make someone feel afraid.

Involved

Being part of something. For example, being one of the drivers in an accident.

Jump leads

A pair of thick electric cables with clips at either end. You use it to charge a flat battery by connecting it to the live battery in another vehicle.

Junction

A place where two or more roads join.

Liability

Being legally responsible.

Manoeuvre

Using the controls to make your car move in a particular direction. For example turning, reversing or parking.

Manual

By hand. In a car that is a 'manual' or has manual gears, you have to change the gears yourself.

Maximum

The largest possible; 'maximum speed' is the highest speed allowed.

Minimum

The smallest possible.

Mirrors

Modern cars have a minimum of three rear view mirrors: one in the centre of the windscreen, and one on each front door. Additional mirrors may be required on longer vehicles, or when towing a high trailer such as a caravan. Some mirrors may be curved (convex or concave) to increase the field of vision. The mirror on the windscreen can be turned to anti-dazzle position, if glare from headlights behind creates a distraction.

Mobility

The ability to move around easily.

Monotonous

Boring. For example, a long stretch of motorway with no variety and nothing interesting to see.

MOT

The test that proves your car is safe to drive. Your MOT certificate is one of the important documents for your vehicle.

Motorway

A fast road that has two or more lanes on each side and a hard shoulder. Drivers must join or leave it on the left, via a motorway junction. Many kinds of slower vehicles – such as bicycles – are not allowed on motorways.

Multiple-choice questions

Questions with several possible answers where you have to try to choose the right one.

Glossary

Observation

The ability to notice important information, such as hazards developing ahead.

Obstruct

To get in the way of another road user.

Octagonal

Having eight sides.

Oil level

The amount of oil needed for the engine to run effectively. The oil level should be checked as part of your regular maintenance routine, and the oil replaced as necessary.

Pedestrian

A person walking.

Pelican crossing

A crossing with traffic lights that pedestrians can use by pushing a button. Cars must give way to pedestrians on the crossing while the amber light is flashing. You must give pedestrians enough time to get to the other side of the road.

Perception

Seeing or noticing (as in Hazard Perception).

Peripheral vision

The area around the edges of your field of vision.

Positive attitude

Being sensible and obeying the law when you drive.

Priority

The vehicle or other road user that is allowed by law to go first is the one that has priority.

Provisional licence

A first driving licence. all learner drivers must get one before they start having lessons.

Puffin crossing

A type of pedestrian crossing that does not have a flashing amber light phase.

Reaction time

The amount of time it takes you to see a hazard and decide what to do about it.

Red route

You see these in London and some other cities. Double red lines at the edge of the road tell you that you must not stop or park there at any time. Single red lines have notices with times when you must not stop or park. Some red routes have marked bays for either parking or loading at certain times.

Red warning triangle

An item of safety equipment to carry in your car in case you break down. You can place the triangle 45m behind your car on the same side of the road. It warns traffic that your vehicle is causing an obstruction. (Do not use these on motorways.)

Residential areas

Areas of housing where people live. The speed limit is 30mph or sometimes 20mph.

Road hump

A low bump built across the road to slow vehicles down. Also called 'sleeping policemen'.

Rumble strips

Raised strips across the road near a roundabout or junction that change the sound the tyres make on the road surface, warning drivers to slow down. They are also used on motorways to separate the main carriageway from the hard shoulder.

Safety margin

The amount of space you need to leave between your vehicle and the one in front so that you are not in danger of crashing into it if the driver slows down suddenly or stops. Safety margins have to be longer in wet or icy conditions.

Separation distance

The amount of space you need to leave between your vehicle and the one in front so that you are not in danger of crashing into it if the driver slows down suddenly or stops. The separation distance must be longer in wet or icy conditions.

Security coded radio

To deter thieves, a radio or CD unit which requires a security code (or pin number) to operate it.

Single carriageway

Generally, a road with one lane in each direction.

Skid

When the tyres fail to grip the surface of the road, the subsequent loss of control of the vehicle's movement is called a skid. Usually caused by harsh or fierce braking, steering or acceleration.

Snaking

Moving from side to side. This sometimes happens with caravans or trailers when you drive too fast, or they are not properly loaded.

Staggered junction

Where you drive cross another road. Instead of going straight across, you have to go a bit to the right or left.

Steering

Control of the direction of the vehicle. May be affected by road surface conditions: when the steering wheel turns very easily, steering is 'light', and when you have to pull hard on the wheel it is described as 'heavy'.

Sterile

Clean and free from bacteria.

Stopping distance

The time it takes for you to stop your vehicle – made up of 'thinking distance' and 'braking distance'.

Supervisor

Someone who sits in the passenger seat with a learner driver. They must be over 21 and have held a full driving licence for at least three years.

Tailgating

Driving too closely behind another vehicle – either to harass the driver in front or to help you in thick fog.

Thinking distance

The time it takes you to notice something and take the right action. You need to add thinking distance to your braking distance to make up your total stopping distance.

Third party insurance

An insurance policy that insures you against any claim by passengers or other persons for damage or injury to their person or property.

Toucan crossing

A type of pedestrian crossing that does not have a flashing amber light phase, and cyclists are allowed to ride across.

Tow

To pull something behind your vehicle. It could be a caravan or trailer.

Traffic-calming measures

Speed humps, chicanes and other devices placed in roads to slow traffic down.

Tram

A public transport vehicle which moves along the streets on fixed rails, usually electrically powered by overhead lines.

Tread depth

The depth of the grooves in a car's tyres that help them grip the road surface. The grooves must all be at least 1.6mm deep.

Turbulence

Strong movement of air. For example, when a large vehicle passes a much smaller one.

Two-second rule

In normal driving, the ideal minimum distance between you and the vehicle in front can be timed using the 'two-second' rule. As the vehicle in front passes a fixed object (such as a signpost), say to yourself 'Only a fool breaks the two second rule'. It takes two seconds to say it. If you have passed the same object before you finish, you are too close – pull back.

Tyre pressures

The amount of air which must be pumped into a tyre in order for it to be correctly blown up.

Vehicle Excise Duty

The tax you pay for your vehicle so that you may drive it on public roads.

Vehicle Registration Certificate

A record of details about a vehicle and its owner, also known as a log book.

Vehicle watch scheme

A system for identifying vehicles that may have been stolen.

Vulnerable

At risk of harm or injury.

Waiting restrictions

Times when you may not park or load your vehicle in a particular area.

Wheel balancing

To ensure smooth rotation at all speeds, wheels need to be 'balanced' correctly. This is a procedure done at a garage or tyre centre, when each wheel is removed for testing. Balancing may involve minor adjustment with the addition of small weights, to avoid wheel wobble.

Wheel-spin

When the vehicle's wheels spin round out of control with no grip on the road surface.

Zebra crossing

A pedestrian crossing without traffic lights. It has an orange light, and is marked by black and white stripes on the road. Drivers must stop for pedestrians to cross.

Answers to questions

Answers to questions

1 C	2 B	3 D	4 C	5 C	6 C
7 C	8 B	9 C	10 B	11 A	12 A
13 D	14 B	15 A	16 B	17 B	18 B
19 C	20 B	21 C	22 D	23 D	24 D
25 D	26 C	27 C		28 D	

Section 2 – **Attitude**

29 D	30 A	31 C	32 D	33 D	34 B
35 B	36 A	37 D	38 A	39 B	40 A
41 A	42 C	43 A	44 D	45 D	46 D
47 B	48 C	49 B	50 C	51 A	52 C
53 A	54 C	55 C	56 B	57 D	58 B
59 C	60 B	61 A	62 B	63 B	64 C
65 B	66 D	67 C			

Section 3 – **Safety and your vehicle**

68 A	69 C	70 C	71 B	72 D	73 C
74 D	75 A	76 C	77 D	78 B	79 B
80 D	81 B	82 D	83 A	84 A	85 D
86 A	87 A	88 B	89 B	90 C	91 A
92 D	93 A	94 B	95 D	96 D	97 D
98 B	99 B	100 B	101 B	102 A	103 C
104 D	105 D	106 B	107 B	108 B	109 D
110 C	111 D	112 D	113 C	114 A	115 A
116 B	117 D	118 C	119 A	120 A	121 D
122 C	123 B	124 B	125 B	126 D	127 C
128 A	129 D	130 A	131 B	132 D	133 C
134 D	135 D	136 B	137 B	138 C	139 D
140 C	141 D	142 B	143 C	144 A	145 A
146 D					

Section 4 – Safety margins

147 D	148 D	149 A	150 B	151 D	152 B
153 D	154 C	155 C	156 B	157 B	158 C
159 C	160 A	161 D	162 A	163 A	164 B
165 D	166 C	167 B	168 B	169 D	170 A
171 C	172 A	173 C	174 C	175 B	176 C
177 C	178 D	179 C	180 D	181 B	182 D
183 A	184 A	185 A	186 C	187 B	188 B
189 C	190 C				

Section 5 – Hazard awareness

191 C	192 C	193 A	194 D	195 C	196 C
197 C	198 D	199 B	200 A	201 A	202 A
203 C	204 C	205 B	206 C	207 D	208 B
209 B	210 C	211 A	212 D	213 D	214 C
215 B	216 C	217 B	218 A	219 A	220 A
221 C	222 A	223 D	224 B	225 C	226 C
227 A	228 B	229 B	230 B	231 A	232 D
233 A	234 C	235 B	236 B	237 B	238 C
239 D	240 C	241 C	242 A	243 B	244 A
245 B	246 C	247 C	248 A	249 C	250 D
251 C	252 C	253 D	254 B	255 C	256 B
257 D	258 A	259 A	260 D	261 D	262 B
263 D	264 D	265 A	266 C	267 A	268 B
269 D	270 A	271 B			

Section 6 – Vulnerable road users

272 D	273 D	274 B	275 D	276 D	277 C
278 D	279 D	280 D	281 B	282 D	283 D
284 C	285 C	286 C	287 A	288 D	289 C
290 D	291 D	292 C	293 D	294 A	295 D
296 C	297 C	298 D	299 D	300 B	301 A
302 C	303 C	304 C	305 A	306 D	307 A
308 A	309 B	310 B	311 A	312 A	313 C
314 B	315 D	316 A	317 D	318 D	319 D
320 C	321 B	322 B	323 D	324 B	325 B
326 D	327 C	328 B	329 C	330 A	331 C
332 C	333 B	334 B	335 D	336 B	337 B
338 C	339 D	340 A	341 D		

Answers to questions

Section 7 – **Other types of vehicle**

342 A	343 A	344 B	345 B	346 D	347 B
348 B	349 A	350 B	351 B	352 D	353 D
354 A	355 D	356 A	357 A	358 B	359 C
360 B	361 D	362 B	363 D	364 D	

Section 8 – **Vehicle handling**

365 A	366 A	367 D	368 D	369 A	370 C
371 C	372 D	373 C	374 D	375 D	376 C
377 C	378 C	379 B	380 B	381 D	382 D
383 B	384 C	385 C	386 A	387 B	388 A
389 B	390 D	391 C	392 C	393 A	394 C
395 D	396 B	397 D	398 D	399 D	400 C
401 C	402 C	403 D	404 D	405 A	406 C
407 A	408 A	409 C	410 B	411 D	412 B
413 D	414 C	415 B			

Section 9 – **Motorway rules**

416 D	417 D	418 A	419 C	420 C	421 C
422 A	423 C	424 C	425 C	426 C	427 C
428 C	429 B	430 B	431 A	432 B	433 D
434 C	435 A	436 A	437 D	438 B	439 A
440 A	441 C	442 B	443 B	444 D	445 A
446 D	447 D	448 B	449 D	450 D	451 D
452 C	453 A	454 D	455 C	456 D	457 B
458 D	459 B	460 C	461 D	462 A	463 B
464 B	465 A	466 D	467 C	468 B	469 C
470 D	471 A	472 B	473 A		

Section 10 – Rules of the road

474 C	475 D	476 B	477 A	478 C	479 D
480 D	481 A	482 B	483 A	484 B	485 A
486 D	487 A	488 D	489 C	490 A	491 C
492 C	493 B	494 A	495 C	496 A	497 D
498 B	499 A	500 B	501 A	502 B	503 A
504 D	505 A	506 D	507 B	508 C	509 B
510 B	511 B	512 D	513 D	514 C	515 D
516 D	517 D	518 D	519 C	520 C	521 D
522 A	523 A	524 C	525 B	526 A	527 D
528 A	529 A	530 D	531 D	532 D	533 A
534 A	535 A	536 D	537 D	538 A	539 A
540 A					

Section 11 – Road and traffic signs

541 D	542 D	543 A	544 A	545 B	546 D
547 B	548 D	549 D	550 D	551 A	552 C
553 B	554 D	555 A	556 B	557 B	558 C
559 A	560 C	561 B	562 C	563 D	564 C
565 C	566 D	567 A	568 D	569 D	570 B
571 A	572 A	573 A	574 B	575 B	576 A
577 D	578 A	579 C	580 A	581 B	582 C
583 B	584 D	585 A	586 A	587 C	588 D
589 A	590 C	591 B	592 D	593 B	594 B
595 C	596 D	597 C	598 B	599 C	600 D
601 B	602 A	603 A	604 C	605 D	606 A
607 C	608 C	609 B	610 A	611 C	612 A
613 A	614 D	615 D	616 B	617 A	618 D
619 C	620 C	621 B	622 C	623 C	624 A
625 B	626 D	627 B	628 B	629 A	630 D
631 A	632 B	633 B	634 D	635 C	636 B
637 C	638 A	639 B	640 A	641 B	642 B
643 A	644 C	645 A	646 B	647 B	648 B
649 A	650 A	651 B	652 D	653 C	654 B
655 C	656 A	657 A	658 C	659 B	660 C
661 A	662 B	663 A	664 D	665 B	666 B
667 A	668 B	669 A	670 A	671 C	672 C
673 B	674 B	675 B	676 B	677 A	

Answers to questions

Section 12 – Documents

678 C	679 B	680 B	681 A	682 C	683 A
684 A	685 C	686 A	687 A	688 B	689 C
690 C	691 b	692 D	693 D	694 B	695 A
696 B	697 A	698 D	699 B	700 D	701 B
702 C	703 B	704 C	705 D	706 B	707 A

Section 13 – Incidents, accidents and emergencies

708 A	709 A	710 A	711 C	712 B	713 D
714 B	715 B	716 B	717 D	718 D	719 B
720 A	721 C	722 B	723 D	724 A	725 A
726 A	727 D	728 A	729 B	730 B	731 B
732 D	733 D	734 D	735 C	736 D	737 B
738 B	739 B	740 D	741 B	742 B	743 A
744 B	745 C	746 B	747 C	748 C	749 A
750 B	751 A	752 B	753 C	754 B	755 A
756 D	757 D	758 D	759 B	760 D	761 A
762 D	763 C	764 B	765 A		

Section 14 – Vehicle loading

766 D	767 A	768 D	769 D	770 C	771 A
772 D	773 B	774 D	775 A	776 A	777 A

Personal information

My driver number

Driving instructor's name and
phone number

Driving instructor's number

Theory test date and time

Theory test pass date

Theory test certificate number

Driving school code

Practical test date and time